STAGING SHAKESPEARE

GARLAND REFERENCE LIBRARY
OF THE HUMANITIES
(VOL. 798)

STAGING SHAKESPEARE
Seminars on
Production Problems

edited by
Glenn Loney

City University of New York
Brooklyn College &
CUNY Graduate Center

GARLAND PUBLISHING, INC. • NEW YORK & LONDON
1990

Library of Congress Cataloging-in-Publication Data

Loney, Glenn Meredith, 1928–
    Staging Shakespeare: seminars on production problems
/ Glenn Loney.
        p.   cm. — (Garland reference library of the humanities ; vol.
798)
    Includes bibliographical references.
    ISBN 0–8240–6613–8 (alk. paper)
    1. Shakespeare, William, 1564–1616—Dramatic production—
Congresses. 2. Shakespeare, William, 1564–1616—Adaptations—
Congresses. I. Title. II. Series.
PR3091.L6   1990
792.9—dc20   89–71404
                                                              CIP

Printed on acid-free, 250-year-life paper
Manufactured in the United States of America

This book is dedicated to the
memories of Joseph Davidson and
Wilson Lehr, Professors of Theatre
Emeritus, who did so much to
develop theatre studies and
production at Brooklyn College.

PARTICIPANTS

Clive Barnes
Anne Righter Barton
Bernard Beckerman
Cicely Berry
Suzanne Bloch
Muriel C. Bradbrook
Robert Brustein
Richmond Crinkley
Edward Downes
Frank Dunlop
Bernard Gersten
Alfred Harbage
C. Walter Hodges
Richard Hosley
John Houseman
James Earl Jones

Michael Kahn
Károly Köpe
Michael Langham
Ming Cho Lee
Siegmund Levarie
Stoddard Lincoln
Margaret Linney
Glenn Loney
Donald Madden
Alois Nagler
Richard Pasco
Richard Peaslee
Ian Richardson
Virgil Thomson
Glynne Wickham
Franco Zeffirelli

ACKNOWLEDGMENTS

This book has been made possible by the cooperation of Brooklyn College of the City University of New York. The text has been edited from transcripts of discussions and addresses on problems of producing Shakespeare's plays, all delivered at a conference at the college, in conjunction with the Royal Shakespeare Company's staging of *Richard II* at the Brooklyn Academy of Music. All the participants have approved this text for publication, some of them making pertinent improvements in the transcripts to provide more factual detail and remove conversational redundancies. The College and the Editor wish to thank all the participants and organizations who have contributed to this work. It is, however, regretted that, for reasons of space and economy forced on the publisher, some of the material has had to be abridged or omitted. Special thanks are owed to the late Professor Nancy Wynn, of Wells College, who prepared the transcripts, and to Augusta Siegel, whose assistance in reproducing text material was invaluable. Thanks also to Ming Cho Lee, for his generous permission to use his slides to illustrate his comments, and to C. Walter Hodges and Oxford University Press for permission to reprint cuts from *Shakespeare's Second Globe*. Thanks as well to Lawrence S. Epstein, M.Phil, and Felicia Ruff, students in the Ph.D. Program in Theatre at the City University Graduate School, for book layout and text formatting.

CONTENTS

INTRODUCTION

The Shakespeare Housing Problem—A Plague on Both His Houses?

Although these discussions on staging Shakespeare's works in various performance forms occurred some time ago, the distinction of the participants and the value of their contributions is such that it is important to make the texts of the panels available for scholars, students, and theatre professionals.

Dualities and dichotomies dominated the discussions of Shakespeare and his works at the Brooklyn College Shakespeare Conference. In addition to the obvious value of bringing together well known Shakespearean scholars with noted performing arts personalities to see how effectively the analytical could combine with the practical, the conference was also intended as a salute to the performing arts, involving as it did members of the Royal Shakespeare Company then performing at the Brooklyn Academy of Music, distinguished American artists, and Brooklyn's own faculty and students in theatre, music, and dance.

Any such meeting of academic minds with pragmatic performing talents would be apt to provoke some disagreements and divisions. Nor were the Brooklyn seminars a disappointment in this regard. Attention was often forcefully directed to the difference between Shakespeare's plays as texts and as stage or film-productions. Dr. Bernard Beckerman, author of *Shakespeare at the Globe*, wittily viewed this dichotomy as a kind of Shakespeare "housing problem." Moderating "Shakespeare: Playwright and/or Poet," Dr. Beckerman emphasized the duality in modern considerations of Shakespeare's works in terms of the Bard's "two homes." One of these homes is appropriately the theatre, in which the plays had their first vibrant life. They were, after all, primarily written for production, for performance, not for publication. (Had publication—with its attendant subsequent literary dissection by critics and scholars—been Shakespeare's major intent in writing such masterpieces as *Romeo and Juliet, Henry V, Hamlet,* and *King Lear*, would he not himself have prepared a definitive edition—at least in Stratford retirement years?)

Although Shakespeare's theatre-home has often been remodelled, redecorated, and recreated in ways which might astonish him, his plays have survived in it most sturdily. After Shakespeare's death, however, literary carpenters and Bardolators began—modestly at first—building another home for Shakespeare. This is, in Dr. Beckerman's phrase, the "ramshackle mansion of teaching and criticism in which Shakespeare also dwells. . . ." Today, it is a structure not unlike California's Winchester Mystery House, a rambling, hodge-podge collection of many, many rooms, some of them severe in their disciplined design, others carelessly decorated, and some luxurious, fanciful, even bizarre. But whatever verities or vagaries are urged by the critics who have created these various rooms for their honored master and friend, William Shakespeare, it is, Dr. Beckerman stressed, in these chambers that most of the public first meets him. Not in his theatre-home. And, although Dr. Beckerman, who was both a scholar and a stage-director, was kind enough not to underscore the fact, this initial encounter with Shakespeare is often the vaccination that protects a student against any further Shakespeare fever. Those who have met him at his other home, the playhouse, frequently have a much more pleasant experience and become lifelong friends, visiting him as often as he is at home to them.

Thus there is a duality in Shakespeare's work—but not one that he intended or possibly even envisioned. The plays, or most of them, are among the greatest dramas available to the modern stage. At the same time, they are among the greatest challenges facing the literary or historical scholar-critic. No matter how much is known, there is more that needs to be discovered. No matter how many convincing, authoritative analyses of the plays exist, there is always room for another thoughtful interpretation, especially one which helps contemporary readers, players, and audiences gain an understanding of the works.

But therein lies a problem. Dr. Beckerman articulated it this way: "Often people choose to know only one kind of Shakespeare and find it difficult to talk to people who live with him at the other home. We either talk past each other, or we don't quite understand the same words in the same way." He wasn't saying that this misunderstanding is willful, only that it occurs. The discussions which follow in this book frequently illustrate that, sometimes with passion, often with elegance and wit, and certainly with some chapter-and-verse citations.

It is sometimes charged by the theatre practitioners that Shakespeare scholars don't even like to come to the theatre; that they prefer their Shakespeare lifeless on the printed page; that, for them, the plays lose their validity in a contemporary performance; or that the theatre, if it no longer threatens moral profanation to contemporary audiences, certainly practices textual profanation on Shakespeare's plays. To which scholars respond variously, as suits their attitudes and beliefs. Some there are who don't care much for plays in performance, but they would argue that Shakespeare's works are anything but lifeless on a page, for the person who has the wit to make them come alive in his mind. Others do enjoy going to the theatre, but they are often, like Bernard Grebanier, in his fascinating survey of Shakespearean interpreters, *Then Came Each Actor*, understandably appalled at what some unschooled and unskilled actors do the Bard's works in performance.

The Shakespeare canon is a staple of college and university theatre in the United States, as well as the mainstay of some thirty-five American and Canadian Shakespeare Festivals, many of which are studied in some detail in *The Shakespeare Complex*, by the Editor and Patricia MacKay. It doesn't always follow that a professional actor will interpret Shakespearean characters with greater insight and skill than a student. Unfortunately, even some Equity-card holders are indistinguishable on stage from college sophomores. But a really well trained and talented performer has an edge on amateurs, at least in matters of technique. What the professional may lack, however, is the guidance of a director—or even an expert production consultant—who is deeply steeped in Shakespeare scholarship. What this means is that it is often possible in college productions to emphasize points in Shakespearean plays which have been elucidated by scholars but which will be entirely lost in professional productions, in which neither director nor actors are aware that there is a point to be made. What may be lacking in the college production, though, is that degree of skill, that sparkle of talent which makes the professional work less embarrassing to watch. But that only stresses another dichotomy in dealing with Shakespeare's work: What do you want from the plays? A colorful, slick show? Or a thoughtful, provocative explication of meaning?

The answer might well be that no one wants the dichotomy. Why can't a production be both colorful and thoughtful, slick and provocative, and in every way an explication of the text, visually and aurally? Those scholars who prefer to concentrate on meanings of minor words, as they would have been understood in Shakespeare's time, are not much help to performers, however. An actor who wants to follow Hamlet's advice about speaking speeches trippingly, simply cannot do that, if he is trying to project forgotten meanings of archaic words during performance. At the same time, though, an actor who is too lazy to study his role's text—and sub-text—carefully, with the helpful guidance of the many brilliant critiques which are available on both major and minor plays, can also give a bad performance. Lack of study, of preparation, no matter how technically skilled and confident a player may be, can prove disastrous. True, instinct and long human experience can help an actor find the vital heart of a Shakespearean role, without having to read Harbage, Dover Wilson, or even Coleridge. But in relying only on inspiration and past experience, he may lose some of the heart-muscle of his role. Then, of course, there is that arrogance of attitude which assumes that no thought, no experience, no technique—and often no talent, though that is not mentioned—is necessary for one to stand on stage and "do his own thing" to Shakespeare. That, if Shakespeare's people and plots are really "relevant," then their immediacy will be at once revealed by the simple act of saying the lines, of moving about the stage, of reacting to others the way one "feels." This attitude toward performance of Shakespeare in performance is a peculiar phenomenon which reached its height during the mini-Romantic Revival of the late 1960's and early 1970's, but its seeds lie deeply buried in the soils of late Lee Strasberg's Method greenhouses. Productions which were achieved through such means—a number of them sponsored by Joseph Papp, so widely praised for his New York Shakespeare Festival—frequently failed to help audiences understand the plays or to enjoy fully the riches therein contained. Some claimed, it is true, that they had pleasure in watching such productions, but these votes of approval came all too often from those who had little or no experience of live theatre and little practice in analytical thinking.

There is no reason why audiences should be encouraged to check their brains at the door when they come to see a Shakespearean play. Why should one's enjoyment of a play in performance be less, if he wants to think about what he is seeing and hearing, than if he merely mindlessly responds to colors, movements, noises, and novelties?

In the discussions that follow, it will soon be apparent that some participants, as Dr. Beckerman deplored, are talking at cross-purposes with one another. Some scholars do show a bias here in favor of the text on the page, as opposed to contemporary performance. On the other hand, some theatre practitioners show either contempt for or indifference to any information or insights scholars can share with them. In general, however, there is a spirit of co-operation, of trying to discover how the scholar and the practitioner can help each other have the fullest possible intellectual and emotional experience from Shakespeare's plays. When that happens, duality, rather than dichotomy, is the theme, as it is in the discussion of the Royal Shakespeare's production of *Richard II*, in which director John Barton developed his staging around the concept of the king's "two bodies." The Elizabethans, historian Ernst Kantorowicz contends, believed that their king was different from them, not so much in his wealth and power, but in his possession of two bodies: one was flawless, abstract, and immortal; the other was fallible, individual, and mortal.

Shakespeare—or his work—like *Richard II* has two bodies. One of them is the text, not as a printed object, but as an immortal abstraction of human experience, never to be completely revealed, never entirely explicated for all men and all time. The other body is the specific scholarly study of a drama or the particular production of a play. These are temporal manifestations of Shakespeare, of his kingship, if you like. They are written or are performed, and they, in their turn, are superseded by others. The one major difference between Shakespearean scholarship and performance is that print has permanence; living theatre does not. Filming or video-taping live performance doesn't really record the actuality, though a performance, such as Zeffirelli's *Romeo and Juliet*, specifically designed for the cinema medium, does have a permanence similar to print.

Ideally, the scholar and the practitioner should work together—and it need not be a one-sided arrangement: the scholar always helping the director, the designer, the performer to get more from Shakespeare. Is it not possible that in a really good performance, the scholar might receive new insights, further inspirations for his researches as well?

In this collection of discussions, despite the differences of bookmen and theatremen, there is clearly a great interest in making Shakespeare's vision of man in his universe more widely accessible to the public, both in publication and in performance. And, for that reason, there is much here which will be of practical use. Obviously, no producer wants his *Titus Andronicus* or his *Winter's Tale* production to drown in academic speculations on line-readings. No costume-designer wants her frocks foundering in footnotes. But that is not a real danger from these lively, informed, good-natured shadings of information and experience.

A word of caution, however: some participants—not scholars—make a few statements about Shakespeare, his plays, his times, and his intentions, which cannot be supported by the known facts. Where possible, to avoid embarrassment, such comments have been edited out of the original transcript. In some cases, however, the comments are inseparable from the point being made by the participant. To remove the misstatement would seem to be playing schoolmaster to acknowledged professionals who have generously allowed their comments to be published. So some comments must be taken with a grain of salt and checked against standard Shakespeare authorities. Most errors are promptly challenged by other participants. The present collection doesn't represent the entire content of the Shakespeare Conference at Brooklyn College. There was only limited space for the materials in this book, so every discussion has been cut to some degree as well as edited. Several contributions were regretfully omitted for lack of space or because permission to publish was not received.

Purists may object to the very broad way in which Shakespeare's name is used by some contributors. Shakespeare is not only the name of a playwright, but it also covers all his plays as well. Thus, one "acts Shakespeare," but the speaker means "in his plays," not the actual character of Shakespeare. Or one "designs Shakespeare," "produces Shakespeare," and now and then tries to devise new ways to "sell Shakespeare to the public." By extension, "this Shakespeare thing" in some cases really is a blanket-term for Elizabethan plays, theatres, and life. William Safire, Edwin Newman, and others may mourn the decay of English usage, but this editor is not going to fight the disease by rephrasing the participants' habitual way of paying homage to Shakespeare and his works. Only where meanings or intentions have been vague or misleading has rephrasing been attempted. In most cases, this was done by the participants themselves, checking the transcripts of the discussions. One or two practically rewrote their entire impromptu oral contributions. This accounts for the contrasts between conversational and essay style in some discussions. The Brooklyn Conference was reviewed in *The Shakespeare Newsletter,* which noted that the conference was designed to bring scholars and theatre people together to help each other achieve a mutual desire: to see Shakespeare well performed. "But," observed the reviewer, Professor Melvin Goldstein, of the University of Hartford, "this sense of teamwork was rapidly dispelled by the participants themselves, who divided into two large camps: those who condemned 'novelty' productions of Shakespeare because they destroy Shakespeare's text (language and poetry), and those who claimed that if Shakespeare is to be for all ages, he must be made to relate to the tastes of our times." After summarizing various discussions, he concludes: "Lest this review of a splendid conference leave the reader with a feeling that it amounted merely to antagonisms between worshipers of the word and worshipers of interpretation, I hasten to add that the general tone of all involved was one of serious questioning and interest among people who saw themselves as comrades in arms, trying to serve best the cause of Shakespeare. The intensity and passionate level of the discussions indicated positive sharing of genuine feelings about matters that mattered very much to all those present." I join with my colleagues at Brooklyn and with the scholars and artists represented here in hoping that, as you read this book, you will agree with the sentiments above. More than that, though, we hope your own experiences in reading, in producing, or in seeing Shakespeare's plays will be informed and enhanced by these discussions.

Glenn Loney
New York

Staging Shakespeare

SHAKESPEARE AND THE MODERN THEATRE

Robert Brustein

The way in which Shakespeare is produced in each age, suggests
Robert Brustein, is an indication—however unconscious—of
how that age regards itself. In this talk, Brustein, former Dean of
the Yale School of Drama, surveys some of the ways of the past
in staging Shakespeare, moving on to a detailed consideration
of trends in Britain and America in the last few decades.
Brustein argues forcefully for periodic renewals of approaches
to Shakespeare on the stage. He cites some of the work at the
Yale Repertory Theatre, a professional producing company, of
which he has been not only Artistic Director but also a member
of the acting ensemble.

His credentials as a critic are well known: he has long been
a drama critic for The New Republic *and has written critiques*
for the New York Review of Books. *In 1962, he won the George*
Jean Nathan Award for his drama criticism. While on a
sabbatical from Yale, Brustein served as guest critic for the
London Sunday Observer, *where he succeeded in irritating a*
number of smug British theatre people by being frankly and
circumstantially critical of their work.

That is characteristic of Brustein. He has never been afraid
to express his considered opinions boldly—and with
considerable style. When he took over the Yale School of
Drama, recalls alumnus Bernard Barrow—Ryan of Ryan's Hope
and Emeritus Professor of Theatre at Brooklyn College—

Brustein had the Green Room painted red! He has been doing the same thing metaphorically in his criticism for years. Among his books: The Theatre of Revolt *(1964),* Seasons of Discontent *(1965),* The Third Theatre *(1971), and* The Culture Watch *(1975). Currently he is driving force behind the American Repertory Theatre at Harvard.*

*   *   *

Some years ago I wrote an article called "No More Masterpieces," in which I surprised myself, as an erstwhile professor of dramatic literature and actor, by coming out in favor of a much more elastic and radical approach to the classics than was commonly being practiced on the stage, particularly in the producing of Shakespeare. It seemed to me that we had reached some kind of a dead-end or turning point in our staging of such familiar works as *Hamlet, Macbeth*, and *Midsummer Night's Dream*—works that most educated people have been reading throughout their high school and college experience, and that the pious and reverential approach to Shakespeare then in vogue, in which the soliloquies are really crooned rather than acted, was in as much danger of putting dutiful husbands to sleep as certain Wagnerian operas.

Now, to recapitulate my argument, I wrote that we had reached an end of a cycle in our staging of Shakespearean classics and that we were desperately in need of some renewal on the American stage similar to that which was currently being undertaken in England at that time, 1966-1967-1968. Now, such renewal ideally should take place every 10 or 20 years and, indeed, it has been taking place throughout human history in one form or another. In fact, it was only in recent times that the Shakespeare canon of plays had taken on some of the quality of sacred, untouchable texts; possibly because only in recent times has literature begun to take on some of the inviolability of biblical scripture. For some people it has replaced biblical scripture.

In the Restoration period, a play by Shakespeare and his contemporaries was treated with about as much respect as the first story idea for a Hollywood movie. John Dryden, whose admiration for Shakespeare was second to none in his critical writings, had no compunction whatsoever about translating his great predecessor's works into an idiom that he found more acceptable to his age—a very formal and very decorous age. He made a hash out of *Troilus and Cressida*. He collaborated on an operatic version of *The Tempest*, with the aid of Thomas Shadwell and William Davenant, of which only the music is memorable—Henry Purcell's music. And he rewrote *Antony and Cleopatra*, as you know, into a play called *All for Love* so as to make it no longer a spiralling, colossal epic, but rather a very well organized, rather unglamourous moral lesson, during which Antony's wife, accompanied by her children, arrives on stage to plead beautifully for the preservation of their marriage. Nor was Dryden at all unique in this particular way of approaching Shakespeare. With the exception of *Hamlet* and *Macbeth*, which remained more or less untouched throughout this period, every other play of Shakespeare was, at one time or another over the next hundred and fifty years, subjected to some change.

As Verdi was later to do with *Othello* and with *Macbeth*, Henry Purcell, the great English composer, adapted *The Tempest*. He adapted *A Midsummer Night's Dream* into *The Fairy Queen*—into operas, that is to say. Colley Cibber revised *Richard III*, adding new characters and a famous line which is still mistakenly attributed to Shakespeare: "Off with his head, so much for Buckingham." That was written by Cibber, not by Shakespeare. In a later version by Nahum Tate—a notorious version which held the stage for about a century and a half—*King Lear* was given a happy ending, which found Lear conquering the forces of Goneril and Regan. It found Cordelia marrying Edgar and everyone but the villains living happily ever after.

Now, nobody in his senses would hold that such versions, however apt they were for their own time and to their own audiences, were any kind of improvement on Shakespeare. I mention them only to emphasize my point that previous ages were significantly less reverent towards dramatic literature than our own age has been, even to the point of bowdlerizing and mutilating some of the finest texts for the sake of adapting them to the sensibility of their times. And, indeed, it is some measure of the sensibility of each age as to exactly how Shakespeare is changed for that age. Really, Shakespeare functions as a kind of barometer of each age and tells us more, in the way he's produced, about ourselves even than we tell ourselves. It's even a measure of a certain age's sensibility that it refuses to change Shakespeare.

In the Romantic period, when the word "masterpiece" was first invented, and when a large public began to seek for cultural improvement through books, plays, newspapers, and magazines, Shakespeare, for the first time, became an object of zealous devotion. It was at this time, during the late eighteenth and nineteenth centuries, that Shakespeare began to develop into that unknown and rather stilted stranger known as The Immortal Bard, and thus sanctified, began to be produced in the most conventionalized possible manner. The famous roles became material for the declamatory acting of actor-managers. Scenery became ponderous and very extravagant. Lighting was full of chiaroscuro; much of that lighting is caught in the famous portraits of the actors of the time. Costumes were made of velvets and brocades with flowing headpieces and beautifully carved daggers and swords. It was the beginning of the so-called historical Shakespeare in which audiences were somehow persuaded that they were seeing an authentic reenactment of the play, precisely as it was written to be played—even though we know that Shakespeare's plays had not ever been performed in his own time inside a proscenium stage as they were in the nineteenth century. They were performed on a bare stage with a minimum of props and with costumes that continually violated historical accuracy. Shakespeare's Cleopatra, for example, was known to have worn a hoop skirt.

But even the so-called historical Shakespeare was really a form of adaptation. It is a fact that no actor can play a role without somehow imbuing that role with his own time. The very accents with which he reads verse, the very way he looks, the very way he wears his hair, the very approach to the part—if it's heavily psychological for example—is somehow introducing notions from his own time. So, even the so-called traditional or historical Shakespeare is an imposition, subtle though it may be, of an age on Shakespeare.

The movement of historical Shakespeare found its culmination in twentieth century England in the institutionalized Shakespeare of the Old Vic Company and the Stratford Memorial Theatre. Both of these institutions could boast of genuine achievements, particularly the Old Vic during the great days when Olivier was with the company. In the late forties and the fifties, he joined a company consisting of Ralph Richardson, Joyce Redmond, Harry Andrews, and Peggy Ashcroft, and they did those great productions of *Oedipus* and two parts of *Henry IV* and *Uncle Vanya*, organized under the supervision of Michel Saint-Denis and Glen Byam-Shaw. But, more often, and as soon as Olivier left in fact, these companies were dedicated more to memorializing, perpetuating the past in some kind of marble, than they were to illuminating it.

As a result, they ended up looking more like museums than they did like living, organic theatres. For example, The Old Vic, once it had been abandoned by Olivier and his companions, degenerated into a collection of effeminate leading men and genteel finishing school ladies who offered a Shakespeare calculated to rouse nobody from his sleep, and who were ultimately absorbed into the quasi-official National Theatre without the slightest protest from anybody. The Stratford Memorial Theatre had value for years only as an attraction for tourists and for schoolchildren who had already paid their dutiful fealty to Mary Arden's house and Anne Hathaway's cottage and Shakespeare's grave and now were ready for a play. That is, until Peter Hall transformed this company in the sixties, taking the name "Memorial" out of the name of the group and also out of the atmosphere, renaming the group the Royal Shakespeare Company, leasing a London theatre in addition to the Stratford theatre, beginning to produce new plays, and adding those to the repertory.

What happened in the sixties, particularly to the Royal Shakespeare Company, was the injection of a new and revolutionary spirit, a spirit from Germany—the spirit of Bertolt Brecht and his company, the Berliner Ensemble. What Brecht showed the English through his own example was the possibility of refreshing the past by fortifying it with a new vision; rejuvenating a classical idea by discovering for it a strong, modern equivalent. Like the poet, T. S. Eliot, Bertolt Brecht was a writer who used literary fragments to shore up against his own writings. His own work is virtually a pastiche of plundered literature. In fact, Brecht worked very much like Shakespeare worked, striving not so much for originality of plot as for originality of conception: *Hamlet* is a reworking of an earlier popular play, probably by Kyd, and *The Threepenny Opera*, as you know, is a modern version of Gay's *The Beggar's Opera*. *Edward II* is a kind of new look at Christopher Marlowe's Elizabethan work. *Trumpets and Drums* of Brecht is a modern adaptation of Farquahar's *Recruiting Officer*, and *The Caucasian Chalk Circle* is an elaboration of the old Chinese play, *The Circle of Chalk*. Looting his way through the past, as Brecht did, he emerges as one of the great buccaneers of literature. As he remarked when he was accused once of plagarizing the work of a contemporary without his acknowledgment: "In literature as in life, I do not recognize the concept of private property."

Given Brecht's manner of working, it was inevitable that he should turn his attention to Shakespeare, as he did towards the end of his life in the great uncompleted work called *Coriolanus*. Brecht, basing his work partly on translation and partly on adaptation, pushed the work towards an economic interpretation of the main character as an expression of the rising power of the price of grain—something that we might respond to ourselves now that prices seem to be rising and changing people's attitudes. It was also inevitable that the style of the Berliner Ensemble should be based on a distillation of epic Shakespearean production. After a visit by the Berliner Ensemble to Great Britain in the fifties, the Brechtian manner was soon transferred to English production of Shakespeare. Settings at the Royal Shakespeare Company became spare, simple, abstract, using metal, wire, and aluminum, instead of canvas and wood. Costumes were now being constructed out of burlap and leather, instead of velvets and brocades, and they had the look of real, threadbare, worn clothes. The acting grew more terse, more ironic, more detached, and the style of the new plays introduced by Peter Hall into the repertory at the Aldwych in London began to influence the style of the old plays at Stratford and vice versa. The most obvious example is Peter

Brook's famous production of *King Lear* with its Beckett-like atmosphere.

Now, the argument that I advanced at the time was that American theatre should begin to experiment with Shakespeare in ways similar to those that were then being tried in England. I think it's somewhat ironic some years later, that not only has American theatre advanced along these lines but it may have advanced a little too far, while English classical theatre seems to have retreated. It was with some dismay that I observed, in my capacity in 1973 as a drama critic in London, that the Royal Shakespeare Company both in the Aldwych and at Stratford had repealed the Brechtian revolution that it had undergone under Peter Hall and returned to the sumptuous, over-produced, over-costumed, even somewhat declamatory Shakespeare that was left over from a previous age. This was particularly true of the Cecil B. De Mille-like production of *Titus Andronicus* that I saw in 1973, with its extravagant effects, its over-emphasis on the new mechanical stage that Stratford had just installed, and I don't suppose that it's any accident that some of the new plays that were being produced at the Aldwych, most notably John Arden's play, *The Island of the Mighty*—a long-winded, overwritten Arthurian epic—would reflect much of the same gaudiness and excess in production as the Shakespeare plays were reflecting at Stratford. So, again we were getting that interplay, but not quite to my satisfaction.

The John Barton production of *Richard II* was something else again, because I think it was graced by a strong and intelligent informing idea, but even this production, in my opinion, was marred by an over-sumptuous physical production—distracting, and was, in spite of its real achievements, a far cry from the genuinely startling originality and understatement of Peter Brook's productions with that company in the past. The productions of Shakespeare at the RSC, coupled with some of those that I was seeing at the National Theatre and in some of the regional repertory companies in England, suggested that once again, for reasons I have not sufficiently plumbed in my own mind, English Shakespearean production was becoming overly preoccupied

for the moment with externals, outsides, appearances, and it
momentarily lost sight of what Lear had called "the thing itself."

In the United States, on the other hand, the thing itself was
also in some kind of obscurity; also in eclipse. Since I've been
commissioned to discuss American Shakespeare production
primarily and most particularly Shakespearean production at
the Yale Repertory Theatre, perhaps I'd better get off the
indelicate, not to say inhospitable, subject of the English and
turn to our own faults and foibles; for the fact is that the new
look in Shakespeare in this country has been attempted by a
number of directors and companies, and the cry of no more
masterpieces, which had been bawled out by a number of
people including myself, has been answered, perhaps to an
extent not originally anticipated nor even desired.

I would prefer not to cite specific examples but rather to
suggest several so-called radical approaches to Shakespeare
which I find personally interesting—and others which leave me
with less enthusiasm. In the latter category, the less interesting
ones, I would cite the process common to much institutional
Shakespeare known as "jollying-up." Actually, it's an English
phrase and was imported from England. This is a form of
streamlining purely for novelty's sake. The jollying techniques
are particularly adored by directors who are doing the play for
the fourth or the fifth time. They're exhausted with it and,
therefore, they undertake to amuse themselves during a chore
they don't particularly enjoy: not by trying to penetrate the play
more deeply, but rather by changing its external physical
environment; not by determining a truly modern equivalent for
the action, but rather just by redesigning its costumes, props,
and settings for no discernible reason. In short, another way to
avoid the thing itself for the sake of its outsides.

This jollying-up technique, which you probably recognize,
was originally associated with the venerated name of Tyrone
Guthrie—also responsible, of course, for many genuinely
impressive Shakespeare productions. But it soon became
immensely popular with many of the classical repertory
companies, not only in England but in America: not only at the
Old Vic and at Stratford, but at the Bristol Old Vic in England,
and in America at the Minneapolis Theatre—the Guthrie, the

old Phoenix Theatre in New York, the original Phoenix, and in fact, everywhere Guthrie visited. Jollying-up reached almost epidemic proportions with the American Shakespearean Festival at Stratford, Connecticut, in its earlier regimes where the play was almost invariably placed during some time and in some geographical location totally foreign both to the spirit and to the letter of the work. You remember these: *Measure for Measure* in nineteenth century Vienna, *Twelfth Night* in Brighton during the Napoleonic wars, *Much Ado About Nothing* in Spanish Texas during the time of the Alamo, and so on. When an interior idea accompanied these exterior trappings and justified them, as in the very controversial Guthrie production of *Troilus and Cressida* which analogized the corruption of the Trojans through images from turn-of-the-century Europe, then I thought such an approach became acceptable and coherent. But it was rare, indeed, when the jollying techniques illuminated plot, theme, or characters in the slightest way. They were simply "outsides."

A more recent approach to modernizing Shakespeare was that of the improvisational performing groups, who generally improvised their own scenes and characters on the basis of the momentary psychic or political needs of the company members. This is the kind of classical production associated with Richard Schechner's group, with the Living Theatre, and with some of the early Shakespeare productions of Joe Papp, beginning, I suspect, with his own initial production at the Public Theatre of *Hamlet*. The impulse behind that particular evening was courageous enough to rescue the play from the seminar room, to withdraw it from history, to obliterate our knowledge about it, and to obliterate the memory of all those beautifully spoken, handsomely costumed productions that stand like a wall between us and the immediate experience of the play and the action. But, while I respected the bravery of this kind of attempt and still do and many of the attempts that followed, mere irreverence is not enough to sustain the evening because even absurdity has to be organized toward some recognizable point. The trouble with these Shakespeare productions, in my opinion, was that they contained too much of the spirit of the time and not enough of the mind of the time.

While the self-expression of the actors and directors substituted for the intentions of the author, they always bordered dangerously on self-indulgence.

Now, it's time to disclose my own particular bias, which I've not been concealing very effectively, for Shakespeare productions that function as poetic metaphors, metaphors that are keys that help us to open and enter the heart of a play. My objection to historical or traditional or academic Shakespeare, Margaret Webster Shakespeare, whatever you may call it, is that it reduces the great plays to conventionalities, lulling us with the familiar and creating studied artificialities, instead of those experiences—as if we're just experiencing the play for the first time. Another of my biases, as you may have gleaned, is that I think there is no sin worse in the theatre than boredom. One is willing almost to countenance anything other than to be bored in the theatre. It's our great illness.

But I have an objection, too, to radical Shakespeare whenever it threatens to substitute another form of externality for the significant heart of the theme and of the action. It has been said of Shakespeare—it's almost a cliche now—that he was not of an age, but for all time. It is the job of modern producers, I believe, to discover as selflessly as possible precisely how to preserve both the agelessness and the contemporaneity of every Shakespeare play.

To give some examples close to home, no matter how stumbling they may be, I would like to mention how we tried at Yale to investigate from time to time the problems of modern Shakespeare production, not to mention production of the classics as a whole. There, we actively encouraged our directing students, always to the outrage of the acting department, that in addition to the new plays they did (and by then the acting and directing departments had become amalgamated, so the outrage was internal), to develop a classical production according to a concept that they found meaningful to the play and to themselves, and that they be prepared to expose this concept to the rest of the class to debate, to argument, before they even began to evolve the production. The concept had then, of course, to be realized visually, through the scenery with the designers, and with the actors. But whatever the outcome in actual production, the habit of finding a metaphor for the play that expresses something meaningful to all those concerned with it, as well as for the audiences, was being instilled at a very early stage.

In our own professional company, the Yale Repertory Theatre, this process was extended further, so that no production was ever chosen simply because an actor wanted to play that role—it's not enough reason for putting on a play. But rather because the production as a whole will make some poetic, not didactic but poetic, metaphoric, complicated statement to the audience.

My own production of *Macbeth*, for example, was an attempt to adapt that play to a world conditioned by the space age and by such movies as *2001*, which had now entered our consciousness and was revolving around as part of our world. Finding a new function for the three weird sisters was inspired by Banquo's line when he first encounters them: "What are these so withered and so wild in their attire that look not like the inhabitants of the earth and yet are on it?" Well, it was my contention in production that the witches were not the inhabitants of the earth, but rather visitors from another world who had materialized on earth in our midst at some primitive time in our history in order to change the line of succession of Scotland consciously through Macbeth and, by that change, to alter human history, for what purposes we don't know.

This fanciful idea I hope did not obscure our concentration on the internal functions of the drama, which I hope remained solid, substantial. But it did help us to find solutions for certain problems of the play: the identity of that mysterious third murderer who now became one of the space creatures—one of the sisters who had the capacity to materialize in human form, saving Banquo's son from the other two murderers so that he might accede to the throne at some future date. Similarly, we effected an economy through the concept by having Duncan and the porter played by the same character. We had King Duncan come back on stage after his murder in the form of a porter, who is now in some kind of hell, obviously, answering the knocking at the gate, resurrected by the weird creatures now as their controlled thing to do their bidding. The masque of

Fig. 1. The Critic Scans Shakespeare. *Macbeth* in a 1971 production at the Yale Repertory Theatre, directed by

kings which Macbeth is shown at the end thus became a filmed montage of kings all played by the same actor—Banquo, which you can do in film—wearing the royal robes from eight different figures from primitive times right down to the modern period. The visual realization of the aim of these creatures to alter Scottish history and, by so doing, of course, to affect English history, because James IV is to become James I of England, will lead to our own time.

I hope the idea for this was not just an expression of my own passion for science fiction or a jollying-up translation into a different environment, but rather that it grew out of the conviction that *Macbeth* is about time, ultimately—about its passing, about its inevitability, about its uncontrollability: "Tomorrow, and tomorrow, and tomorrow. . . ." We set the play in the most primitive period possible, when men wore skins and ate their meat raw, against a background very much like Stonehenge, with three huge dolmens—the home of the creatures—where they materialize as if they were space ships. They materialized in projections. The idea was stolen from Arthur Clarke's beautiful book, *Childhood's End*—an idea that primitive men were once visited by intelligent extra-terrestrial creatures long, long ago, who then vacated the earth after having worked their will on us, leaving us with myths which were memories of their visit. And my notion: one of these myths was Macbeth.

For various reasons, most of this was not clear in the production—mostly technical reasons. The idea was really too complicated to be realized through our equipment, which was limited. I have occasionally longed, in my weaker moments, for the kind of technology that you see at Disney World, where Disney has developed, in his haunted-house exhibit, three-dimensional transparent images which are projected right before your eyes—dancing, drinking, carousing in a room full of ghosts. Three-dimensional ghosts! Imagine what that would be like on stage. But it's also one's hindsight, since, if a concept needs a lot of technology to realize, it's probably not worth doing.

In a production of *The Tempest*, directed by Moni Yakim and Alvin Epstein, we tried to amalgamate the timelessness and contemporaneity of Shakespeare by grafting on the text the music Purcell had written for the opera of the play some 70 years later. It worked. Thus, the music became an extension of Prospero's magic, as well as being very beautiful in itself, and the entire work took on the stately and statuesque quality of a masque. Instead of one Ariel, we had seven, both male and female, led by the beautiful Carmen de Lavallade, dressed in an elastic gauze-like fabric that looked—when the Ariels were around Prospero's feet—as if they were mists swirling around him. The gauze functioned as an imprisoning fabric for those graceful sprites, thus leaving them both immobilized by their costumes, as Ariel is imprisoned until she is set free; yet, because of their number, Ariel is capable of being here, there, and everywhere all at once. At the end, when Prospero does set Ariel free, de Lavallade, high up on the stage, emerged naked from her costume like a chrysalis from a cocoon, as the orchestra played the lovely concluding strains of the opera.

In another vein, we did a version of *Hamlet* in our production of *Watergate Classics*, a satirical review which attempted to turn the "no more masterpieces" idea to political purposes; in this case, demonstrating how such works as *Oedipus*, *Waiting for Godot*, *Krapp's Last Tape*, *Iphigenia in Aulis*, and others contain material which prophesies and illuminates and works ironically in relation to our presidential dilemmas. This particular *Hamlet*, written by Jeremy Geidt and Jonathan Marks and retitled *Samlet*, cast Sam Ervin in the part of the prince trying desperately to revenge himself on King Claudius with a gavel. Haldeman and Erlichman are Rosencrantz and Guildenstern, obviously continually being confused with one another. John Mitchell now becomes the king's chief councilor, Felonius, giving larcenous advice to his protege, John Dean, who is Laertes. A trio of the players, including John Wayne, Sammy Davis, Jr., and Frank Sinatra, enact the death of Spirago in order to catch the conscience of the king. Meanwhile, the ghost of Uncle Sam hovers in the background crying for revenge and, after the king has triumphed over everybody including Sam Ervin—inept and absented-minded at the end—the ghost of Uncle Sam turns to the audience and says, "Remember me." Now, of course, this is a review sketch which can hardly be put forward seriously as a production of *Hamlet* but it embodies, nevertheless, the idea that Shakespeare is a vast storehouse which can be raided for virtually any purpose and somehow that storehouse remains full.

I would like to close with the thought, in spite of my own strictures on the kinds of production I don't like, that we try to develop more toleration as theatre people in regard to Shakespeare experimentation, even when it goes awry. I'm not suggesting we lower our standards, nor am I taking back my own criticism of certain approaches to Shakespeare production in the expectation that it is going to be something definitive. Treat it rather less as a total recreation of the work. That is impossible because we know too much about the work, and there is too much controversy about each work to be definitive. Treat such productions as intelligent directorial essays on the plays. Changing Shakespeare is not the same thing as desecrating a painting. If an artwork is permanently damaged—if you put a moustache on Mona Lisa—a dramatic work continues to exist, regardless of what you do to it. As a text, as a platonic idea, it's still there.

The theatre should be a place of dialogue, where each production of a play inspires enough excitement and enough controversy, even in opposition, to engender another production of that play in reply. It is this continuing dialogue that keeps masterpieces alive on the stage, just as the dialogue among Shakespearean critics, which is full of controversy, keeps these plays alive, partly on the page. In short, I would like to see an answer now to Peter Brook's radical approach to *A Midsummer Night's Dream*: one, say, that rescued that play from acrobatics and returned it to romance. Or, I'd like to see a reply to his *King Lear*, which reminded us that this action took place within a thundering universe where the protagonist was almost as mighty as the storm he was defying. This is not to speak in disparagement of those two fine Brook productions, but rather in respect to them. It is as a stimulus to thought and feeling that productions have their true success, and not simply as objects of our praise or blame, our veneration or attack.

I must say that what I miss most in American theatre today is a critical atmosphere and an audience atmosphere in which productions are interpreted for what they are trying to say. It's like pulling teeth to get any critic to do this. Maybe they are able, but they don't do it. To find out what the production is trying to say, and to judge it on the basis of whether it said that effectively, or whether it's worth saying it that way, rather than treat them as objects either of excessive blame or excessive praise—hits or flops. This adds nothing to our experience except our capacity to say we saw it, or we didn't see it, or we left it alone, or what have you. We need this atmosphere in which critics and audience discuss the production, trade ideas about the production, rather than simply trading opinions about the production. Opinions are a dime a dozen. This is perhaps the same kind of atmosphere in which we'll begin to find some provocative productions formulated. For it is in the context of such theatrical intelligence and imagination, rare as it is, that Shakespeare shows us he is not just for an age, but for all time.

*   *   *

THE ROYAL SHAKESPEARE *RICHARD II*

Anne Righter Barton
Richard Pasco
Ian Richardson
Glenn Loney, Moderator

Surely mediocrity and boredom are two of the theatre's chief enemies? The production of Richard II, *directed by John Barton, which the Royal Shakespeare brought to America, avoided both, but its unusual visual aspects and its emphatically urged intellectual concepts did not make it universally admired. Partisans and foes were sharply divided, as they had been earlier over the RSC's Peter Brook* Midsummer Night's Dream, *though for rather different reasons.*

In this discussion, Anne Righter Barton, standing in for her husband, John Barton, explains his approach to the drama, at the same time acting in her capacity as a critic and Shakespeare expert to take issue with some aspects of the production. Ian Richardson and Richard Pasco, who alternated the roles of Richard II and Bolingbroke for the RSC, offer their own reactions to Barton's vision and discuss the experiences and skills they brought to their interpretations. The interaction of playing both classics and modern dramas in the Royal Shakespeare's Stratford and London homes is also explored.

Anne Righter Barton is currently a Fellow of New College, Oxford, and has been a professor of English literature at Bedford College, University of London. Her book, Shakespeare and the Idea of the Play, *is regarded as an important, authoritative study. She has contributed introductions for all the comedies in the Riverside Press's edition of Shakespeare's plays.*

Richard Pasco's many roles for the Royal Shakespeare have included not only Shakespearean ones but also characters in dramas by such a diverse group of playwrights as T. S. Eliot, Maxim Gorky, Bernard Shaw, John Webster, and John Arden. He also played Jimmy Porter, in John Osborne's Look Back in Anger, *as well as Cardinal Richelieu on television.*

Ian Richardson, who took leave of the RSC to star in the Broadway revival of My Fair Lady, *created more than thirty roles for the Royal Shakespeare. An awkward first for Richardson was a dividend of playing Marat in Peter Weiss's* Marat/Sade: *he was the first actor to appear nude on a Broadway stage.*

The moderator, Glenn Loney, is a professor of theatre at Brooklyn College and at the Graduate Center of the City of New York.

* * *

BARTON:

I should begin by saying that although I am John Barton's wife, and I'm standing in for him on this panel, my voice is emphatically not to be identified with his. I don't consider it to be my wifely duty to agree with or even to like all of my husband's productions. In saying this, I would also like to add that I do not, in any sense, either expect him to admire or even to use in the theatre the ideas and the theories about Shakespeare's plays that I develop in my own critical articles and books.

We do talk together a great deal about the plays that we're working on. We argue, we criticize, and very often we agree to disagree. But we do constantly try out our interpretations on each other and sometimes we adopt and build on one another's ideas. For me, this is marvelous when it happens. I think that it's true for most academics who work on Shakespeare, or indeed on drama in any form, without themselves having any practical connection with the theatre—we feel a certain sense of guilt and unease. I think it's all too easy for us to lose sight of the essential factor: the extra dimension of the stage. We begin to talk about the play as though it were a novel or a non-dramatic poem. When one's critical ideas, when an insight about a scene or character does prove to be something that can be made to work on the stage, it's immensely reassuring. One begins to feel that one is no longer working in a vacuum, that there may be something to the idea after all.

If John had been able to be here, almost certainly he'd say that he could not speak about his conception of *Richard II.* I think he'd say that what he had to communicate he'd expressed, or tried to express, in the production itself. That it may have got across to the audience, or it may not, but that basically it had to stand or fall as a theatrical experience. He'd add, too, that he wasn't himself satisfied with the production because he is never satisfied with any production he does. He'd say, I think, that there are a number of moments in it that require reassessment. And he'd agree with Mr. Brustein who has said that there is no such thing as a definitive production of any play by William Shakespeare and also that there's no such animal as a production that is finished; one that's settled and definite, correct and fully achieved. If a production is alive, it's constantly changing; it's growing, modifying and correcting itself, much as a living organism does.

I think I'd like to introduce another parenthesis here. I'd say that one of the great privileges of being a scholar married to a theatre director is the opportunity to watch the development of a single production over a span of time, to be able to go back and see it over and over again. If you see a production six or seven times, as I have had the chance now to do over a period of months, you come, I think, to understand how difficult and how limiting it is to try to make a judgment—any overall assessment—on the basis of a single performance. By the way, you understand how diabolically difficult it is to be a good drama critic. Performances simply vary enormously from night to night, and, of course, so do audiences. So, too, does one's own state of mind, one's capacity on a given occasion to respond to or to take from the experience being offered on the stage. I, myself, used to be far more arrogant, far more sure about my own ability to evaluate and judge a performance seen once than I am now.

What I want to do briefly now is to talk about the style and some of the methods that are being employed in the production of *Richard II*. I underline again that what I am going to say is not necessarily what John Barton would say.

Richard II is a very great play, and it's a play that seems to me still meaningful for us now. But it's not an easy play: it's not easy for the actors; it's not easy for directors, and certainly it is not easy for a modern audience. I think that of all Shakespeare's English history plays, it's certainly the most relentlessly Elizabethan. What I want to do, then, is to state what seem to me to be the three major problems that any director faces in staging this play, and then to talk a bit about the way in which John Barton tried to solve them.

In the first place, this is a play which concentrates, or is focussed on, a difficult, remote idea of sacramental kingship. This is an idea which was never native in America and which is pretty remote in England in the present day. Now, as a working method, John customarily reads a great deal of critical material before he goes into rehearsal. He steeps himself in the background of the play, but when he gets into the rehearsal stage, he stops. He tries as much as possible to forget the critical work he's been reading, or at least to let it sink down to a kind of subliminal level. Simply, what he tries to do in rehearsal is to build the production as a cooperative effort between actors and director—an effort in which the actors themselves collaborate in building the final structure.

This production of *Richard*, however, is slightly different from any other production that John has done, in the sense that it is a production that does have a single book behind it as a germinating idea. As it happens, it's not a book of literary criticism at all. It's a book written by the American historian, Ernst Kantorowicz, at Princeton, and it's entitled *The King's Two Bodies*. It's a study of the Elizabethan doctrine of kingship—the ideas about the king which were in the air the Elizabethans breathed. And the ideas which Shakespeare himself, as well as a number of his fellow dramatists, employed in writing plays about English kings. The Kantorowicz idea which he's gleaned from a number of sources—parliamentary papers, letters and documents, law reports—is a complicated one, but I want to at least try to summarize it because I think it helps to explain what is going on in the production.

Elizabethans believed that the king had two selves or two natures or bodies. One of these bodies was like the one that all of us have: an individual self, subject to death, subject to time, subject to passions, to errors and mistakes. But the king was also invested with, at the moment of coronation, a second body—a body-politic. This body, in which the king is incorporated with his land and his people—things which cannot, by their nature, die—this body is immortal and flawless. It is not subject to errors, to passion, to mistakes. I think you can see how even some of our ordinary usages preserve this idea: the cry, "the king is dead, long live the king," is a way of talking about the transference of the king's body-politic from one body natural to another. The royal "we" is another way of expressing this idea—the use of the first person plural rather than the singular.

The whole idea is a parallel with the incarnation of Christ, another figure who possessed two bodies: who was both human and divine, a god-man. But the difficulty arises from the fact that with Christ this incarnation is perfect; it's something that happens, not within finite time, but within eternity. This is not true with the king. The king is a man within whose hollow crown death sits. And when he's divorced from his body-politic by death, there will be no resurrection on the third day.

There's also another problem: the coronation, the moment of anointing, is supposed to weld his two bodies together, but this marriage may not be, and indeed, usually is not perfect. Often there is incompatibility between the king's body-politic and his body-natural; between the kind of person he is, the individual he is, and the role that he's asked to play. The mask may slip from his face and may reveal, beneath the mask of kingship, an individuality, a personality at odds with it. I think this is very much what one sees in the opening scenes of *Richard II*. The mask is continually slipping from Richard's face: when he jests callously about Gaunt's death ("Pray God we may make haste and come too late"); when he seizes Hereford's movables and goods, and when he's led by flatterers. This is an individuality at variance and at odds with the king's body-politic. Of course, it doesn't go unnoticed as the play progresses. The idea of divorcing the king's body-natural from his body-politic suggests itself to Northumberland and others, and, of course, this is what they proceed to do. I think that when Richard compares himself with Christ, as he does on a number of occasions later in the play, this is not a bit of self-flattery—not a bit of fatuous comparison. He is, in fact, making a very precise analogy between his own twin natures and the twin natures of Jesus.

After the deposition, however, Richard finds himself in an intolerable position. He's neither a king nor is he a private individual. "Not all the water in the rude, rough sea can wash the balm off from an anointed king." He remains a king, and yet, Henry IV has replaced him. What then is Richard? The man one sees in the second half of the play is a man who has no name, no title: "No, not that name was given me at the font." A man who is engaged in a desperate struggle for identity, grappling between the halves of a sundered self, a self that was once double and incorporate. This position is obviously a tragic position, and, I think, it's one that Shakespeare explores brilliantly in the play. Other Elizabethan dramatists dealing with deposed kings had done something like this. What I think is unique about *Richard II* is that Shakespeare saw that not only Richard's position was tragic, but that the position of the man who replaced him, Henry Bolingbroke, is tragic as well.

When Richard holds the crown and asks Bolingbroke to seize the other side of it and talks about the two buckets in the well—the one down and filled with tears and the other empty and flaunting triumphantly in the air, in a sense, this is the central image of the play. The bucket down and full of tears is Richard; the bucket on top of things is Henry IV, and yet the image is double-edged, because what goes up must come down. The two buckets are, in effect, engaged in a parallel action. Their position is ultimately the same. This is very much a point that the production is trying to stress. It also says something about why John Barton decided to have the two actors learn both roles—to have two actors alternate Richard and Bolingbroke. I think it's a way of underscoring the idea that although these two men as individuals are intensely different (they're different in attitudes towards words, towards personal relationships—they are different people), nonetheless they are united by the fact of kingship. The burden they bear is the same—there is an affinity between them. They share something with each other that they share with no one else in the play.

I talked a bit about the parallel between the double natures of the king and the double natures of Christ. There is another parallel that I want to mention briefly because I think it's important: the parallel which links the double nature of the king with the double nature of one of the humblest of his subjects, the actor. After all, the actor, too, is a man who has a twin self. There is a difference between Laurence Olivier as Laurence Olivier and a double-natured being who is Laurence Olivier temporarily incarnate in the part of Othello. But I point out that, in fact, we measure the success of an actor by the extent to which he is able to submerge his private individuality within that of the role he plays. If we remain aware all the time that this is Laurence Olivier on the stage, something is wrong with the performance. What one wants is the whole, the sense of the twin natures united and indivisible. In a sense, the end of the performance is a little like the king's death. Laurence Olivier once again becomes a single-natured individual. But something worse than this can happen.

A performance can be broken up by violence or because the actor in some way is inadequate to fulfill his role, and this is a kind of analogy to the deposition of the king. What I'd like to stress is the way that this parallel haunts the play of *Richard II.* Theatrical imagery follows Richard throughout. Ironically, it also follows Bolingbroke. You remember when York describes the two men riding into London together, he describes them as two actors; Henry IV is the well-graced actor, the man people cheer. Richard, riding behind him, is the man upon whose head rubbish is thrown. Both of them are seen in terms of the stage. I think this is why the production has chosen to stress, in the first half of the play, the theatricality with which Richard plays his part as King; because kingship is a part as Queen Elizabeth herself knew. She once said the princes were like actors—they stand on a stage in sight of all the world.

This idea that I've been talking about—the king's two bodies—may seem remote and rather abstruse. It's not so remote that we can't translate it into an analogy fitting for our own time. Although I think it's without the overtones of the mystical, nonetheless, we're all too familiar with the way in which an individual may behave or reveal a nature at odds with the high office which he embodies, with which he has been entrusted. When this happens in real political life now, as in *Richard II*, trouble is almost certain to ensue.

Let me pass now to the second problem of the play which is its verbal style. As it happens, this is the only play by Shakespeare which contains not a single line of prose. It also has almost no comedy. It's true that York makes us smile a bit, but I think we scarcely roll about in the aisles at York's doddering and fumbling movements.

More important is the fact that it's an oddly homogeneous play—one in which everyone speaks the same verse, stylized, intensely formal. This applies even to characters like the groom or the gardeners—people who belong to the lower classes, and there are very few of them in the play. There's a sense in which the very articulateness of all these people, the way in which they are constantly anatomizing their emotions and their griefs, is something alien to us now. There is an adage which says, "He that can say exactly how he burns is in no great fire." But in this play, people say all the time precisely how they burn: whether it's the queen in her garden, King Richard at Flint castle, or old Gaunt playing grimly and punning on his name in the moments before he dies. We may find this more alien than a play like *King Lear* where characters are constantly aware that they have no words to express their experience, that language breaks before the enormity of events. The result in *Richard II* is that the verse in its imagery becomes a character in the play, and it must be made to tell in the production.

This particular production has tried to help its audiences—audiences which are not, and cannot be, as acute as Elizabethan audiences about picking up verbal links, patterns of imagery, although the patterns of imagery in this play explain and express its structure. Simply, there are a number of key words, almost talismanic words, in this play: words like earth, crown, blood, snow, or horses. I know that the hobby-horses in this particular production have been criticized and I think myself that we see too much of them. I'd be much happier if they went from at least two of the scenes, but I'd emphasize that they're emphatically not a theatrical gimmick nor do they represent any kind of false attempt at realism. I think we see that in the modulation that one gets from the red and blue, all-sugar-candy horses of the tournament scene at Coventry—horses which express and reflect the chivalric, medieval, already anachronistic court of King Richard—to the great, black, sinister horses on which Henry IV's henchmen ride, horses that seem to come from some Tolkien land of Mordor, and are contrasted in their turn with the white unicorn upon which Richard returns from Ireland—an already extinct, if beautiful beast. This modulates down at the end to the wooden figure, rudely carved, of roan Barbary which is brought to Richard in his prison.

This is important because it translates into visual terms something that is embodied in the language of the play, something about its structure that we might otherwise have missed. And so, I think, is the bowl of earth on the forestage, the snowman, the golden regalia of kingship, the skull, and the use of masks. These are all visual equivalents to and reinforcements of things buried in the language of the tragedy which are less available to us, unaccustomed as we are to picking up verbal connections of the kind that Elizabethans were good at.

The third and final problem has to do with the difference between the Elizabethan passion for English history and their knowledge of it, and our own relative ignorance and disinterest. Any director is going to find the first scenes of *Richard II* positively hellish. Why should Edward have been so inconsiderate to have had seven sons that we can't conceivably get straight in that first scene? Unless, of course, we've been dutiful and read the program notes. I think it's enormously difficult to straighten out those seven sons, let alone the relationship existing between their descendants before us on the stage. I think also there's a great problem over the death of Humphrey, Duke of Gloucester, constantly talked about and yet never made explicit for us. Who is right: Mowbray or Bolingbroke? Who did kill the Duke of Gloucester, and why is there such a fuss being made about it? Of course, the one important fact is that it was Richard himself who was at least

largely responsible for the death of his uncle. It's a fact that
Elizabethans didn't need to be told—they knew it. But, unless
you listen to the play with enormous care, it's a fact you're likely
to miss.

There's a similar problem about the end of the play:
Shakespeare's audience would have known what happened next
in the story; they would have known that all of Carlisle's
prophecy of doom and disaster was going to come true; they
would have known the truth of Richard's own prediction that
Northumberland would prove a traitor, that the man who made
a king would know how to pull him down again. They knew that
Henry's whole succeeding reign would be one of rebellion and
civil war, and that his dynasty would ultimately be swept away
from a throne it had no right to possess. This knowledge of the
future is one that's meant to color the way we respond to the
whole last act of the play. When Henry talks about making a
voyage to the Holy Land, "To wash this blood off from my
guilty hand," in the last line of the play, Elizabethans would
have known that he never made that journey because he spent
the remainder of his reign fighting down rebellion, and that he
finally died ironically in a chamber called Jerusalem, in
England.

But what do you do with an audience which largely lacks this
kind of knowledge? I suppose the most really controversial part
of this production is bound up with John Barton's attempt to
solve this problem, by which I mean the insertion of certain
lines taken from the second part of *Henry IV*—lines which are
inserted in the last movement of *Richard II*. In these lines we see
the King Henry who really belongs to a later time, to a later
play: a tragic, sleepless man already experiencing the torment
and the burden of kingship, and, of course, in this production, a
man who goes himself—following some irrational impulse—to
visit the imprisoned Richard at Pomfret castle in the disguise of
a groom. He goes to attempt there some kind of silent
communication, some rapprochement with the man he now
sees as a fellow victim, a man destroyed, like himself, by the
crown.

But these are incontrovertible changes to the play that
Shakespeare wrote, and I am not prepared to defend them.

Personally, I would rather that the lines from the second part of *Henry IV* were not there. I would rather that the groom was a groom and not Bolingbroke in disguise. They seem to me to be effects that are gained at the cost of other effects which are more germane to this particular play, to its shape and structure. But I would defend their seriousness of purpose, the intention to elucidate and make clear to an audience an idea which is present in the text, and which for a modern audience needs a kind of pointing up that it did not need for Elizabethans.

I want to end by saying how much I agree with what Robert Brustein has said about the chimera—the false ideal of a traditional or "straight" Shakespeare. Every age reads and interprets the plays from its own vantage point in time. This is inevitable, and it seems right. There can be no such thing as a definitive production of a play by Shakespeare. And I would also argue that a production cannot be any good unless it is, in some measure, controversial. The only production which every member of an audience will go away liking equally, will be able to find no fault in, is a production in which the entire audience was sound asleep. We ought not to go to the theatre to have our prejudices and preconceptions confirmed. We go to find out truths about the plays and also about ourselves which we did not know about, which we would not have found out without this experience. With an author like Shakespeare, the number of these truths is seemingly inexhaustible. Some of you will have liked the production of *Richard II;* some of you will not. It doesn't really matter. What matters is that the production should, as it has already, take its place in what Dean Brustein has described as "that continuing dialogue between productions of a given play, reaction and response, acceptance and modification," that dialogue which is such an exciting and vital part of the modern theatre.

LONEY:

I think that John Barton would be very pleased had he been in the wings and been able to hear this! Now, I'd like to ask our actors to tell us how they worked in the rehearsal period with these various images. Richard Pasco and Ian Richardson alternate in the roles of Bolingbroke and Richard. I told Ian that

I had the good fortune to see the play in Stratford, and I saw him as Richard. Then on opening night in Brooklyn I again saw him as Richard. He said, "You're fired! I adjure you: you must come and see it on an evening when Richard is playing Richard!" Could we begin by asking Richard Pasco to tell us about rehearsals and how he worked with Ian?

PASCO:

I must say this before I say anything else; it is very difficult to analyze my own rehearsal processes and my own approach to a part because I largely work through my instincts. I am an actor who likes being directed. There are many actors who object to being told what to do by a director, but I place myself—I hope mostly with confidence—in the hands of my director and I say, "Please show me and tell me." I am privileged to work with John Barton, because I think he is one of our very finest directors ever. I have been in the theatre since I was sixteen, and I have learned more through working in four or five productions with John Barton during my time at the Royal Shakespeare Company than I have in my entire professional career. Having said that, I would like to say that John and I first worked—alas, without Ian—on what I can only describe to you as a miniature production of *Richard II*. It was a production which was done in 1970 for the Theatre-Go-Round section of our company. That is part of the RSC's work, to take the plays of Shakespeare and recital programs to theatreless towns in England, and sometimes abroad, to university campuses and so on. We were asked by our artistic director to do a production of *Richard II* for this purpose.

John was extremely excited and, for some time, had been wanting to do a production of *Richard II*. I was fortunate enough to be the actor selected to play the part. So, in this production, we had a cast of only twelve or fourteen people. There was a lot of doubling, trebling, even quadrupling of parts with much hurried changing of wigs, beards, and make-up behind screens on the stage. In this production, John first began to be able to put into practice the many ideas that he had long toyed with in the privacy of his study. Of course, Richard II is a part, perhaps like Hamlet and King Lear, that every actor wants an opportunity to play at some time—if he has been given by God a reasonable enough approach to looking like a king.

So, before we came to this production, John and I had that initial little "canter" through the play together. When we were given the go-ahead to do a major production, John had, I think, this absolutely brilliant idea of the doubling of Richard and Bolingbroke. He rang me up, as is his wont, sometime around one a.m. one morning. He said, "I have the most extraordinary idea which I want to put to you. I want to invite Ian Richardson to double the part with you—what do you think?" Then he went on and gave his reasons as Mrs. Barton has explained to you far better than I could ever do.

So, when Ian and I then met, we had never worked together before. We had admired one another's work in all media from a distance but we had never had the opportunity to work together. We knew that, professionally speaking, we were sticking our necks right out. We knew that we were going to be perhaps like two race horses put side by side and told, "You win or you lose— you're better, or you're not so good." Fortunately, this didn't happen. The end product of all this time and brain-washing was that the critics, on the whole, and our audiences acknowledged our production and our performances as an entity. I have found it, and I think Ian has found it, one of the most rewarding experiences of our careers.

We started rehearsing with Ian—having known that I had played Richard II—coming to the first rehearsal knowing his lines as Richard, which I think is a very remarkable thing to do.

RICHARDSON:

Actually, Dick, if I can pop in there . . . You see, what happened was that Barton said to me, "Look, why don't you . . ." And I said, "No," and he said, "Oh, come on, have lunch," and I still said, "No." Then Dick Pasco was invited to an occasion in John Barton's study, and by some marvelous means the telephone rang, and John had to leave the room. Sometimes, you know, in our studys in England we don't have the telephone there . . . Actually, John does have the telephone there, but for some reason, he had to leave the room. While he left the room, Dick Pasco said to me, "Now, come on, come on, do it." And I did it.

Frankly, it was the most marvelous thing that had ever happened, but I was terribly aware and acutely conscious that he had played it before. Therefore, there was a lot of the groundwork, and he knew the street map, if you know what I mean. He knew where the stop-lights were; he knew the neighborhood very well, and I was a total and complete stranger. What I did was have a long series of sessions with John Barton in which he outlined to me his interpretation. Then he suggested that I should go away with the interpretation very much in the forefront of my mind and memorize every single word that the king says. Well, this I did.

I arrived at the first day of rehearsal terribly tentative, as you can appreciate. As Dick has told you, we hadn't worked together before, although we knew and admired each other. John suggested that Dick should get up there and recreate move-for- move, business-for-business, exchange-and-inflection for exchange-and-inflection exactly what he had done. I was invited to sit there and decide whether I wanted to go along with it or not. We thought that this was going to be a disastrous kind of set-up. But, in fact, the most marvelous, miraculous thing occurred: I opened my big mouth and said, "I hate what that scene is about there," and Dick said, "Why?" And we stopped. What looked as though initially was going to be a tentative, non-productive relationship became a really working relationship in the most exciting form.

We haven't made differentiations in our performances just for the sake of doing it. The differences have come about because Richard Pasco has gone through a series of life-experiences which, in many respects, are similar to mine, but in others are totally different. After all, when we come to perform parts, we call upon experience to feed the reality and bring the breath of life to any part that we play. Inevitably, one line—a reference to a tree—will have a certain imagery response in a kaleidoscopic collection of photographs in Dick's imagination as he says it. To me the tree is simply a thing where my dog lifts his leg. Inevitably, the way my reference to a tree comes out will be different. These differences occur; they are inevitable, and they are what make theatre magic and my relationship with

Pasco and Barton one of the most exciting experiences I've had as a professional actor.

PASCO:

I can only say that I agree with him. I mean that!

LONEY:

Might I ask you, because you have both acted modern plays in the framework of the Royal Shakespeare program: how does this, in your feeling, feed back into playing at Stratford in Shakespeare?

PASCO:

I think that it's extremely helpful because I feel that the text, Text (capital T), of any play, whether it is Gorky, T. S. Eliot, Shakespeare, or whatever it may be, is the Bible for us working in the Royal Shakespeare Company. This is the thing that we constantly go back to when we get tied up in knots in rehearsal and in the privacy of our own work. We go back to the text when we are trying to make sense of scenes and situations, exploring character, and we think: why does he do this or think that or say this? Why does he move here or there? What are his relationships? All the actors' problems in the rehearsal process inevitably must come back to the text. I find that with the ability to be able to work in both modern plays or non-Shakespearean plays, this somehow feeds one's response to coming back to the Shakespearean text.

RICHARDSON:

I would agree with that completely. However, I would like to add a rejoinder, and it's simply this: you must treat Shakespeare, from an actor's point of view, with healthy disdain.

PASCO:

Hear, hear!

RICHARDSON:

Because, if you enter a choir-boy-filled cathedral atmosphere with Shakespeare, you are going to strangle him out of existence. The only thing that we have to remember is that if you open up a modern play, you will find that modern authors will say—in italics—"Pause, he looks troubled," or—in italics— "disdainfully." In other words, the playwright indicates your performance in italics. Shakespeare does not. He indicates your performance in the structure of his text. You'll find that, whereas a modern author would heavily underline a word that had to be stressed, you'll find that word at the end of the poetic structural line as indicated by Shakespeare. Now, the curse of our English language which we share, Briton and American, the curse is the downward inflection. In order to make ourselves fundamentally strong when making a statement, we always come down. The ball on the tennis court must come down. The cricket field is the same. In every respect we try to get things down, and the language has gone along with it.

A social stigma of disgrace can be that we have an over-elaborate vocabulary. I have found this: people have looked at me as though I am some kind of nut because I am capable of stringing four or five words—verbs, nouns, and adjectives— together. We have to realize when we approach Shakespeare that this was not a problem at that time. Consequently, we have to learn a new habit. It's not really so difficult; it's just that instead of going down, we have to keep going up! Let me show you what I mean. Oberon, in *A Midsummer Night's Dream*; here's the downward inflection:

    I know a bank where on the wild
                thyme
                      blows,
    Where oxlips and the nodding
                violet
                    grows,
    Quite over-canopied with
              luscious
                woodbine,

With sweet musk-roses, and
                        with
                        eglantine.
Well, thank you and good night! Now we must learn the habit of
just lifting it:
                                blows,
                        thyme
I know a bank whereon the wild
                                grows,
                        violet
Where oxlips and the nodding
                                woodbine,
                        luscious
Quite over-canopied with
                                eglantine.
                        with
With sweet musk-roses, and
                                (Act II, Scene 1, 249–52)

LONEY:

Audience questions about Barton's *Richard II* seem to divide
themselves quite neatly into two groups: 1) What was wrong with
this abominable concept? and, 2) Why so many gimmicks? Let's
begin with the first group. This one asks, "How on earth can any
audience, whether American or not, grasp all these points that
Anne Barton so brilliantly brought out, making the performance
meaningful, if it sees the play before getting the explanation? I
saw the play and thought it was simply horrendous, but now, I
would really like to see the performance again."

BARTON:

I think that's one of the nicest things anyone's ever said to me.
All I can say is I hope you can see the performance again.

QUESTION:

How much were the actors in *Richard II*, and at the Royal
Shakespeare Company in general, involved in the creation of
the concept of the production and the specific stage business
used? Was the director the dominating, decision-making power?
Also, how much, if any, improvisation was used during
rehearsal? What rehearsal techniques were used?

PASCO:

I'm speaking personally here—I don't really know what
improvisation is. As an actor, it doesn't mean anything to me.
The director says to me, "you're a tree—improvise being a
tree." That doesn't do anything to me at all. To try to answer the
question: no, we didn't use improvisation, thank god, in
rehearsals of *Richard II*. I think the actor-director relationship is,
at its worst, a fight and a battle of wits. Today, maybe rightly or
wrongly, it is a director's theatre that we are working in and not
an actor's. It is a director's and a designer's theatre and not an
actor's theatre. But, when one is working with a director like
John Barton, then it is a totally different matter. It is not only
John's great theatrical flair, but also his academic background
which can help those of us not fortunate enough to have had
academic life and training. One can go to John and ask him
about these particular problems that come up in the play and in
rehearsal and trust him completely. An actor must trust his
director, and I do trust John.

We were involved completely in the concept. I mean, John
didn't keep us in the dark at all. He said, "I want to do this—can
you do it?" We would discuss it; we would put it into practice in
the rehearsal room, and if it worked, it worked. If it didn't work
for us actors, and John still wanted to do it, then we would
somehow meet one another half-way, and this is possible with a
director like Barton. It isn't possible with other directors. Maybe
Barton is lucky with his actors as well. But it is a uniting of
creative minds: the actors who have to go out there and do it;
the director who, on the first night, has his work done and all he
can do is either drink himself crazy in the bar, or stand in the
back of the circle and watch with his knees rattling. How much

were we involved in the creation and the concept of the production? Entirely! And the specific stage business used? Entirely. Was the director the dominating decision-making power? Well, in the final analysis, yes. The director must be the final word and the referee in the battle of rehearsal.

RICHARDSON:

Dick, may I just come in there? You see, it's simply this: the director has the overall conception. But the moment you are handed the play and there is the part that you are going to live with and try to interpret, inevitably, you must give that role more thought and weight of your reading-time than the director gives to the conception as a whole. Therefore, it's perfectly inevitable that you as the actor, with one role to perform, come each day to rehearsal with ideas and interpretative thoughts about that role, and possibly the response from the person who plays any particular scene with you. Now, it is not possible for the director to have this immediate insight, because his mind is not invited to channel itself in that direction.

What you find happens, and, thank god, it does with the Royal Shakespeare Company, is that the director will acknowledge overall interpretative control, but be perfectly sensible and sensitive to the fact that you may have certain moments that you wish to bring into focus at any given time— moments which may have escaped his notice in the overall conception. With Barton, with whom I have worked since 1960, I have found this particular working relationship a remarkably rewarding one. He is initially a scholar. He is a Cambridge don. You can have the best of both worlds because you can tap his brain without any danger of that brilliant mind losing sight of the inevitable theatricality of what has got to take place in the play. So, you've got it made—you couldn't go far wrong.

However, there are problems. Let's not try to kid you. John frequently gets on his high-horse about some intellectual pointing of a line, and you sound like some kind of a computer: you know, like that film *2001*, that delicious thing that used to say, "I'm going, I'm going." I remember John once asked us both to point out to the audience (I'm talking about Bolingbroke, now), the fact that when he leaves the stage, he's going to go away and come back a much wiser guy. For those of you who haven't seen the play, Bolingbroke is banished because he unfolds a dangerous situation, and the king has to get him out. But the king, because he is the cousin of Bolingbroke, doesn't dare risk more than six years—he gets him away. Now, John wanted us to say to the audience; "I'm going but I'm coming back, and when I do, you'll see exactly how I worked." The line is, "Now must I serve a long apprenticehood." It's simple—it's the statement. But, sometimes John will have us say, "Now...............must I serve a [Pasco joins in] LOOOOOOOOONG apprenticehood." Okay, let him say that with his lips. We get the point; we relish it and digest it, and we regurgitate it in our own way. He's the greatest interpreter of Shakespeare in the Western Hemisphere.

PASCO:

I think there were some other good questions in connection with this. "How does this production differ in rehearsal techniques from the earlier RSC productions of the *Wars of the Roses* and *Henry IV?* Presumably, the questioner means the major history cycle in 1964. I think Ian was in the company then?

RICHARDSON:

I was here in New York, playing at the Martin Beck in *Marat/Sade.*

PASCO:

Rehearsal techniques differ from generation to generation, year to year. We're all learning something all the time. I feel that I have learned a great deal about my performances of Richard II and Bolingbroke by simply being here in the United States. Audience reactions to our performances are totally different from the audience reactions that we have experienced in Stratford. Last night I was playing the king, and Ian was playing Bolingbroke, and I said to him, "On certain lines and words I've got laughs that I've never had before. What's wrong—what am I doing? Is my wig wrong, or something?" He said, "No, for god's sake, don't you understand it is the political implications of this play at this time [the Watergate scandals] which are white hot?"

Concerning the rehearsal period, we were rehearsing virtually two plays because we were both playing two roles. We were fortunate enough to have a rehearsal period of something like twelve weeks.

RICHARDSON:

Don't think it was twelve weeks just getting to one guy. It was six weeks getting to one guy and six weeks getting to another.

PASCO:

I should also bring in our colleagues in the company. Ian and I were only working on two major roles. Our colleagues, by that time, were also playing every night in as many as two other productions. So, they needed the time, as we did.

LONEY:

There are two questions here that rather go together: "Doesn't the concept of changing actors for the title role get lost for the vast majority of the audience, who will only attend one performance?" "Should there have been more advance notice of the necessity to go at least twice to really understand the concept of the production?" "How do you know beforehand who is playing what part?"

RICHARDSON:

Well, if you find out, let us know because we frequently don't know.

LONEY:

How does that work? Do you flip a coin?

RICHARDSON:

No! It should be there in the program. We arrive, and sometimes Dick thinks he's going to do the king, and I think that

I'm going to do the king, and we have to check out on the playbills at the front of the theatre to find out who actually is. But it's simple. We alternate. I did the benefit; Dick did it last night, which means I've got to do it tonight, and Dick will do it tomorrow at the matinee; I will do it in the evening, etc., etc.

PASCO:

Let me tell a story here. The entire company enters as a company of Shakespearean actors who are going to do a play, and we are all dressed in identical costumes. One line of characters enters stage left and walks straight down the stage. Another line enters from stage right, walks down stage, and then the two lines face another. If we are playing the king, we enter stage right; if we are playing Bolingbroke, we enter stage left. Before the curtain goes up, while the stage managers are preparing to let things happen, we congregate in the wings. One night, Ian and I found ourselves both stage right. I said, "It's me." He said, "It's not you; it's me," and I said, "It isn't; it's me." He had to send the stage manager to the front of the house to see who was doing it.

LONEY:

So, if you go to the production and you see Ian coming down on the left again, get up and leave. You can say, "Right, I have seen this production; I must come another evening."

RICHARDSON:

Let's put it another way. In England, there is a very strong group of people who are Pasco fans, and obviously, they are interested in seeing his performance. I'm happy to say that I have my little group, too, who might possibly be interested in seeing mine.

BARTON:

Because of the simplicity of the costumes, you two don't find yourselves in danger of the situation which I gather once happened in a production where Othello and Iago were doubling the roles. They happened to be two actors who, unlike

Ian and Dick, detested one another—they did not speak off the stage. Before the production, both of them met in the lavatory costumed as Othello. They said nothing, but five minutes later both appeared on the stage dressed as Iago.

LONEY:

Since we're on the topic of playing the role, there are several questions here that go naturally together: " How much research do you do on your own, and what do you look for in the main: historical facts, other interpretations, other actors, literary criticism, etc.?" "Was Richard's character based on the play or on historical fact?" And this is addressed specifically to Ian: "Where did you get your interpretation from?"

PASCO:

"How much research do you do on your own?" I don't want to go into a long thing again about the fact that I have not had an academic background, but I haven't, so just forget that. I was thrown out of school when I was fifteen, and I've been self-taught ever since. I have a very small, modest collection of books of criticism of performances by other actors. I go to these books, as I believe John Barton does, of course, in a totally different way. I try to find out as much about what Hazlitt, Coleridge, and others have written about the play. I also read accounts of other actors' performances in the past, going right back to Irving and Garrick and Kean. Of course, now we are talking about Shakespearean roles.

I read so that my box here [points to head] that is going to take in Richard or Bolingbroke is being filled up with certain facts, certain warnings, certain red triangles saying, "Watch this; watch that; be careful of this; do that; don't do this; remember this; remember that!" I have an amalgam in my head of various facts and ideas before I come to rehearsal. If it is possible, I always like to get the director on his own, over a lunch or dinner-table and talk to him. So I do that particular bit of work on my own.

Next: "What do you look for in the main: historical facts, other actors . . .?" I've answered that. We look for what is in the text—what Shakespeare has written. For all our theorizing and analysis, for all our probings, both private and public, we must eventually come back to the text. If there is a particular problem that seems totally insoluble during some part in rehearsal, simply going home that evening and sitting quietly, reading the scene very often solves it for me.

RICHARDSON:

My question was: "Where do you get your interpretation?" And, "Do you believe in Coleridge's statement that Richard's character is the same in Act V as he is in Act I?" No, he is not. The second half of that question leads me to a simple explanation of how I came to the interpretation. It suddenly occurred to me that here was a man who performed the part of being a king superbly well. It suddenly occurred to me that he was never without an audience surrounding him at any given moment, until Act V. He talks about places where he wants to stage his next appearance, and clearly talks about clothes that he's going to wear and his golden crown and all the rest of it. It seemed to me that the overall idea was a man performing a role.

I come in on Dick's question only briefly to say that historically I did acknowledge that Richard became king when he was very, very young; so that unlike Bolingbroke, he was thoroughly well-groomed and trained for it, much in the same way as the Prince of Wales probably is for the time when he becomes King Charles III.

Now, the next thing I discovered, purely working with John Barton, was that the play fits, in terms of Richard's ascendancy and descendancy, into three categories. There's the first area where I quite purposely go out of my way to make the audience think that I am the most impossible human being who's ever walked. When I leave as king to go off to Ireland, you should not really feel at all sympathetic. When he comes back, he comes back to a situation of total rebellion and suddenly finds that his props are being taken away—the clothes that he would normally wear are not going to be available, and, in fact, the whole role of being king is no longer an attractive proposition, so he gives it away. Please examine your text because you will find that at no point does Bolingbroke demand the crown. On the contrary, Richard gives it. He doesn't want it any more under those conditions.

Finally, he discovers a nonentity, he says, having broken the mirror and having left himself with only the frame around which the glass was where he saw his image, the image of anyone that he cared to reflect it towards. The glass is broken. Richard as the monarch par excellence is likewise broken, and at that moment, he comes to terms with nothingness. In a happy frame of mind, all on his own for the very first time in the prison, he says that nothing is what he has come to terms with, and "nor any man that but man is with nothing will be pleased till he be eased with being nothing." Now, how to latch these three central sections onto the kaleidoscope of the actor's mind? I remembered *Tom Brown's School Days* and a character called Flashman, chief prefect, spoiled brat, who holds young Tom up against the fire, burning his backside, being spiteful and vicious, and eventually, of course, brought to a realization that he is an adult and about to leave Rugby school and face the world. That was point one.

Point two I based on a purely textual image. As the king returns from Ireland, Aumerle says, "How do you like the air after your late tossing on the seas?", and it suddenly occurred to me that if they'd had a stormy passage physically, coming from Ireland back to England, I could make a parallel. The events that happened to the king between his arrival back in England and his giving away for the crown are metaphorically a storm. You'll notice when you read it or see it that one moment he's up and then he's down, just like riding the waves, and I use that.

Then I thought that I wanted to show the king at his most relaxed; for once, having dropped his performance and being a real human being with whom one could make contact. It was just fortunate that at the time I read a book called *Nicholas and Alexandra* which is about the last czar of the Russias and his ill-fated queen—if you remember, they were assassinated, or so we're led to believe. Anyway, there was a situation where you had a monarchy which was rather similar to the Richard II monarchy in that it was full of protocol and proper behavior. And there is her hemophiliac son upstairs, and she can't get to him until she has gone down this long line of nodding from right to left. When they are taken away, you find in the book, it says that the joy of the czar at being able to sit there in his suspenders at the breakfast table, not having to wear all the medals and the accoutrements of royalty, was such a confounded relief that, for the first time in his life, he was a happy man. I used this image for the prison scene—that Richard is happy at the moment of his assassination.

LONEY:

We have two things that go together here. The first is a comment followed by a question: "This performance of *Richard II* is the simplest and most intelligent I can imagine. Admirably lucid. Do you speak differently as a company to American audiences: for instance, more slowly and carefully? Do you make any adjustments for U.S. listeners, or is Stratford mostly for American tourists anyway?" And: "I saw the play at Stratford, and it disturbed me that portions of the play, especially the more familiar speeches seemed to be done in a more realistic or active style than the rest of the play. Why is this, or am I wrong?"

PASCO:

No, we don't speak differently as a company to American audiences. I don't think we come here and say we're going to perform differently, because you do understand the English language. We have performed in Japan where they do not speak the English language, and this is an extraordinary experience. I've also played, as I know Ian has, to Russian audiences where they do not understand the English language, and this has been quite extraordinary.

If I may digress for a moment and tell a little story: I was playing in *Look Back in Anger* in Moscow, where I went in 1956 to play five performances of that play at the Moscow Youth Festival. Those of you who know this particular play know that it is full of what we call very "in" jokes for our society at that time—the mid-fifties. In London, the actor would deliver a line, and the laugh would almost beat the delivery of the line. In

Moscow, on the first night, I spoke the line as Jimmy Porter and there was total silence. After about what seemed like two minutes, but in fact was possibly six seconds, a laugh began to grow. They then got the point—they had heard on their simultaneous translations. After the first performance—Ian will understand as a fellow actor—one's whole timing had to change; so that one was saying such and such a line as one would say in England—laugh! But in Moscow, one would say such and such a line and . . . . . . laugh!

RICHARDSON:

I was doing *Merry Wives* in Tokyo where they had this instantaneous translation and my experience was quite different and frankly more frightening. That was, before I said the laugh line, I got the laugh.

PASCO:

No, to answer the question, we do not speak differently to American audiences.

RICHARDSON:

And, why should we?

PASCO:

Why should we indeed? More slowly and carefully? We speak carefully—we hope we are audible in the damned theatre. It's a beautiful theatre to play in, I may say. It is somewhat daunting for all actors to see an enormous auditorium as the Brooklyn Academy of Music is, but we have discovered after only two performances that it is a very warm auditorium. As actors, we can make contact with the audience, even though it is so enormous. This has something to do with acoustics, and acoustical experts must really answer that question. Now, "Is Stratford mostly for American tourists?"

LONEY:

Try and get a ticket!

PASCO:

I can't comment on that. I don't think it is.

RICHARDSON:

No, it's not. Stratford is a festival performed in a town which has a certain attraction as the birthplace of William Shakespeare. As a complementary part of your visit, you may come and see our plays, and we hope you do. But whether we aim our sights at an American audience, or a German audience, or a Japanese audience is neither here nor there. It's a festival which takes place, and we hope to attract audiences. It's as simple as that. Really.

BARTON:

You go to universities and schools all the time.

RICHARDSON:

Exactly. There are institutes working on the more academic aspect of the works. There's a very nice tie-up because frequently the actors are invited to go along and meet the students—who are on a much more academic plane—and talk about the problems from the actor's point of view. We have a very nice rapport.

PASCO:

Here's a good question about seeing the production at Stratford and being disturbed by the fact that portions of the play, especially the more familiar speeches, seem to be done in a more realistic or active style than the rest of the play. "Why is this, or am I wrong?" The realistic or active style is possibly that, in the more purple passages of the play—"For god's sake, let us sit upon the ground and tell sad stories of the death of kings"—we don't "sing" it. We don't adopt a style in our work at the RSC which is now slightly old-fashioned. That is the ooooold waaaaay of taaaaaaalking thuuusss. Our approach is to relate the text of the plays to our own times, as I have said.

RICHARDSON:

Dick, may I remind you of something which will help? John said, "How can you play a king who puts on an act, unless we find out the areas where he doesn't act? There must be moments when he's actually making contact with someone and being truthful." I asked John who he made contact with. John said, "The audience." Together we worked out that some of his moments were where suddenly, out of a great sort of mishmash of wonderful performed style, he says "O god, O god . . . this tongue of mine!" And he's being truthful.

PASCO:

Within the Royal Shakespeare production, John has encouraged us, and generally we work to involve the audience much more than is usual with the proscenium arch, where we have this great gap between us. So one of John's ideas about his production was that we should play a lot more to you; that we should, in fact, as the king does at the setting up of the play, when he bows to the audience and makes that statement that he wishes to involve you, the paying public. He says, "Face to face and frowning brow to brow, ourselves will hear the accusor and the accused really speak." "Ourselves" meaning the audience and me. In the deposition scene, he takes the mirror and, before he looks at his face, he says, "Ladies and gentlemen,"—in parenthesis— "Therein will I read," to the audience. There are many, many moments throughout this production where the deliberate aim of the director is to bring you onto the stage with us.

RICHARDSON:

Especially at the end of the famous speech about kingship, where he says to the audience, "For goodness sake, don't take your hats off. Put them back on. Don't stand up and bow; don't treat me any differently than you would treat your neighbor; because, I, like you, live on bread, and I taste grief and I need friends." That is all at John's directorial insistence, shared with the audience. So, in answer to your question about shifts to "realistic" style, these are the moments where the king is actually sharing with his audience.

BARTON:

There are a number of questions which relate to specific production details that I might try to answer. A couple of people have obviously been bothered by Northumberland as a kind of vulture, an obscene bird of prey on stilts. I think what's being done here is an attempt on John's part to pick up a movement in the play at large. If there's any one line that lies behind that, it's Richard's line, "From night-owls' shriek, where mounting larks should sing," a line which is really about the displacement of the birds of day. The displacement of good, fair, bright things, with the harbingers of night and death. In the movement of the play, we do see the bright colors. This is something worked out in the color pattern of the production—the earlier scenes giving place to a world of blackness. It's a world of death. It's also a harder, more iron world because Henry's kingship is going to be a different kind of kingship from Richard's. It's going to be a more efficient kingship in many ways, but it's also going to be more ruthless, more steely, darker. This is what John was trying to get across. I think there is parallel movement, too.

This leads to another question: "Why the mask?" The mask expresses the dual nature of the king—his impersonal self, the body-politic. When he takes it off, we see the face beneath, the individual incarnate in the role. It's a way of trying to make that visually explicit to an audience. As the play goes on, Richard does come nearer, as Ian and Dick have been saying, to us in the audience. For me, he begins, in the scene with the queen, to speak to someone in human and personal terms. I find that scene immensely moving. When the queen appears in black, again we have this movement towards black and away from the pale green—the floating, gauzy, gossamer garments she wore before—with her hair shorn, almost a shaved head. I find their leave-taking touching and intensely human, despite the continued formalism of the verse. For me, it is made more moving and frightening by this figure of Northumberland, the man who got bigger and bigger and less and less human as the play went on. I don't think I've ever confronted John with this: I think one of the things subliminally behind this is his reading of Tolkien. He's enormously fond of *The Lord of the Rings* and, in fact, did refer to the black horses that Northumberland and his henchmen ride—the concept of the "black riders." Those of you who have read Tolkien will remember that towards the end of *The Lord of The Rings,* the horses give way to black birds. I think that, subliminally, is what triggered that particular thing.

For me it works, particularly in that scene, throwing into sharp relief the desolate and lonely humanity of a husband and wife parting forever.

A final point; two people have asked about the snowman. Again this is a visualization of the mockery king-of-snow image which Richard uses before, melting before the sun of Bolingbroke. I think John uses that in that particular moment in the play because it is a watershed in the play. It is a very clear-cut structural break, the moment in which we realize that Henry IV, the de facto king, is going to sit on this throne—perhaps not with comfort—but he's going to stay put. We realize that even a man like York, weak but honorable, is going to throw everything he has behind Henry IV, despite the fact that he continues to feel compassion and human sympathy for Richard. Nevertheless, he will go so far as to be prepared to sacrifice the life of his own son in order to back Henry's kingship.

You must remember the garden scene, the way the garden is talked about, the diseases of the realm. I think it's a moment in which we are being made to see a turning to spring, despite the black riders. From this point on, the verse of the play alters significantly. In fact, in many productions the scene between Aumerle and the Duke and Duchess of York is cut. It's cut because it's the only scene in the play, I suppose, that is genuinely comic. It's inevitably comic, I think, because of the rhyming couplets: lines like "Happy the vantage of a kneeling knee, good aunt stand up . . . Say it in French, *pardonez moi . . .*" and so on. It's a sudden, jarring note in what I've talked about earlier as the homogeneity of this production. It's something new, a tone, a note, almost like something in music we haven't heard before. This melting of the snowman is an effort to signal this final movement of the play in which something new is happening.

LONEY:

There are several other questions that deal with technical matters in the production. "Was the production designed for an extremely narrow house? The sightlines are especially bad." And, "The set for *Richard II* is very striking, but I found that no matter what the scene, the two staircases are always very obvious. Since they are not used too often in the production, what exactly is their purpose or significance?" Also, "I thoroughly agree with the intellectual concept of this production; however, since I found the staging too obvious, contrived, and artificial, I would appreciate knowing more about how the actors felt about the physical concept. Was there disagreement?"

PASCO:

Yes, I think one can be perfectly honest and say that the setting is not entirely satisfactory. I say that with great respect because it is designed for us by two extremely respected designers [Tim O'Brien and Tazeena Firth]. Inevitably, there must be at some point in the process of rehearsal, not enough of something one way or another. In this instance, I think it may have been a hand-over from the Theatre-Go-Round production. John had an almost Elizabethan Globe playhouse stage with the upper and lower levels. In this production, we had to have an upper and lower level, and in order to carry out certain of the images, we wanted this extremely high level. There are moments, for instance, when the king stands in the lists, and he is like a sun-god, standing above everything, in total command of himself and his court. Therefore, we wanted a very high level. We also wanted a slightly lower level. When this lift was decided on, this elevator, this bridge which moves up and down, it was also incorporated for theatrical effect in the great moment of the play, "Down, down I come like blistering phaeton." Indeed, the whole stage and the actors involved do come down, physically speaking, to the floor level. The two staircases on either side had to be there because actors have to get up there. They can't be flown up, and there have been certain sight line problems. These were overcome at the Royal Shakespeare Theatre in

Fig. 2. *Richard II*: Set for the Royal Shakespeare production, showing stepped inclines for moving platform. (Photos courtesy Royal Shakespeare Company/Brooklyn Academy of Music)

Stratford. Here, we are playing in a different house, and there are different sight-lines and, of course, difficulties. We quite appreciate that.

*   *   *

Fig 3. *Richard II*: Richard Pasco as King Richard in the Royal Shakespeare Company production. Grooms (l. and r.) Lloyd McGuire and Wilfred Grove. (Photos courtesy Royal Shakespeare Company/Brooklyn Academy of Music)

Fig 4. *Richard II*: Ian Richardson (standing) as Henry IV, Richard Pasco (seated) as the deposed Richard. (Photos courtesy Royal Shakespeare Company/Brooklyn Academy of Music)

Fig. 5. Shakespeare Scenes: The Shakespeare Memorial Theatre, Stratford-upon-Avon, seen from the rear. (Photo: Loney)

SHAKESPEARE: PLAYWRIGHT AND/OR POET?

Alfred Harbage
John Houseman
Michael Langham
Bernard Beckerman, Moderator

The question posed for the distinguished participants in this discussion may seem odd, even meaningless. Of course, a Bardolator will answer, Shakespeare is a playwright; who ever doubted that? And certainly he is a poet; is he not the greatest poet in the English language? So, if Shakespeare is both poet and playwright, just what is the problem? For there is a problem, as a number of the other discussions in this book make clear. Are Shakespeare's meanings, means, and intentions the same for us today as they were for him? If not, why not?

The moderator, Bernard Beckerman, clarified the question and the problem to which it relates with a homely analogy: that is, that Shakespeare and his works live in two "homes." Not everyone is aware that he now has two addresses, which is in any case none of his own doing. As Professor Beckerman phrased it: "One home is the theatre into which he was born and in which he has lived in quite different styles over the centuries." But, said Dr. Beckerman, "There's another home which did not exist when Shakespeare first wrote. Over the years, rooms have been built, additions made—extensions, annexes, and now we have a ramshackle mansion of teaching and criticism in which

Shakespeare also dwells, and where a large part of the population first comes into contact with him."

This discussion was an attempt to bring people from both houses together for a productive visit. The participants were Alfred Harbage, late Emeritus Cabot Professor of English at Harvard, a noted Shakespeare scholar and a beloved teacher, former professor at the University of Pennsylvania and Columbia University. Among Professor Harbage's many important writings on Shakespeare are Shakespeare's Audience *(1941),* Shakespeare and the Rival Traditions *(1952),* Shakespeare: a Reader's Guide *(1963),* Shakespeare's Songs *(1970), and* Shakespeare Without Words *(1972). He was also the general editor for* The Complete Pelican Shakespeare *(1969). The late John Houseman became well known to millions of film fans for his roles in* Three Days of the Condor, Rollerball, *and* The Paper Chase, *for which he won an Oscar for Best Supporting Actor. But that work was only a by-product of his long career in theatre and films, documented in such memoirs as* Run-Through *(1972). Houseman and Orson Welles came to prominence in the 1930's with their Federal Theatre work and the Mercury Theatre, which followed it in 1937. In 1956, Houseman became Artistic Director of the American Shakespeare Festival, in Stratford, Connecticut, a venture he helped found. In 1959, he left to head the UCLA Theatre Group. In 1965, he became director of the Drama Division at the Juilliard School, continuing until 1976. He turned the first graduating class into the Acting Company, and he was the Artistic Director of that young troupe.*

Having spent most of the 1970's as Artistic Director of the Tyrone Guthrie Theatre in Minneapolis, Michael Langham is well qualified to talk about Shakespeare not only in his two homes, the theatre and the scholarly mansion, but also in his theatre-homes in three nations, America, Canada, and Great Britain. Langham worked under Sir Barry Jackson at the Birmingham Repertory from 1948-1950. His directorial talents earned him invitations to direct at Stratford-upon-Avon, where he staged Julius Caesar, *and at the Old Vic, for which he produced* Othello. *He was briefly Artistic Director of the Glasgow Citizens Theatre, but was summoned from that job to a*

*similar position in Canada at the Stratford Shakespeare Festival.
His* Timon of Athens *and* The Merchant of Venice *were
admired productions at Stratford. Currently, Langham is head of
the drama program at the Juilliard School. The late Bernard
Beckerman, the moderator, has been chairman of speech and
theatre at Hofstra University, after which he was brought to
Columbia University to create an advanced theatre program.
Later, he was made Dean of Fine Arts. He is widely known as a
Shakespeare expert through such studies as* Shakespeare at the
Globe *(1962).*

*   *   *

HARBAGE:

I am a person of extreme age. My career covers . . . well, let's
just say I am a very old fellow, and coming here required a
good deal of courage. What possible use could I be? Then I
listened to some of the discussions and it made me realize that
perhaps I do have a function. That is, about ten or fifteen
minutes worth of function. Subjects are being discussed here
with a potential of passion held just below the level of
explosion. I've been discussing them for a long time. Now I can
return to them and say a word about them, all passion spent.

How old and inescapable the issue is! I'm not talking about
interpretation, but about an underlying question. In the
production of a Shakespearean play, what is the relative
importance of what we hear and what we see? The issue arose in
Shakespeare's own day. It's been continuous; it's increasing
yearly in its applicability, its difficulty. And it is inescapable.
When I received the topic from Professor Beckerman, it
contained—as it still does—one of these "and/or" formulations
which invites witticism. I hoped he would make this pun, so that
I wouldn't be tempted to make it. We have to eliminate the
Witch of And/or. Or, like Saul's Israelites, we'll be slain.
Eliminating this and/or, I found something peculiar about that
title. It didn't matter how you read it—Playwright and Poet,
Playwright or Poet. It struck me that if Shakespeare saw it, he

would not know what we were talking about. But it doesn't mean that we haven't something to talk about.

Investigating the reasons for my sensation, I looked up "playwright" in the *Old English Dictionary*—being a man of research—and I found the first recorded occurrence of that word comes 70 years after Shakespeare died. Then I tried the word "dramatist"; same, about 65 years. They simply didn't have the words dramatist or playwright in his time. Occasionally they used a word close to it, but only in a contemptuous sense, and it never took hold: it was "playmaker." Their word for what Shakespeare was—and Jonson, Dekker, Heywood, and the rest, whether they had written verse or prose—was poet. Jonson was a poet; Shakespeare was a poet; Dekker and Heywood were poets. Some poets wrote for a musician; their songs would be set; some wrote for readers; some wrote for players. Now we get the essential second member for the combination. There is the poet and the player, and immediately when you had this combination, you began to have antagonisms. They would not have called a writer of plays a playwright—a maker of plays, because no one man can make a play. It's an illogical word. It takes the cooperation of a writer and a player to make a play. A poet can write a script for a player, but he can't write a play. A play is the thing which is produced with the cooperation of a poet and a group of players. The poet wrote what they called "book of the play."

I say antagonism arose immediately. Part of it was simply that the poets thought the players got too much of the money. This accounts for the first allusion to Shakespeare: Greene's attack upon the players. As pride in authorship increased, poets began to feel that the players did not always cooperate in the way the poets wanted them to cooperate. You soon begin to hear the "What have you done with my song?" type of complaint. Shakespeare is speaking from the point of view of the poet, as Hamlet talks to players.

Why should this issue have arisen? Since I am an old schoolteacher, I'm going to use a pedagogical device. We have seen *Richard II.* In conversation afterwards we said, "Did you see so-and-so's Richard II?" Do you notice anything peculiar about what I am saying? The Elizabethans would have. They did not speak of seeing a play. When Christopher Sly is taken to attend a performance of *Taming of the Shrew*, he's told that "they thought it good you hear a play." And then in *Midsummer Night's Dream*, when Duke Theseus is told of the *Pyramus and Thisbe* piece, he says, "I will hear that play." In the prologue to *Henry V*, which is one of the most spectacular of the plays, Shakespeare asks the audience "gently to hear, kindly to judge our play." In the opening chorus of *Romeo and Juliet*, we are asked for patient ears. And when Hamlet is about to put on the play for Claudius, he says, "We'll hear a play tomorrow," and later we have the question asked, "Will the king hear the play?" I know of only two instances where the word "see" is used. Again, they're both by Shakespeare. In *Hamlet* there is a reference to the king hearing and seeing. Naturally, there's a dumb show in the Mouse-Trap play—and that he can only see. Then there is a reference in *Antony and Cleopatra*. Cleopatra doesn't want to be taken to Rome to "see some squeaking Cleopatra boy my greatness in the posture of a whore." In this particular instance, the emphasis is upon something seen. But normally, Elizabethans thought of plays as something heard. This, in spite of the fact that we know that this was a period of pageantry, during which one did both see and hear, and they delighted in costumes and movement. Nevertheless, it's a signal that we're much closer to the pre-Gutenburg period—to the period of dominant aural transmission—in Shakespeare's time than we are now. The normal way of talking about attending a play in his time was that one go and hear. The normal way of talking about attending a play now is that one goes to see.

This represents a change in human sensibility. We are much more eye-minded than they were. Between the visual and the aural in the drama—although all of us want both, their tendency was toward the aural; ours is toward the visual. No one is responsible for this except time, which makes these changes. This presents you with the question: what are you going to do with texts which were written for an aural generation, in which the language is so rich and pictorial? What are you going to do? For audiences of today, we can say that the ideal performance is one in which the author is like a musician. He writes the score, and the players, like performers, are very true to that score. The director or producer is like a conductor who assures proper coordination and balance between these two necessary parts. The analogy doesn't hold. You could produce a perfect production of that kind, and it would now be a popular failure. Where does the responsibility lie? I don't like to say in audiences; it lies in the times. I'm quite sure that if aural emphasis (what one hears) was now increased at the expense of visual emphasis (what one sees), audiences would feel cheated, as if they had bought symphony tickets by mistake. The director is actually driven—he must please. Because there's not only the player and the poet; there's also the audience, and that audience must be pleased. Whom can we blame for trying to please the audience?

A show must be provided. Striking visual effects must be provided, or we must abandon the production. I no longer feel angry with producers who seem to me to over-produce the play or over-decorate. I feel a great deal of sympathy for them. And this seems to be an accelerating thing. Almost no one wants to hear words anymore. At any rate, that seems to me to be the issue, and poets aren't to blame, or actors, or directors, or even university professors. It is time, mutability, that brings about these changes. You see, I haven't said a word about interpretation. It's an entirely different subject.

I have a great many illustrative notes here, including something Dekker said. He told what he wanted an actor to do, and he compared his own function as to that of a composer. Then he talked about the actor who introduces false notes and his own crotchets, if he departs from the provided score. I will read just one note from Dekker: what he wanted his collaborators to do. He is the poet, and there are the players. What is a good poet and a good player? This appears in the prologue to *If This Be Not Good*:

> That man give me whose breast, filled by the muses with raptures, into a second them infuses, can give an actor sorrow, rage, joy, passion, which he again by self-same agitation commands the hearers, sometimes drawing out tears, then smiles, and fills them both with hopes and fears.

The actor is one who not only speaks the words trippingly on the tongue and suits the action to the words, but who communicates the poet's emotions to the audience so the audience feels those emotions.

Dekker doesn't say a word about costumes, setting, business—any of those things. Emotion communicated by spoken words was thought of in Shakespeare's time, I think, as the essence of drama. It is so no longer, and whom are we to blame, if we blame anybody, for the over-stuffed productions? I am willing to excuse almost any production at all which is not morally offensive.

BECKERMAN:

Professor Harbage has stated the dilemma. We'll turn to the directors for the solution. First, we'll hear from Michael Langham.

LANGHAM:

I don't have a solution to the present problem of disrepute into which the spoken word has fallen. I think it dates from the colonial days. So many promises were made and broken by governors in those days that language became immediately suspect. Anyone who spoke well was consequently suspected of some ulterior motive. That has continued, reinforced by great help from politicians, right down to today. I don't know how one changes that except by revolutionary methods.

The title of this debate rather suggests the question: Were Shakespeare's plays meant for theatrical performance? Do we regard them as such today, or were they meant for private reading? Are they best appreciated in a theatre where there is frequently, and inevitably, going to be some distortion of what they're about, or in the mind of the reader where private distortions may prevail? To me it is significant that Shakespeare never seems to have shown even the smallest interest in having his works published. The first authentic publication of his works happened after his death. It was the work of two character actors in his company who went through a lot of dog-eared and dirty old prompt-scripts and finally came up with the first folio. This suggests to me that Shakespeare regarded his plays primarily as raw material for theatrical performance, not as reading matter. And certainly not as a fertile hunting ground for captious scholars. He makes this view abundantly clear in the only play where I would say he had something distinct and definite to say on the subject, *Love's Labour's Lost.* I tried to get a copy of Shakespeare's works from the desk at my hotel, but they didn't have one. As I recall, talking about people who work with books, he says this:

> Small have continual plodders ever won,
>   Save base authority from others' books.
> These earthly godfathers of heaven's lights
>   That give a name to every fixed star,
> Have no more profit of their shining nights
>   Than those that walk and wot not what they are.
> Too much to know is to know naught but fame;
> And every godfather can give a name.
>
> (Act I, Scene 1, 86-92)

As you know, the play is about name-giving godfathers who "go over the house to unlock the little gate." Over and above this, in my view Shakespeare was a dramatic (meaning theatrical) poet, exploiting rhyming verse, blank verse, prose; exploring them like an Elizabethan maritime adventurer over all seas until inspiration might lead eventually to his theatrical goal, which I believe was the expression of a totality of life. In the same sense, a painter might feel that to present the look of a person either in profile or in full-face is inadequate; it being a kind of lie because the painter only sees that person when his head is moving and therefore is impelled to present him in both profile and full-face at one and the same time. As with Picasso, so it was with Shakespeare's unceasing attempt to express more and more fully a revelation of humanity; he is not concerned with surface conversation between characters, though he does have the skill to make these conversations, these rhythms, sound rather like everyday speech; he is not concerned with what is happening on the surface of their minds. He is concerned with what is happening inside their minds. This is one of the principal reasons for his frequent use of the soliloquy—which is not speech so much as thought; it is as if you were to cut my head open and look inside now while I am speaking to you, you would discover far more about me than I know at this moment, for you would see into my revelation of subconscious thought rather than the pronouncement of conscious intention.

I don't think it's necessary for an audience even today to begin to understand Shakespeare's methods of work nor even the contemporary political scene or the political significance of what he wrote in order to be put under his spell. I refuse to accept that the day of language is over. I firmly believe that, granted sufficient assault on its debasement, it can be reestablished as one of the most glorious things that we've inherited. I think we simply have to work hard and with great skill to reestablish the fact that it's a joyful thing to find words with which to express oneself. Shakespeare's text is built on this assumption: that each character has an overwhelming passion to explain precisely and exactly what he's thinking, and thus what he's feeling. This requires a sort of intellectual glee in the actor, which will give him the power to infect people with the simple joy of utterance. It is not helpful for audiences to be aware of the methods Shakespeare is using, because his appeal is frequently to their subconscious. If they are consciously aware, while listening to a Shakespearean play of the methods used (of the persistent imagery of a play, of its metaphors, of its antitheses and so forth), they won't allow him to reach them subconsciously. But for us, the interpreters, whether students, scholars, scholars or members of the theatrical profession, it is absolutely essential that we understand his methods—or at least try to, for there is seemingly no end to this search.

In this respect, we in the theatre can usefully separate poet and playwright from time to time and occasionally unite with Shakespearean scholars in profitable collaboration. But this must end up in the most important collaboration of all which is the collaboration between author and actor.

There is a certain body of so-called Shakespearean criticism which represents a somewhat bizarre and bloodless hobby. I think this should be eschewed. But if one is working on the works of a poet, one can, for example, become usefully involved in consulting the psychologist or psychiatrist. I am not very interested in Freud; I am more interested in Jung. The most important things in our lives perhaps are the things that happen in our minds when we're asleep. These things are probably more important, in terms of understanding us or understanding what is happening to us, than what occurs in our minds in our waking hours.

Someone asked me, wasn't it difficult to regard Shakespeare as anything other than old-fashioned because of what Freud had shown us since? It rather implied: what would Freud have given to Shakespeare, had he been available at the time?—completely forgetting that Shakespeare gave an enormous amount to Freud. On this particular subject, I remember a peculiar production of *Othello* with Ralph Richardson in the title part and Laurence Olivier as Iago. The facts were these: It was 1937. Ernest Jones was writing the "definitive" biography of Sigmund Freud, who was then all the rage in London's intellectual circles. Guthrie was working at the Vic on a production of *Othello*. Hitler was in power in Germany, building a state based on the superiority of the Aryan race, backed by a party that was quite extensively homosexual.

Guthrie went to Ernest Jones and asked, "Isn't *Othello* a play about homosexuality? And about the polarity of black and white? Isn't Desdemona confused by a Freudian mother-complex? Isn't Cassio . . . ?"

Jones, as I understand the story, responded unhesitatingly: "Of course, why has no one thought of this before?" So Guthrie advised Olivier to consult with Jones. After a lengthy session, Olivier became convinced of the rightness of the interpretation.

But how about Othello? How about Richardson? How would this straightforward, trusting man react to such a scheme?

Both Guthrie and Olivier decided that Richardson wouldn't begin to understand it. And they kept him, with misguided protectiveness, in ignorance of the main thrust of their intentions.

Well, throughout the first night performance that I saw, it was remarkable how Richardson kept avoiding all possible physical proximity to Olivier. As Guthrie later explained, he was terrified of a repetition of the kiss Olivier had implanted on his lips in the last scene at the dress-rehearsal.

This is an example of a director getting over-excited whenever he finds something that is suddenly very relevant to the time he's living in. I think it is more trendy than relevant when it imposes a whole red-letter interpretation on a play. Relevance! Yes, I guess we are discussing the relevance of a poet and a classic. I think that if a classic deserves the name classic, then it has continually to prove itself by showing that it carries with it something from a past age which still speaks to us in our understanding of our age or of the perpetual human condition. If plays or any other works of art can't stand up to the test of a particular age, then perhaps they should be put aside. Maybe they'll come back later, as happened with *Troilus and Cressida*, which was performed in Shakespeare's lifetime and then performed not at all until the beginning of this century. Not that anyone thought it was a bad play, but only in this century did we discover in performance what a marvelous relevant play it really was. Its attitude towards war, its disillusionment about government, and its preoccupation with disease brings it very close to our contemporary experience. The terror of syphilis was spreading throughout Europe at the time it as written; there was no known cure for it, in much the same way as there is today as yet no known cure for cancer. Generally speaking about classics, I think they can have the power to distract us from our preoccupation with our own tiny moment in time and make us aware of being part of the human continuum, and I think this awareness makes us a wiser, richer society.

As I just mentioned with the example of *Othello*, some directors do show a sort of hysterical concern for being relevant to an extent that often destroys Shakespeare's works or intentions and makes him seem an indifferent writer. It's not always done out of ignorance. Sometimes it is a willful attempt to undermine every treasure we've inherited, which is a desperate throw. Nevertheless, whatever the motive for such interpretation, it's still part of (as we are students, scholars, actors, directors) the age-old, endless, loving battle between Shakespeare and posterity.

BECKERMAN:

Now we turn to John Houseman.

HOUSEMAN:

It seems to me that we in the theatre are particularly fortunate at this time, because if anybody had wanted to make a prediction about 50 years ago, it might very easily have been said that the spoken word was falling into disrepute as a means of human communication and that print was entirely dominant. The spreading influence of the press, the increasing literacy, and the printing of cheaper books—those all indicated that the spoken word was becoming less and less important, and that print—communication through the eyes—was becoming man's dominant if not his exclusive means of communication.

Then, by one of those historical accidents, the scientists came along and invented electronic reproduction, and immediately, for better or worse, the spoken word once again became the principal means of communication in the modern world. It's not quite the same as what Mr. Harbage was speaking about, but it does affect the theatrical situation. Technically, it affects us in slightly different and rather disagreeable ways. (I'm not talking about television having stolen our audiences, because I don't think that is true. I think ultimately it'll help them.) But the mechanical reproduction of sound—the ability to control volume, to listen to the spoken word through amplification as though you are in the room with the speaker, and your ability to turn the knob if you are not hearing him clearly—has made it, in some ways, more difficult for audiences to listen to spoken words in the theatre. The actor tends not to "speak up"; too often the theatre—particularly old theatres with the double balconies—are tortures for those who are trying to listen to what's going on the stage. That is only the fault of the actor. I sincerely believe that a modern audience does find it more difficult to listen, to make the effort to hear what is being said by an actor. The word is not being poured into the ear as in television; the actor has to make the effort to fill the space; the audience has to make the effort to hear and participate in what the actor is saying: these are problems for the director or actors which certainly would not have existed in Shakespeare's time or even in the nineteenth century. That's a technicality, and amplification can take care of that to some extent; so can our increasing acoustical knowledge and our tendency to build smaller theatres.

But I think people in the theatre are getting back into the habit of hearing dramatic texts, of hearing poetic images, of hearing situations rather than just watching them. I sincerely believe that the combination of visual-aural elements used in presenting Shakespeare's plays to contemporary audiences is entering a creative new phase. I'm not myself an enormous admirer of modern stage design as generally practiced; it seems to me that all kinds of evils, including elaborations of interior decoration, have followed nineteenth century Romantic archeological preoccupations onto the stage. But less and less are we finding it necessary to create great illusions on the stage, so that what is seen is becoming less important than what is heard. Of course, that makes it much more easy to get back to the original relationship between audience and actor that must have prevailed in Shakespeare's day.

The fact that many of the words don't mean the same thing, that many of the images have changed, that the whole ethical and religious concept has changed—all these things do create problems. Any of us who has ever directed a Shakespeare play knows that the great challenge occurs in the first 10 or 15 minutes of a production. One has to make sure that an audience, accustomed to prosaic, naturalistic communication, does not get thrown by an alien language and a totally different convention of speech. Once you get over that, I think audiences are probably more capable of following the Shakespearean action expressed in words than perhaps the nineteenth century, which was enormously concerned with lyric flights—treating Shakespearean texts as excuses for arias. Today, I think we are coming closer to the relationship of playwright-actor-audience than at any time in some centuries.

Those of us who have worked in festivals are aware that we were playing Shakespearean plays to audiences of whom probably 50 percent had never been exposed to a Shakespearean play, except for forced reading in early grades at school, and probably another 25 percent who had never seen a play at all. God knows all of the productions were not clear; they were not all of them good; our concepts were frequently confused. But we did always get the impression that those audiences went out with a kind of revelation of discovery of the potential greatness of the theatre—of a direct communication between the stage and audience that they did not suspect existed. That, of course, was visual to some degree, but it was principally aural.

Anybody who has worked with Shakespearean texts knows that there are certain verbal miracles that have to do not only with the dramatic situation but also with the aural quality of the piece. In a play like *Lear*, one suddenly becomes aware not just of the obvious puns, the onomatopoesisms—all the things that are fairly contrived and recognizable as contraptions, but one suddenly is amazed at the repetition of certain words, certain sounds, and these all contribute to the enormous, violent impression that a Shakespearean text makes on an audience, if it is delivered with any kind of clarity and with any kind of understanding.

I agree that you are in grave danger if you start too many scholarly investigations. That's not what I'm talking about. Those words in the English language spoken to an audience about four centuries later still manage to create much of the impression that was intended, even though the intonations and style of acting may be different. How much one conveyed to his audience is, of course, problematical. We have no idea, and it is idle conjecture. What is absorbing is the problem of the relationship between actor and audience and, at the same time, the relationship of the visual and the aural. Michael Langham mentioned that *Troilus and Cressida* had not been performed for centuries. There are far more popular Shakespearean plays which have undergone the same fate. One is *Measure for Measure*, which was virtually abandoned in the nineteenth century and which was certainly detested if it was done. It was always considered a cynical, rather repulsive, rather foolish play. It was not until the whole morality of our time changed, from the euphoria of the nineteenth century, that one began to find this play communicable. This is a mysterious play anyhow.

G. Wilson Knight has made elaborate studies of how it's all
derived from the gospels and has to do with the second coming
of Jesus Christ. I have not found this helpful in producing the
play on Broadway, but certainly many things in it do directly
communicate to the audience and are recognizable, even
though they may not be 100 percent comprehensible.

The same is true of *Lear*. When *Lear* was done in the
nineteenth century, it was a star-vehicle to a great extent. It was
much admired as a library drama and appreciated as a great
poem, but as a play it was considered repulsive and even
foolish. Nobody understood what this old man was about or all
those awful people. It took the atom bomb and daily examples
of man's inhumanity to man to make *Lear* an immediate,
popular, and potent play for modern audiences. This was
certainly due not to the scenery or even to the great romantic
presentations of the heath scenes, but simply had to do with the
words—words that compel recognition between the characters
on the stage and the audience, profoundly conscious of the
situation existent in the world today—the conceivable
possibility that mankind would be wiped out, civilization
destroyed—the return of man to the bestial condition. All that
seemed inconceivable to the nineteenth century, which was
expecting a millennium at any moment, with the Industrial
Revolution making it nice for everybody—eventually. Today that
play has a terrible and immediate meaning. The poetry of it
may, in some cases, be beyond the comprehension of a
contemporary audience, but the sum of what that play says
through those words is not.

That brings up another question that I would like to touch
on lightly. We cannot reproduce the exact circumstances of
Shakespeare's theatre, but we try on fairly open stages to cut
away the obfuscations of over-production. We are playing in
medium-sized houses to a limited number of people. Now the
question is: what about taking this to much larger audiences?
When those words are transmitted electronically and when the
image is put onto a screen—either movie or television—can
you achieve, in indirect communication with a mass audience,
the same kind of emotion and the same kind of perception and

vision that you can give with actors on a stage talking to a small audience?

I believe you can tell the story and even bring the words to the audience, but the transcendental, poetical aspect that we have been talking about is probably not achievable in mass media. I think the poetical aspect must rely on direct communication. With the enormous spread of the regional theatres all over the country, with the habit that audiences are getting into of seeing a catholic range of plays, and with that style, I think the fate of the actor playing Shakespeare and of actors trying to reach their audience through Shakespeare is better today than it has been at any time for many generations.

BECKERMAN:

We've had considerable agreement at the starting point, but if I may, I'll go into an area that you point out, the matter of interpretation. Is a critical interpretation, like the one you mention of G. Wilson Knight's, a different kind of animal from what a director means by "interpretation" of a play? Are they related in any way? Is one merely one kind of creative act and the dramatic presentation another kind of creative act?

HARBAGE:

First, I want to say how comforting I have found the remarks of Mr. Langham and Mr. Houseman. We are in agreement. I think of a good director in his best productions as one who really does preserve as much of that aural distinction as possible. I have seen and enjoyed and felt grateful for productions by both. There is only one thing I would question, and that is the last remark, that it is now getting easier or that people are coming back to a greater perception of the aural quality. This must have happened very recently. You used the illustration of television. I think television is a visual art. It succeeded radio, virtually eliminated radio, where you had nothing to do but listen. Who now listens to radio? We all look at television.

HOUSEMAN:

When I was talking about television, I meant the electronic media. While I don't think that the beauty of language is necessarily enhanced by what we see on television, our sense of the potency of language is. In previous generations, you read a President's speech or saw statements of important persons in print. Today you hear it spoken, and this isn't a question of quality. This is just a question of the concrete fact that you are hearing spoken words in important moments of our lives, instead of relying almost entirely on print.

HARBAGE:

I didn't answer your previous question. This is about the function of criticism or its use to the producer. You see, when the poets stopped speaking for themselves, then people began speaking for them, or thought they did. It is interesting that all the famous critics take as their point of departure their dissatisfaction with what the players do. Dr. Johnson said Garrick didn't understand Shakespeare. The first fine characterization of a Shakespearean character, Maurice Morgann's book on Falstaff, was written because Morgann didn't like what the actors were doing. Lamb didn't like what they were doing with *Lear*. Coleridge despised the productions of his day. At least—to some extent—these eminent critics really were speaking for the poet. Mr. Langham and Mr. Houseman would now agree with what Johnson said about Garrick, with what Morgann said about the actors, with what Lamb said. Lamb didn't like Lear hobbling about on a crutch. Morgann didn't like Falstaff constantly squealing in fear. This was not because the interpretations were wrong, but because they were incomplete. Falstaff is much more than a coward; Lear is much more than a feeble old man. What they were could only be preserved by what we hear, not by a bit of "business." I absolutely agree that the worst thing that a producer can do is shape productions to twentieth century criticism. The law of diminishing returns has set in, and much modern criticism is misleading.

LANGHAM:

Unfortunately, I find myself in agreement. As to the question of winning an audience back, I don't think that it's really happening as fast as Mr. Houseman seems to think. It's a long process.

HOUSEMAN:

The elements of winning them back exist. It certainly hasn't happened. I agree with you.

LANGHAM:

The problem with distracting an audience by encouraging them to see, to look, rather than to listen is inevitable. It was probably true of the Elizabethan age. I can't believe the Elizabethans were so spare. They covered everything up many times over, never stopped decorating, although they had a non-picture frame stage at least for the first part of Shakespeare's career. The greater part of the population was illiterate, and people liked being read to—that was one part of the tradition. Now, we can't just say, "Sorry, you've got to listen to the word," and take away everything they've got to look at. We must balance it gradually. We can do that well just now, because many of the lyrical plays require that the words be accompanied by something lyrical in terms of movement and style and cut of clothes.

As for critics reacting: often with well-known plays, anyone who directs a well-known play must expect, if you are not going to stay in a rut, that most critics will react to it with a definite preconception. Therefore, you have a standard chance of 75 percent of losing out with them.

I heard something that is beside the point, but it absolutely delighted me. I was talking to an Irishman (does that remark come from Shakespeare?), and we were discussing that second-best bed that Shakespeare was supposed to have bequeathed to his wife, Anne Hathaway. The Irishman said to me, "What do you think the best bed was?" and I had never thought about it. He said, "It's the grave." It's obvious and it's beautiful.

QUESTION:

Mr. Houseman, I saw your *Measure for Measure*. There was a bit of cutting here and there and also definite directing towards the comic element. It doesn't have to be done that way. How do you, as a director, make the decision about which lines are going to be left out and why you are going to move it towards the comedy?

HOUSEMAN:

The second question is really the vital one. This is a problematical play. If you are going to take the first part of the play seriously and grimly, then the end of the play, by any standards of our kind of theatrical consistency, becomes absurd. It is a kind of a circus and series of tricks cooked up by the Duke. It's almost insulting to the audience, it seems to me. The question of finally marrying Isabella is one of those fine Shakespearean finales, where he winds everything up, but working backwards. I think you have to let that work into the front of the play.

I've done the play three times, and I happen to adore it, but I'm convinced the charm and merit of that particular play is this razor's edge between comedy and tragedy. In the great scene between Isabella and her brother, she says, "I'd give you my life; I'd lay it down as lightly as a pin," and you know this poor fellow is worrying only about survival and living and he'll take any means. She makes this remark, and he says, "Thanks, dear Isabel," and this gets a big laugh. It's impossible to avoid the laugh. As far as I'm concerned, the trick of the play is not to play for farce. If we went overboard for comedy, which is possible, I take the blame for that. The play should be constantly poised between the comic and the terrible. That scene is followed by one of the most extraordinary speeches about death that has ever been written, and it is preceded by the Duke's explanation to Claudio about life not being worth living and death being preferable. In this play, the balance has to be kept constantly swinging—always within the bounds between comedy and taking the play seriously. Some people have felt I've gone too far on the side of comedy, but I cannot but believe that that is not how the play was intended. I also believe that in Shakespearean times it was probably easier to achieve that rather contradictory tone between the tragedy in the beginning and the comedy at the end than it is for us today.

As far as the cuts are concerned, ask Mr. Langham—he's cut plays: I've cut plays; Tyrone Guthrie cut plays; Peter Brook has cut plays. Everybody who has ever done a Shakespearean play has tended to cut plays, unless he's doing a full-length *Hamlet*. Some are easier to cut than others, but the cuts are arbitrary and may be strongly disapproved of by members of the audience who know the play.

QUESTION:

A few years ago at Stratford, Ontario, I saw *Timon of Athens*. In that play there was an addition to the text. There was an opening scene which was extraordinary: it was musical: Duke Ellington was in the loft. When I read about it before seeing it, I was surprised and bewildered and mildly outraged. But when I saw it, somehow it worked. At what stage does a director make that particular decision and how and why? How does he make an addition to the play that he considers vital?

HOUSEMAN:

Mr. Langham will answer specifically. All I can tell you is: if it works, it's legitimate. I don't mean "works" just in a vulgar sense. If it offends too many sensitive and intelligent persons, then it's not working. If it clarifies the meaning or movement of the play, then it seems to me that it is working, and it might work this year and not work at all ten years from now. I think this is very delicate.

LANGHAM:

I once put a scene into *The Merry Wives of Windsor*. It was about four minutes long, and nobody noticed. Quite a few scholars saw it—if they did notice the addition, they kept very quiet about it—for there was a symposium going on at the same time! In the case of *Timon of Athens*, the textual change was minimal. At the beginning of the play, we put in a minute street scene of about eight lines to build up something that was missing—I think it had something to do with Alcibiades being banished—but there was a good reason for it. Of course, there is so much corruption in so many scripts, one can always make oneself feel easier by saying, "Why, this must have been missed out by mistake, or it hasn't been passed on to us."

Unless one is going to be pedantic about it, if a particular passage is completely beyond the means of the majority of the audience, I think one is justified, not in oversimplifying it, but in making it a little more available. It may be due to obscure, archaic words or to the actual form of the sentence. I don't think such adjustments are unjustified. Some of the plays are very long and that may be one of the reasons why they have to be cut. People now don't have quite the endurance they used to have, or else people's bladders have shrunk. I prefer to see a play without a break in it, and for all we know, that may have been the way they did it in Shakespeare's day. But then the audience wasn't locked in its chairs; the people were able to move around.

BECKERMAN:

When William Poel tried to return to a more Elizabethan staging and Granville Barker started working in the Savoy, there was a tremendous effort to speed up the speaking of the actor. When the plays came over here, there was a complaint that the audiences couldn't understand. I believe that Tyrone Guthrie tried to speed up the speaking of the actor, still having not only the sense but the feel of the language.

LANGHAM:

I think that the speed of speech is very much related to the speed of thought. Almost all of Shakespeare's writing is written off the top of the head, so to speak. When you embark as an actor on a phrase of Shakespeare's, you don't know, as you often do with a modern play, what you want to say before you say it. But you have the germ of an idea, and you embark on that idea-journey right up until you find the conclusion of the idea, which obviously comes at the end of the phrase. Each phrase will then have that degree of spontaneous life, white-hot from the mind. Often this will come in rushes of mental agility.

If you are playing Shakespeare in a great big barn where you have to thump everything over, word-by-word, this approach becomes impossible and renders a great disservice to the author. It makes him seem like a heavy writer, whereas his plays are always light in texture—even in a work like *King Lear*. To treat Shakespeare in a ponderous, heavy, considered way is almost always destructive. Rapidity of speech is obviously easier if you're in a small house. I think it's very damaging to play Shakespeare in large houses.

QUESTION:

With all deference to both gentlemen, it seems to me that you've resolved the problem by simply walking away from it. You haven't talked about how criticism can illuminate a play or how a play can illuminate an act of criticism. Has Professor Harbage ever seen a production of a play that has changed his critical attitude towards it? Or has Mr. Langham ever read a criticism that has changed his conception of how to produce a play?

HARBAGE:

I have seen a number of productions which illuminated a play. In some respects, what was said in the eighteenth century is true—that actors are the best critics of Shakespeare. This business of detecting and communicating an emotion can be extremely important. What I dislike is when I see a performance of Shakespeare in which I perceive which critic the director has been reading. Then there's something wrong.

LANGHAM:

When I started in the theatre, I did find that almost all commentaries really turned me on, especially the more famous ones. Now I get a lot of illumination when responsible literary people write about a production I've done, and they see that I've done something that I had no intention of doing or no awareness of having done it. And then I want to go to work on that and make my purpose clearer.

QUESTION:

Were you ever influenced by the so-called Freudian phase in production?

LANGHAM:

No. I am a shining example of not being influenced.

QUESTION:

How did those who were involved in it finally come to a realization that Jones was wrong?

LANGHAM:

I think they realized that on the first night.

QUESTION:

How much of the criticism do you desire your actors to expose themselves to?

LANGHAM:

Journalism, or other kinds of criticism?

QUESTION:

General criticism of the superior critics. You say you're turned on by them yourself.

LANGHAM:

Sometimes. As far as actors are concerned, I only feel defensive for them if they've been vehemently abused. Talking about journalism, there aren't many critics who are really respected by actors, but they can hurt actors when they hold them up to ridicule in public. Many critics who write for newspapers and magazines are extremely ill-informed about their subject, and all of us suffer to some extent because they are ill-informed. The public suffers, too. As far as criticism and research goes, when the actor finds he's going to do a certain play, there is voluminous material to refer to. There were, for example, certain significant events happening just before and during the writing of the work which may well have had an effect upon its contents. I think theatre people can't do enough poking about and nosing around, but there comes a point when you have to stop that and realize what you've garnered and then get back to the text. I think the more research there is, the better. It's not just criticism; one has to read all kinds of things and look at lots of pictures and sculpture or whatever might be significant.

QUESTION:

Does the directorial responsibility alter in any way when you undertake Shakespeare, as opposed to other productions? Are there unique problems that arise in this case?

LANGHAM:

I just felt infinitely more confident, because I know it's good writing.

BECKERMAN:

I suppose one of the most celebrated instances we've had of a critic influencing production is Jan Kott supposedly having influenced Peter Brook. Certainly Brook's *King Lear* and *Midsummer Night's Dream* have been stimulating productions. Would you regard that as an instance where there was a very positive response to a fresh critical approach?

LANGHAM:

All of us who work in the theatre are in danger of feeling over-hungry for stimulus. When we find something, we're apt to latch on to it. To try to relate the problems of North America with the problems in Poland is hard. Those problems are very alive, and we understand them, but there is a danger of imposing something that's quite foreign into the American scene. I'm not saying that Peter Brook did this. He was more influenced by *End Game* than he was by Jan Kott.

HARBAGE:

I am doing nothing but agreeing today. Something that Mr. Langham said in passing I thoroughly agree with: if you're going to read criticism, read a great deal of it so that the wild parts cancel out.

QUESTION:

Mr. Langham, have you ever had the urge to mingle at intermission with the audience to find out if they're discussing anything other than where they're going for supper after the show?

LANGHAM:

I do it continually. I like to be a fly on the wall and eavesdrop. I've been pretty well humiliated sometimes.

BECKERMAN:

We have all been through the stage of tremendous emphasis on making the play "relevant," by either modernizing it or presenting it in Brechtian fashion. There have also been attempts to give a bare production or a revised text. Do you discern that we are at any particular point now, or are there any special trends in production that we can note?

LANGHAM:

I find it really hard to say. I've been through a long stretch of extremely hard work, and I want to have a gestation period. I know I'll be touched by everything that is happening. It's hard to say what is around the corner because you don't know.

We all complain because we lack contact not only with the Greeks but also with Shakespeare's world, in terms of theatre. Theatrical practice and tradition is only passed on by doing it by imitation, by people seeing what is done. This is really very valuable. I did a production of a play that was based on a production that I had seen in 1955, and I tried to remember every single detail. I tried to remember every detail and reinterpret it in my own way. I knew that the one in 1955 was based on another production by someone in Britain in the mid-30's, and that production was based on a French production in 1922, and something of importance must have come from that thing. I don't think of it as plagiarism. I think of it as immortality or some kind of continuity of really live tradition. I think that there are many instances within the theatrical profession where people feel that it is dirty to do that. I think it is healthy to pass these things on.

QUESTION:

Could you comment about the Guthrie Theatre and how it aids the director?

LANGHAM:

It aids the plays of Shakespeare. If you have no proscenium arch, and the actors are thrust out among the audience, you can build an auditorium of a proportionately larger number of people who are nearer to the actor, than if you have the same number of people who are all going in one direction. You get the combination of a large number of people and intimacy which makes speech less tiresome to cope with, both from the actor's point of view and that of the audience. If it's true that Shakespeare's plays were done in something along those lines—who knows; its all surmise—and that there was an audience on three sides of the stage, perhaps that is why the plays work so well in that environment.

If you have audiences arranged like this, then that means the actors tend to do what they don't do in a proscenium arch, and that is to play much more to each other. Instead of excluding an audience from the experience, this has the effect of bringing the audience more into it. In a proscenium arch, you tend to play straight out, or to the audience. But what suffers is the relationship between the characters. I think a far greater development of relationship between character and character happens on the thrust stage. Certainly the sweep and flow of

Shakespeare's plays are much easier to handle on a thrust stage, because you can overlap and merge as in a film sometimes. The Guthrie is an easier theatre than Stratford, Ontario; it's smaller. It is rather self-consciously asymetrical in every respect; this was a reaction against Stratford which is very symetrical; both theatres of course were designed by the same people, Tyrone Guthrie and Tanya Moiseiwitsch. But I don't think it's the answer. I find frustrations. There are certain get over problems of masking, which are acute with that arrangement of seats. I don't think that the Vivian Beaumont is a fair example of what I'm talking about.

*   *   *

PRODUCING SHAKESPEARE

Frank Dunlop
Bernard Gersten
Michael Kahn
Harvey Lichtenstein, Moderator

Staging Shakespeare certainly presents many difficulties, but the problems of the play-director are as nothing compared with the problems of the play-producer. Many American directors would never have the opportunity to try their hands at directing Shakespearean drama without the producer's knowledge, experience, skill, and instinct for survival. Currently, there are a number of interesting Shakespeare Festivals in America and Canada[1] which owe their existence to the Shakespeare canon, of course, and to the resourceful, determined festival producers. Frequently a Shakespeare producer is born because a director longs to stage the plays and finally realizes that his only hope is to create his own ensemble, raise his own funds, and obtain his own theatre-space. Producer-directors Frank Dunlop and Michael Kahn and producers Bernard Gersten and Harvey Lichtenstein discuss a wide range of Shakespearean production concerns.

Frank Dunlop draws on his staging experience with the Young Vic, a London-based troupe which showed American audiences such lively productions as The Taming of the Shrew *and* Scapino. *They were hardly a traveling Shakespeare Festival, but the Bard's plays were clearly a staple of their repertory, including* The Shrew, The Comedy of Errors, *and* The Winter's

Tale, *their greatest British successes. Dunlop's stagings of* Scapino, Sherlock Holmes, *and* Habeas Corpus *have all been seen on Broadway. Currently, he is Artistic Director of the Edinburgh Festival.*

Bernard Gersten, formerly Associate Producer of the New York Shakespeare Festival, has been Joseph Papp's strong right hand. He was deeply involved in every aspect of production, not only of Shakespeare but of the astonishing variety of old and new plays presented by the NYSF in Central Park, at Lincoln Center, and at the Public Theatre in Greenwich Village. He is currently managing the Beaumont and Newhouse Theatres at Lincoln Center for Artistic Director Gregory Mosher.

The theatres Gersten has overseen are, at least, all in one city. But, producer-director Michael Kahn has been a constant commuter. As former Artistic Director of the American Shakespeare Festival, in Stratford, Connecticut, he had to concentrate his efforts on the summer, late spring, and early fall. During the regular season, even though he was planning ahead for Stratford, he was also, for a while, heavily engaged at Princeton University, where he was Producing Director of the McCarter Theatre, a professional theatre operated under the university's sponsorship. He is—and has been since its founding—a valued faculty member of the Drama Division at the Juilliard School. Currently, he is also in charge of the Folger Theatre in Washington, D.C. When he has some spare time, he may direct elsewhere as well, on occasion for John Houseman's Acting Company, begun with Juilliard's first drama graduates.

Harvey Lichtenstein is one of New York's most interesting impresarios, bringing an amazing range of performing arts events to the several performance spaces of the Brooklyn Academy of Music. But he is not just a master of theatrical booking; he is also an ingenious, resourceful producer at the Academy.

*   •   •   •*

GERSTEN:

Some people in the New York Shakespeare Festival audiences are young enough to think that the Delacorte Theatre was always in Central Park. One of the reasons for thinking it's always been there is because it looks like it's always been there. I wrote a letter to the City Comptroller, saying we needed $120,000 to fix up the wood decking in the theatre. [Major repairs were completed in 1976.] I said the reason it's worn out is that it's over twelve years old [in 1974], and it's had so much wear and tear from the enthusiastic patrons who flock there every summer. The Delacorte was built to open in 1962, but for several years before that, Shakespeare in Central Park was presented on a make-shift, temporary platform at the same site. Bleachers were erected, and folding chairs were set around the stage. That informal arrangement led to a style of production that was finally transferred to the Delacorte when it was built. The Delacorte itself reflected the stage and theatre that took shape in those improvisational beginnings. The productions are still influenced, not only by that size and shape, and the fact that the [2,000 seat] theatre is an outdoor theatre, but also by the nature of the audiences that come there. The fact that it's a free theatre changes the set of rules of the game of producing plays. That is still a powerful factor in presenting Shakespeare at the Delacorte Theatre. The amount of money you have to produce Shakespeare also obviously influences powerfully how you produce your plays.

There is a tension or dialectic that has been going on for us as a producing company in having that massive, seasonal, out-of-doors theatre and also having, as another place to produce Shakespeare, a wonderfully tiny theatre thrust platform, with 300 people banked high around.[2] Mr. Barnes said that it doesn't seem eminently sensible to him to produce Shakespeare in a theatre seating only 300 people, because the economy is self-defeating. There is, of course, a groat of truth in that. The economy is not defeating—merely threatening. But the intensity of working in the space for people who normally have to produce in a 2,000-seat theatre outdoors, competing with airplanes . . . Well, the very fact that we don't hear airplanes in the Newhouse Theatre changed the entire terms of the way we produce.

Our lives are more fun now—more pleasurable, because we are vibrating between the 300-seat theatre where we at least make a brave attempt to produce Shakespeare and the 2,000-seat Delacorte.

DUNLOP:

Why on earth is there a different attitude in producing Shakespeare because it is a free theatre? I just don't understand that at all. When I produce a play it's with everybody in mind. I mean, I hope that it can be performed just as well for those people in the street as for all those people who can pay $12. I don't think of the audience any differently. Secondly, I cannot understand why, when you've got the best kind of big Shakespearean auditorium in New York—the Vivian Beaumont—you're messing about in a basement with 300 seats. I'd have given anything before I had the Young Vic, to be producing Shakespeare in the Vivian Beaumont.

GERSTEN:

I don't know what the difference might be in Britain. I think the difference here has to do with my own experience in Connecticut, for example. At Stratford, during the years I was there—'57 through '59—we were very aware that the mainstay of our audience was subscription. I would guess we sold in those years some fifty to sixty per cent of the total tickets available on subscription. That is factor number one. Factor number two: Stratford, Connecticut, was and is a suburban theatre. At that time, the United States had lots of gasoline, and the main way of getting to Stratford was driving there. Then, it also was a summer festival. As a result of that, Stratford then attracted—and I think to a certain extent continues to attract—a middle-class audience. The theatre in Central Park attracts a cross-sectional audience that to me has always been more interesting than the audience at any theatre that I know. It cuts across age lines and class lines more successfully than any other that I know in the United States. How does that affect the work? Well, it affects your work on one level in terms of the selection of plays. I remember when I was at Stratford, we always had to condition the choice of plays and the balancing out of the season partly in relationship to audience tastes. I think one would have been loathe in those years to do *Titus Andronicus*, *Pericles*, and *Cymbeline* in any one season—one might be loath to do those three plays in any season anywhere! But we had to be aware of a purchase response from the audience; that was a factor in the choice of repertory.

DUNLOP:

Don't you think there is an obsession with having an audience? Even if the audience is coming free, you might not choose those plays, because you want to show that you are getting a lot of people in?

GERSTEN:

True. But in terms of experience, I've always felt much freer, that the audience will tend to follow, and their principal investment is their time. Of course, the audience at Central Park values its time almost as much as a paying audience values its money. Anyhow, I think that the risk factor is greater.

KAHN:

Since he keeps talking about Stratford, perhaps I should mention several things. The Stratford theatre was built twenty years ago by an eminent man basically for a dance company. So I'm stuck with a very, very large theatre. I quite agree with Frank. I think we'd all like to do Shakespeare in the Beaumont. Stratford is an unwieldy, way-too-large, cinemascopic theatre, in which the problems are to create focus and intimacy.

When you said that you work for a free audience, it has meant two things to the New York Shakespeare Theatre. My comment is based on having done, at one time, a production for the New York Shakespeare Theatre. At one point, the New York Shakespeare Theatre, because they thought they had a lower middle-class audience, catered to a sort of non-intellectual group, and there was an overemphasis on physical jokes. I believe that it's as constricting an approach as the one you had in Stratford in '57 through '59, because the audience was middle-class.

The minute you are a non-free theatre, your ability to raise money is obviously different. Not that you don't have to raise a great deal more money than we do. And there is pressure put on us, on me, to pick at least one play a year for the repertory that somehow will make people get into their cars and come, whether it's wonderful or not. So, one chestnut, if you will, is always in the repertory. That actually is a challenge to me in an odd way, because now that I have to do *Macbeth* or *Othello* or *Romeo and Juliet* or something that conceivably will sell a year, it makes me work quite hard to find out why do I want to do it— beside trying to sell it.

The problem for me has always been to find a way to make Shakespeare work in that theatre. Those of you who have been to Stratford know that it's really very, very large and not really conducive to creating any kind of real actor-audience relationship. It also runs into another problem because it is so large: the actor has to have certain skills in order to make his points in that theatre. It's very comforting for an actor to work in the Mitzi Newhouse Theatre, because little things count a lot.

Over the years in America, the training has been towards a kind of greater intimacy of portrayal and the importance of small moments. It's why a great many American actors are really much happier working in films. It has been increasingly difficult to find actors who can make their points, who can create characters, who can fulfill moments in a theatre as large and unfocused as the American Shakespeare Theatre. It's healthy to try, though, because one of the things I would hate to see us get away from is the largeness of Shakespeare.

I was brought up in the Method. I mean, I went to the Actors' Studio—the whole thing. I was brought up in those years when to speak well was considered the mark of a phoney. In life, if you didn't wear a sort of dark shirt and plaid tie that didn't match, you were already a phoney. If you were an actor and spoke well, then you were obviously aping the English, which was a reaction, I suppose, to a lot of not-very-good English actors coming here in the late '30's and early '40's—ostensibly showing us what Shakespeare was. So that generation of actors in my youth did not particularly learn to speak and did not really have any particular interest in playing in a sense larger than themselves. Coming to Stratford was a rather good experience in trying to get beyond that. The new generation of actors is eclectic—they are willing to do both. I don't think that most directors direct for an audience. I don't think you do anymore, either. Perhaps you could do *Pericles* and *Cymbeline* in one season.

GERSTEN:

For diversity.

KAHN:

Yes. Certainly there is no way that I could do *Pericles* and *Cymbeline* and *Timon of Athens* in one season, even if it was in a fountain with lots of naked people, without printing my own counterfeit money to pay the deficit. I don't think that anyone really ever sits down to direct a play for the audience. I suppose I direct a play to communicate to the audience, but I don't think I direct it because I expect a certain audience to come.

DUNLOP:

No, not a certain audience . . . . I direct it for people to be the audience. I don't direct a play to be exactly the way I think it should be for all time. I really do think about that audience at that moment when I'm doing it. I think, when I'm directing a play, my main job is to represent the audience, and I try every time I sit at a rehearsal to question everything that's going on as though I'm hearing it and seeing it for the first time. That's my main job, and if ever I get carried away from that, I go home, give myself a shake, and when I go to the next rehearsal I say, "Now, I am here for the first time."

LICHTENSTEIN:

For what audience, Frank? So far we've mentioned two different audiences that go to Stratford and go to the Park.

DUNLOP:

Human beings.

LICHTENSTEIN:

No, no, no!

DUNLOP:

I'm serious! When I first went to produce abroad, I didn't know the language, and everybody said, "How on earth can you produce in Holland, when you don't know a word of Dutch? How can you understand what people are saying—the rhythms and all that?" I behaved as much like what I think a human being is. It works in Dutch, even if you don't know the language; it works in French; it works in Chinese. I truly believe that.

LICHTENSTEIN:

One of the things that has been written about you is that you started the Young Vic to get young people to go to theatre, and that essentially your approach to Shakespeare and other works .you've done is a pop approach.

DUNLOP:

Not a pop approach. I started a company a long time ago at the Edinburgh Festival called Pop Theatre, but that was meant to be short for popular. Because I was obsessed with the Theatre Nationale Populaire in Paris, who played in an enormous theatre at very cheap prices for very enormous audiences. But you can't translate the name TNP into English, so I just called it Pop Theatre.

GERSTEN:

I have to interrupt you. Why were you obsessed with the theatre? I mean that large theatre with the cheap prices.

DUNLOP:

Because . . .

GERSTEN:

They're just human beings?

DUNLOP:

No, no. I was obsessed with it because they treated the audience like human beings, and all the actors behaved like human beings and not like "Actors." The director, Jean Vilar, was a great human being—he wasn't . . . .

GERSTEN:

Were there audiences and actors in other theatres that weren't?

DUNLOP:

Not a lot.

GERSTEN:

Human beings are not equal!

DUNLOP:

I think they were conditioned to behave in ways that an ordinary human being doesn't. Even nowadays when you go to the theatre, you are expected to dress in a certain way, to behave in a certain way, to keep quiet at certain moments, to be respectful at certain moments.

GERSTEN:

Are you the same person who asked me earlier, in what respect the audience in Central Park differs from any other audience? That's what you're describing very skillfully—the audience in Central Park.

DUNLOP:

I'm trying to describe the difference between an audience which is conditioned and is behaving according to rules, and what ordinary people do. I work for ordinary people, and I wanted to work for ordinary people—people who have never, perhaps, been to a theatre because they were put off by the rules and regulations of the theatre and the conventions of the theatre. I've always worked like that; maybe because I wasn't brought up in any way with anything to do with the theatre. When I went to the National Theatre, I became absolutely appalled at the sort of people who came to every first night and still come to every first night. They were not the people I wanted to work for because of their conventional phoney attitudes.

That was why I then said I'd sooner go off and build a theatre where people are not afraid to go beyond that foyer. They're not afraid to go and talk to the person at the box-office. They're not afraid that if they come and slop around in their seats or don't wear respectable clothes that the people around them are going to go, "Hmmmmmmm, hmmmmmmmmmm." That's what puts so many people off going to the theatre. In the theatre I built, there are no rules and regulations. There's no man standing at the door to make sure that you behave properly. If you want to shout in the performance, you won't be told off. If you want to go the way you are from the street, nobody who sits next to you, dressed up, is going to look down on you.

GERSTEN:

That's fine. Since we play to 100,000 school children a year, it's rather the same thing. But you're talking about a social thing, and if you are choosing to play to an audience that has never been to the theatre, or trying to attract an audience who has never been to the theatre, does that obviously influence the way in which you do a play?

DUNLOP:

No.

KAHN:

We're not talking about how you organize the auditorium. But once they're in there, if you are trying to attract an audience who's never seen a play before, do you find yourself having to produce a play in a special way for them?

DUNLOP:

No. I've done a play for the Royal Shakespeare, *Sherlock Holmes*, by William Gillette [subsequently imported for Broadway and an American tour], because it was a play they very much wanted me to do. I surprised everybody—I did it exactly the same way as I do any play. If I'm doing a play for a commercial management that's meant to make a hell of a lot of money, and the people are going to pay whatever they pay on the front row in New York or London, I still have the same attitude. I do everything as though I'm seeing it, thinking about it, for the first time. If I'm doing *Twelfth Night* for the twentieth time, I don't think, "Oh, that audience has seen it before and so on." I still must do it as though it is being done for the first time. There aren't any overlaying attitudes to it; I don't want to comment on it. I'm not interested in comments—those comments are for the audiences who are sophisticated and who know about the play, who think about the play, who think they know what the theatre's about. I just want to do basic things.

KAHN:

I think that we all think that way. Coming over here today, I thought that's what I'd say about how I work. One has supposedly done this kind of production, and one has done an anti-war production, and one has done a pop production, or a rock production, and you think, "No, I've really just done a play." I've just simply read the text, as I do all the time, over and over again as though it's a new play. I keep trying to tell myself this is by Neil Simon or somebody, and it's never been done before; it doesn't have a history; it isn't in the cultural pantheon; it's just a new play. You want to approach it as a new play, and you want the audience to see it as if it's a new play.

There's something that happens in America but not as much with your English audience. I remember being very upset the first time I worked in Central Park. The audience kept getting up.

I thought, "Oh, they're walking out!" They weren't walking out; they were just going to get frankfurters. They immediately got the thing and came right back—I was very beady-eyed and noticed each person who left, since it was my first large production. I was glad they came back after the commercial or whatever they thought they saw. Sometimes they missed something rather important. I wanted to explain it to them when they came back.

So, I just read the play until I sense how the play is organized and what really is the center of the play. In Shakespeare, the director does have a choice of what to stress within a production, because Shakespeare is so extraordinary in that sense of being ambiguous and complicated and complex but not organized as tightly as some other playwrights. I find now that I can use that freedom.

Certain plays have certain resonances for me during a particular period in my life and I choose those. Perhaps it is selfish, but it has to do with the time in which I live. I was very much interested in redoing *Measure for Measure*—my feelings about the play were different partly because we had just been through a specific kind of summer (the Watergate scandals) in this country. When I did *Henry V* in what looked like the end of the Vietnam War—and wasn't, the play seemed to contain criticisms of nationalism and interested me more that year than perhaps if I had done it thirty years earlier, and we were fighting Adolf Hitler. Of course, when choosing or doing a play, it is partially one's own conscience one is responding to, and also those things that catch me up in a play that I hope I can communicate to the audience.

LICHTENSTEIN:

Does the audience see a certain approach to Shakespeare by theatres that do a lot of Shakespearean production? Does the National have a way of staging Shakespeare, so they all look somewhat the same?

DUNLOP:

The Royal Shakespeare does. They develop what we call a "house-style." This isn't in any way attacking their approach. They try to force everybody's images in one direction: the designer, director, actors. I think this has been happening less, because forcing a house-style means that, after two or three years, the thing is dead because everybody's just conforming to playing in a wide box or speaking in a certain way. Things are not constant from year to year, because everybody is developing and changing.

I think the National Theatre has never had a house-style for doing Shakespeare. One of the great things about Lord Olivier was that he said that theatre had to take in every style and every attitude from all over the world. He believed in saying that this production is this group of people, and they must show their own individuality in it. He didn't say, "It's got to be like this, and the scenery has got to be like this, and the acting has got to be like this." As a result, individual productions were quite startling and fascinating and reached very deeply. Also, as a result, there were a hell of a lot of really awful flops, but I think that's quite a good thing. As for the best, there has been a series of things which measured up to Peter Brook's *Dream*, which was a great individual thing in the middle of the Stratford house-style.

At the Young Vic, there has been no sort of pressure on how anything should be done by a guest director or a guest designer. I think the style came from the building. You can't work against the building, because you're working in architecture. You can't stick up a lot of scenery which says this is a very pretty little street in Verona. You've got a building, and you work in that building as in Shakespeare's day. Therefore, there is a style imposed just by the architecture, but I don't think that's a bad thing.

There's a style that comes from the actors who are used to working within that architecture and with the audience in a certain relationship to themselves. I employ actors—employ is not quite the right word—who have to want to work there, because they get very little money. I tend to gather actors who have an attitude to the audience which is the same as mine. Therefore, if another director comes along, he has to accept people with that attitude, so there is a certain style. But I don't think it's in any way an exterior style. It's something which comes from one person's mind trying to get in touch with another's. That's the basis of all our performances—not a general impression being put on for a lot of people to pass the time.

LICHTENSTEIN:

Would you say then that architecture is the main influence in producing Shakespeare?

DUNLOP:

I think that the reason why the Elizabethan theatre was so remarkable was that at that moment in time the actors and the managers and the writers suddenly found they had built a theatre which was great architecture. Like a great piece of music. So they had a form for which to write, in which to act. That's why I think that the theatre was great. In the Restoration period, there was a form of theatre which was perfect for their writing. Then suddenly the theatre was kicked in the teeth by opera, and everybody began to build permanent solid structures that were really created for operatic productions. That has undermined every Shakespearean production since. You are now forced to do a production either operatically, or to do what Stratford is trying to do all the time—that is, to break this operatic convention. It's very difficult to do, once you've got opera houses.

LICHTENSTEIN:

How do you feel about working in the Opera House at the Brooklyn Academy of Music?

DUNLOP:

Well, we will build you another stage. After working at the Young Vic, which is very like the Shakespearean theatre, we were going to work some of the festivals. The first year around Europe, we were having to go to opera houses. At first, we wouldn't go. Then we sort of "cased the joints," and we realized that we could actually get in the middle of the audience by building the stage out, playing out across the front of the stage, and getting a lot of the audience up on the stage behind us, so that we've got audience on two sides. Now, that's much more difficult than having audience on three sides, because they're two separate blocks. But they presented a very different challenge from the normal operatic theatre convention, and it broke the audience's preconceived attitudes to watching a play. We stopped doing that. We think that we ought not to perform in proscenium theatres at all.

LICHTENSTEIN:

Thinking about this term, "operatic performances of Shakespeare," and the kind of theatre you have in Connecticut . . . With the number of people in the space, do you feel that that's what happens?

KAHN:

I've tried every way to fight that problem. Frank is right and, as I said earlier, I think the theatre at Stratford is really a liability in terms of reaching the audience, in that there is separation. Why don't I change that? I'll tell you why. As you know, over the years the stage has moved, crept out into the audience, and now it's a bastard thrust. The best solution would be to just take it apart and put it all in the middle. What I try to do is reduce the size of the stage in every possible way I can, so that one does not have to do a spectacle to fill it up. That means making a smaller playing area. If there's been any style of production, it's been taking place somewhere in the middle and down front of the proscenium on a smaller stage built on the big one.

I think one of the things an actor has to do, in order to get away from an "operatic" performance in a theatre that seats 1,500 people, is to give the kind of physical performance that communicates much with the body rather than just having to "emote largely."

LICHTENSTEIN:

What about amplification?

KAHN:

We don't have amplification. I've been against it, partly because of my experience in Central Park. In the old days, when the very first line was said, out came police calls, because the mike was picked up. We also had traffic lights. I remember saying to the composer, David Amram, "What is the flute doing there?" He said, "It's not the flute!" We found out a week later it was the traffic lights on Fifth Avenue, when the signal changed. It just went, "Boop, boop, boop."

But I don't like the idea of someone standing here, playing to someone there, and the voice coming from over there. I find that a little startling, and it has a disorienting effect. So I fought amplification a lot.

I also believe that actors should be able to project. While the Globe Theatre was not that large, the actors had to talk over the audience. They had to reach quite a way, and I think that is the actor's responsibility. I don't like class-dividers, where we have high balconies for the poor people and orchestras for the rich—to hell with that. But I think that actors must be able to fill theatres like that, to find ways of doing it. As I said, I think one way is to be more physical and not just stand still and speak terribly loud.

DUNLOP:

One of the troubles in the theatre is that there are actors who think they can go on stage and not work, not perform, and be "overheard" by the audience. I think voice teaching is absolutely appalling all over the world. People are conned by voice teachers who are training actors to make wonderful noises like "AAAAHHH." That isn't what conveys the meaning of what we're saying. One of the great happinesses for me was the first time I worked with Olivier. I said, "God, there is somebody who is doing everything, but I'm considered eccentric when I talk about it." He works on getting over the consonants. It seems an obvious, banal thing to say: I just want to hear the consonants. I don't want to hear those beautiful noises that go with them, because the consonants carry the meaning, and it's very easy, if you play the consonants, to be heard in a very, very big theatre.

I think quite probably what the Elizabethans did was to convey meaning through the consonants. They made every word a unit. That was what they were talking about when they were discussing oratory. It's to do with projecting the meaning, not the wash of emotion. I just spend hours of rehearsal saying, "I'm sorry, I didn't hear that 'B' at the end of that word." I don't talk about psychological things anymore . . .

GERSTEN:

Just consonants?

DUNLOP:

Yes. Olivier does it—if you listen to him, that's the great thing he's doing. You are riveted by the words. He doesn't need a microphone, but I don't think anybody does who speaks in the right way. I've offended a lot of my friends, saying that about voice teaching.

LICHTENSTEIN:

What about dress and decor? Do you have any ideas, any style, any feeling about productions being in a certain dress or decor?

KAHN:

Stratford was certainly the most at fault in this area at one time. One felt when one went to see a production that one wasn't seeing the play—one was seeing Goya or Valesquez or Manet. I think sometimes people just look through an art book and say, "Wouldn't it be nice if we did this Spanish?" And then rush off and find a Spanish painter. I think that that replaced a real engagement with the play. It replaced an idea about the play with a decor idea.

I would try to limit it at the time to three choices: One would be to do the play in the period in which it was written— Elizabethan or Jacobean. Or, to do it in the period it was written about, or to do it in modern-dress—since the plays were obviously modern-dress productions when they were done in Shakespeare's time.

I still react against productions when I feel the choice of setting and decor inhibits the meaning of the play. I'll just use *Much Ado* as an example. I know it was a very successful production. I found that the play began to have overtones of *Ah, Wilderness!*, and *Ah, Wilderness!* is a less interesting play than *Much Ado*. It tended to take away from the richness of the texture of *Much Ado* by pigeon-holing it. I think any rigid concept makes Shakespeare smaller than he is. Even saying, "Well, this is an anti-war play," begins to make Shakespeare less interesting than he is. What is interesting about Shakespeare is that you cannot categorize him that easily. Choosing a period like eighteenth-century Napoleonic, for instance, either reminds you of something else or makes the play less rich. To turn *Way of the World* into Oscar Wilde is a mistake. It seems to make *Way of the World* less interesting and makes you want to see *The Importance of Being Earnest.*

DUNLOP:

I have to plead guilty in advance of what I'm going to attack now. It's something that's forced on directors—again, it has to do with working in this operatic tradition. If you have to put a play on in an opera theatre, where you have to create a picture, you really don't have to think about saving the audience from the boredom of having to look at the same white box five times in a season for five different plays, or to look at the same black curtains. If you decide not to have a decor, that's much worse than having a decor. Once you're doing a picture production, then you've got to make a picture, and that's forced.

I've done terrible, extreme things when I was at the National, because there was a lot of money, and you tend to put on more and more scenery to entertain the audience with what you do with the back wall of that stage. It's something I don't think you can avoid in the sort of theatre one is often presented with. It's appalling that one has to spend so much time, energy, and money. This different, bloody, titillating construction has nothing to do with what goes on between the actor and the audience. But I plead guilty.

I do it because the theatre is wrong for not doing it, and a sheer commercial reason. That affects directors, too. When you are asked to do a production in a big theatre, one of the things that matters, unfortunately, is getting good notices. At the moment, the theatre is conditioned by what the reviewers say. In New York, it's one person; in London, it's three people. Everybody thinks that we've got twenty persons—it's not, it's three persons, and one of those three is the powerful one and can fill your theatre in London as well. So, you have to show him that you've got an attitude toward the play—that he's seeing something different from last night and the night before. So, a lot of the work we do is to impress the critic and also to get another job. The director is busy making a very highly personalized impact on maybe twenty or thirty other people, who will write nicely about him or give him another job. I don't think that's something to be underestimated.

KAHN:

I find settings terribly important. I hate the fact that one has to do them in advance of rehearsal; that one can't make them up around the third week of rehearsal, because that's about when one has some idea about what is needed and what one would like.

DUNLOP:

You can make them up if you are working in architecture.

KAHN:

Yes, and I could make them up if I were working in some other places. It's a repertory theatre, and everything has to be done a month or two in advance. One has to have the designs in, so one has to arrive at the idea. I suspect that's what I try to look for is something that does not say what the play is about. I don't think that the set should make the statement, but should somehow create as neutral an atmosphere as possible. My favorite thing to do is have everything against a brick wall. My bricks get larger or smaller depending upon the play. Perhaps it's because I like Pasolini movies, but I like to find the most neutral setting with a texture that somehow relates to the major color of the play.

DUNLOP:

You are having to make a statement behind the actors.

KAHN:

To occupy the space, at any rate.

DUNLOP:

Once you occupy the space, you must think exactly what you are going to say there. In most big theatres the designer and director have to do the whole of the production and send it in to be made before the first day's work with the actors. This is utter nonsense. You don't know what marvelous things are going to come out of twenty people working together and creating.

KAHN:

You are also boxed in. I suppose if we all got together and said we won't do it anymore . . . but it's become a dire matter of economics. I've gotten more difficult about waiting until later to have my designs in. The later they are, the more expensive they become, because it's competitive to build. The budget goes up, and you have to cut, or there's no time to do it.

At Stratford, Ontario, although the answer seems architectural, it is still a statement. Although it is a playing-area, you finally do everything against brown wood with the same doors. At Juilliard, I have a set that I do everything on, and it's really rather like that. It's infinitely easier, and it makes the rhythm of the plays interesting, but even that is a kind of statement. When you get down to it, even if I did a play in this room, I've made a statement. I've done a play in a sort of garage. Although it seemed neutral to me, the audience, walking in, immediately reacted as if I'd built a set.

DUNLOP:

At Stratford, the statement that's made up on that stage architecturally is an Elizabethan statement. I think it's quite difficult now, because architects don't think very clearly either. But if you get a really good architect, and there are some, he can create a place where you can work. There are some great architects who can make good statements around you.

QUESTION:

Would Frank Dunlop be frank about his reaction to American productions of Shakespeare—if he's seen any?

DUNLOP:

I've not seen very many, and this isn't an American thing; I think it's all over the world. I think they tend to be a bit imitative of English styles of production. That has something to do with critics and sophisticated people who expect a certain kind of Shakespeare performance. I think American performances are best when they're American, not British.

I was asked to go down and do a play to open a place in Oklahoma. George Grizzard and Barbara Baxley came down and we did *The Shrew*. I'm always doing *The Shrew*—it's my favorite play. It was wonderful. I expected the American actors to be thinking and doing mumble, mumble, mumble. This group didn't, and certainly George and Barbara didn't. They spoke Shakespeare and meant it—better than any English actors I'd ever worked with. I think that American actors are the best, which means that they've got a certain specific training. Also I like people who have been in musicals because they have to put over words exactly. I think that sort of American actor is the best in the world, without a doubt.

KAHN:

There is something that I don't have the courage to do yet, and I know why I haven't. There is something really desperate which happened in America called Mid-Atlantic speech. I was trained in it. (I also have not been able to find out where Mid-Atlantic is.) The kind of speech that we were all trained in seems to be colorless for some reason. I went to school and was told not to drawl, but it is the way I talk, and it is reasonably colorful. I have heard Shakespeare read by Texans, or especially Southerners or black actors who are willing to speak black, and the rhythms have been absolutely wonderful to listen to—consonants or not. Someday I want to work with a company where one can really use regional speech.

Now, the reason that I don't at the moment is that I can see chaos with ninety-three regional speeches in one production. I cannot work my way through doing a production of anything with one Southerner, one Texan, one Californian, and one New Yorker, all speaking with a different ear for dialect. And I don't really like saying all the low characters are going to speak Southern, as they used to do cockney all the time. It's really boring, so I don't do it anymore, because that would really cheapen my act.

But someday, I'm going to bring a lot of Southerners or Texans and do Shakespeare and I don't mean that all of this is going to have to be set in the South. There's nothing I hate worse than seeing a lot of people in crinolines doing Shakespeare as they used to do at Stratford, too. It's a problem I have at Juilliard, where I know we will all teach them how to speak well. One has to have a certain kind of uniformity of speech in a production. I'm really struggling with this; I may find myself having enough guts to say screw all that and just get up and do it. Speech training in America really kills interesting ways of speaking, in order to get uniformity.

DUNLOP:

But I think the same about the English actors! All that English flatness is boring, and that's why it's exciting to hear Americans speaking real American. The most exciting Shakespeare I've done was at the Edinburgh Festival. Over half my company were Scots, who do speak differently from the English. They have a much more fantastic rhythm in their speech; so, up in Scotland we were able to play in Scots. I'm sure that Shakespeare originally was played in extraordinary ways, rhythms, and accents. I think good English-speaking Shakespeare is awful.

KAHN:

It's not Shakespeare.

QUESTION:

Can modern-dress add anything meaningful to a production?

KAHN:

It's an extraordinary thing. I did a production of *Love's Labour's Lost*. It was the first modern-dress production I'd ever done, and *Love's Labour's Lost* is a reasonably complicated text for audiences to understand. Literally, because I set it that way, the audience understood everything. I got a lot of letters saying, "How dare you rewrite the text?" I had not rewritten anything. I had added a few lines, because I had decided on modern-dress. I thought it was fair game, since the play was a satire on the Earl of Southhampton's circle. These were obviously recognizable personages in Shakespeare's time. I felt it was perfectly okay for me to substitute recognizable personages of our own time; so it was filled with the Beatles and Truman Capote and Lee Radziwill and Mia Farrow. At least I knew that's who they were.

GERSTEN:

But you substituted common personages for royal personages.

KAHN:

No, no. Lee Radziwill, Mia Farrow, and those people are the royalty of our time. The audience absolutely understood everything. They laughed at Elizabethan puns; it was quite extraordinary. The year before I had done a production that I thought was extremely together—*Merchant of Venice*. I thought it was about money and commerce, and I set it in the Renaissance. Everybody thought it was really rather dear. A lot of people just came because it was Renaissance clothes and didn't listen. I didn't feel it was really my fault, because the people who did listen did understand.

In an odd way, in order to get people to really listen to Shakespeare, you have to break their expectations. In one way or another, this is what we're talking about. Sometimes one goes overboard doing it; sometimes one finds the right way. I'm beginning to think that the best thing that can happen to get people to listen is that when they come in, they think they have tickets for the wrong production. "I came to see *Macbeth*, but I guess I'm watching something else," and so they listen.

GERSTEN:

I remember when I entered the Billy Rose Theatre to see Brook's *Midsummer Night's Dream*, the white light was really blasting onto the stage, from the moment the audience came in. And the audience was sitting there in the reflected light, literally bathed in it. Exactly what Michael referred to was taking place during the fifteen minutes I was there before the play began. Everybody was sitting forward, and there must have been doubts from certain people stunned by the light. One of the things that struck me most sharply about the RSC's *Richard II* was that the whole stage was bathed in grey. I have never seen so goddamn much murk in my life. It depressed me and cast me down. But I sat at that *Dream*, and I half-watched the play and half-watched the people. They were listening to the lines that so often lull audiences to sleep, the lines that they knew they could count on—the measured treads. They listened and they heard. The entire reaction to that production was fresh.

I just want to draw my circle closed concerning our *Much Ado*. I remember when there was a *Much Ado* done with Hepburn and Drake up at Stratford. The New York Shakespeare Festival mocked it because it dared to violate the text and slip in somewhere between Spain and Mexico and make Dogberry a cross between Pancho Villa and somebody else. How that was mocked at the New York Shakespeare Festival! And ten or twelve years later, there we were with Teddy Roosevelt waving a little American flag.

One of the major critics of our time—Nixon—attended that performance, accompanied by large numbers of secret service personnel, and was quoted as saying, "I read the play, but I didn't know they could do it that way."

KAHN:

I started out by thinking that you must make Shakespeare "relevant." That word violently upsets me now. I tried to find ways to make Shakespeare speak in production terms—to have people swinging from the ceiling, loud music . . .

DUNLOP:

. . . and be one-legged.

KAHN:

Yes, one-legged, with a lot of peeing on the floor. Now I've come to find that sort of thing pigeon-holes Shakespeare and makes it smaller and less "relevant," because it replaces Shakespeare's mind with substitutes.

QUESTION:

What good does it do to do a museum piece, if you have nobody coming?

KAHN:

You must be very careful. A museum piece has very little to do with decor. I think there's a lot of fuss about the fact that if you set a play in the Renaissance because it deals with that period, then immediately it's old. You have to be careful about that. One of the most modern productions of *Romeo and Juliet* I ever saw was Franco Zeffirelli's stage production, set in the Renaissance. It was absolutely contemporary and alive—at least up until the last act! It was done absolutely period, but it had to do with a relationship of the director and actors to the text and to the life they created.

GERSTEN:

Of course, but that's always been true.

KAHN:

Classical theatre must not be a museum. It must be investigation.

QUESTION:

I think a lot of that has to do with making choices. I saw the Guthrie production of *The Merchant of Venice*. It was highly traditional and a very good production. I sat in the audience with 1,000 junior and senior high school students and they were riveted by it. It had nothing to do with making it current or updating it. It was just very good acting and good directing. I think that's what counts in the end.

GERSTEN:

There's no substitute. It doesn't matter what clothes you put on, or what clothes you fail to put on. There are no substitutes for the talent of the actors and the skill of the director—then, into the text.

KAHN:

That's the answer.

GERSTEN:

You can always buy costumes without limit—depending upon how much money you have—and decor from now until doomsday. But these are not substitutes. The virtue of our production of *Much Ado* was the relationship between Beatrice and Benedict that transcended any antic behavior of the Keystone cops in the show. Sam Waterston as Benedict realized that part to a greater extent than any of a half-dozen Benedicts I've known and variously liked. He could have worn anything. The couple could have done it in their rehearsal clothes on this platform, and it wouldn't have mattered.

QUESTION:

Let's not separate traditional theatre into one category and put in another category of modern, wild, avant-garde production.

GERSTEN:

It's too neat and packaged. I don't think the reality of preparing plays responds to that kind of packaging. Nobody sets out to say, "I will now do a traditional production!" How would you define it? What defines the costumes as traditional that you mentioned in the Guthrie production of *Merchant*? What fulfilled that production was not that the costumes were traditional; it was the fullness of the play.

QUESTION:

Is there one particular aspect, when you produce a Shakespearean play, such as mood, clarity, impact—one thing that you finally think is most important? One could argue for clarity: if one simply makes clear what is happening in a truthful manner, you will be closest to fulfilling the play. What do you think?

DUNLOP:

For me it's making it clear. My first duty is to see that the play is absolutely clear—to get over what the words mean, what the situations and characters are. And I don't think that any means can be ruled out in order to make it clear. The means I would like to rule out are those which are done for different effects in order to express one's self as an artist.

QUESTION:

But then you walk into Brook's *Dream* and see some amazing effects.

KAHN:

The Brook production was really a kind of watershed production. I saw it in Stratford in the middle of a very dreary season. Suddenly out came the *Dream*. After one got over the white box, one finally realized it was just a rehearsal studio, and that all kinds of marvelous tricky things were rehearsal props in Day-Glo colors. What was astonishing about the production was its clarity, as opposed to other productions where we've seen people throw themselves around and jump from the ceiling. The text was clear—I mean, I heard things in the *Dream*, in that production, that I had never heard in any production of that play before.

DUNLOP:

I think the reason they do those shock things at the beginning is to jolt people sitting there with a conventional attitude. Unless you jolt them, they just sit there. At the Old Vic, *Love's Labour's Lost* was a great example. I was going to co-direct it, and halfway through the first day's rehearsal, I suddenly realized what it was going to be. I went to Larry Olivier and said, "Look, I cannot do this with you because I know what you going to force me do in this production with you." When it came to opening night, there was exquisitely lit decor, all pinks and blues and greens. From the first word, you knew it was going to be beautifully spoken in the English tradition. The whole audience, when it saw them, went "AAAAAAHHHHHH." It was like lying in warm, shallow water, and it was a great experience for them for about —it seemed like ten hours. Most of those people were asleep in the second act, because it was respectful to Shakespeare—the whole operation—you couldn't knock it down.

QUESTION:

Students tell us what is clear and what isn't. When they're bored, we're not getting through—when they're listening, we are. I think that's a marvelous way to begin.

KAHN:

The only danger I fell with that is that one must never speak down to an audience—ever. One must never be a hooker.

QUESTION:

I saw Mr. Kahn's modern version of *Love's Labour's Lost* at Stratford a few years ago. We saw motorcycles come out and young people with masses of curly hair—just at the advent of long hair. We saw the interaction of the majority, and we were getting a little lost by the second act and the Maharishi—the guru fellow with the flowers and all? By the end of the play, we said, "Well, this is interesting, and now we're part of the scene." But it wasn't what we remembered of Shakespeare. In New York, when they did Brook's *Midsummer Night's Dream*, I went with my three married children and their mates. They loved everything. I kept seeing it as a beautiful circus spectacle, acrobatics here, there and everywhere. I know there can be several kinds of Shakespeare, and I love theatre, but I can't see why the tradition has to go by the boards, with the young people establishing their own traditions.

GERSTEN:

I must tell you this—I didn't see Michael's production of *Love's Labour's Lost*, but from your description, I'm so sorry to have missed it. You must understand that everybody who does a Shakespearean play today, unless he has done them repeatedly in conventional fashion, investigates the play every time as for the first time. I'm sure every time Frank does *Taming of the Shrew*, he approaches it in a fresh way. You are quire right when you say it was the period when people were just newly wearing long hair. Hair was only a couple of years old and had not yet arrived as an institution. I've loved great chunks of the audiences who were all different and who remember productions in the 20's, 30's, and 40's. I'm not a blind advocate of youth. The world is a more interesting place because it's not all youth, or old people, or middle-aged people. Our audiences are best when they represent a spectrum of age.

In my experience with student audiences, when they are rotten they can be the worst possible audience. They are responding to each other or playing jokes amongst themselves and not being just human beings in society. When you get some students in a normal audience, it's terrific because they infect that audience. It's very positive.

QUESTION:

You are plagiarizing titles. Shakespeare isn't around to defend *Much Ado About Nothing* or *West Side Story*.

GERSTEN:

You don't have to worry about him. He'll survive all of us. You should try to be as open as you can. What's wrong with a circus? Circuses are fine in the theatre. The day I saw that *Dream*, people, young, middle, and old, were listening to the words and to what was happening to believable, creditable people on stage. The fact that they did some circus tricks incidentally didn't matter a bit.

KAHN:

I never think that I am going to do an avant-garde production or a traditional production. The year that you saw *Love's Labour's Lost*, I also did a very traditional—in your terms—production of *Richard II*. I'm very eclectic. What I tried to say early on is that a play strikes you at a given time in a given way. I don't like directors who say, "Dammit, I'm going to do a white box production, or whatever damn play you hand me, I'm tired of going to a Growtoski production." I get a little tired of that—you give them a *Tempest* or a *Hamlet*, and it's going to come out a version of Growtoski. I find that shabby. I will not do a play that I don't feel I have a reason for doing at that particular time. It will either come out rock-and-roll, or come out whatever, because that play at that moment is important to me.

*   *   *

[1]Analyzed in *The Shakespeare Complex* (1975) by Loney and Mackay.

[2]At this time, Joseph Papp's New York Shakespeare Festival was producing in the Lincoln Center Theatres. He is referring to the Mitzi E. Newhouse Theatre.

Fig. 6. Designer John Napier transforms into a Quasi-Stratford's proscenium arch stage into a Quasi-Elizabethan Theatre: *Much Ado About Nothing* (1976). This basic set was used, with alterations, for Shakespeare repertory. (Photo: Joe Cocks/Royal Shakespeare Company)

The London Merchant. The Swan Theatre. From a model of Francis Kimbrough's production of an Elizabethan stage.

Fig. 8. Designer Ralph Koltai, with costumier Nadine Baylis, gives *Romeo and Juliet* an ultra-modern look for the 1980 Stratford Royal Shakespeare production. (Photo: Royal Shakespeare Company)

Fig. 9. The Forest of Arden as one tree, designed by Hayden Griffin, in *As You Like It* (Photo: The National

Fig. 10. Among the trees—designed by Carl Toms—in *Love's Labour's Lost*. (Photo: The National Theatre)

Fig. 11. Lavish costumes and elemental set props distinguished the Prospect Theatre's *Richard II* in Edinburgh's Assembly Hall. (Photo: Edinburgh Festival)

Fig. 12. Aerial view of the Elizabethan Theatre, inside the surviving walls of a Chatauqua Arena, as reconstructed for the Oregon Shakespearean Festival in Ashland, Oregon. (Photo: Dwaine Smith/Oregon Shakespearean Festival)

Fig. 13. *All's Well That Ends Well* on Ashland's Elizabethan Stage. (Photo: Hank Kranzler/Oregon Shakespearean Festival)

CREATING A SHAKESPEARE THEATRE

Frank Dunlop

Considering how many former students complain that college "taught them nothing," Frank Dunlop's generous praise of his teachers and his explanation of how they have helped him in his artistic career should be music to many dedicated instructors' ears. Trained by the late Michel Saint-Denis, at the Old Vic Theatre School, Dunlop first achieved international attention when Lord Olivier—then Sir Laurence Olivier—invited him in 1967 to become an Associate Director of the National Theatre ensemble, resident at the Old Vic and waiting impatiently for its new theatres to be finished. In addition to mounting some highly effective productions for the Old Vic stage, Dunlop, concerned about attracting young and working-class audiences to the theatre, developed the Young Vic Company.

Here, he discusses some aspects of the development of that troupe and its work, putting special emphasis on the audience-actor space that it created down the street from the Old Vic in a war-damaged building. Dunlop and the Young Vic separated from the parent ensemble. There is some evidence that this was a mutual relief. The Young Vic's Scapino, *staged by Dunlop, was a success both on and Off-Broadway, and the troupe later toured the United States with its athletic* Taming of the Shrew. *Dunlop's R.S.C.* Sherlock Holmes *was well received in London, New York, and on American tour, so his skill as a director has had wide exposure.*

* * *

I have been one of the lucky people in my training. I went to university, and my tutor, Professor Terence Spencer, later became the head of the Shakespeare Institute in Stratford-upon-Avon. Then, I went to the Old Vic school, where I had a thorough theatre training under Michel Saint-Denis. It gave me a fantastic background to work on later. I've been very lucky in that I've never had to drop the relationship with Terence Spencer; so that whenever I have done an Elizabethan or Shakespearean production, I've been able to go back and talk it through with him. I have seen the play from both the practical side of the theatre and from the scholastic point of view.

From those discussions quite a lot of extraordinary results came; sometimes in the over-all conception of a play, but often in details, which had a startling effect on the audience. One of the things which resulted from these discussions happened when we were preparing a Young Vic production of *Midsummer Night's Dream* several years ago. We decided that Theseus and Oberon should be played by the same actor, and Titania and Hippolyta should be played by the same actress. We analyzed why—both in terms of company recruitment and in terms of artistic theory. We did that in a production at the Edinburgh Festival, and it was a great success. Following that, Peter Brook took up the idea and extended it even further to do that magnificent *Dream*, making Puck also the master of ceremonies in Theseus' court, which we'd never thought of. When we did *Love's Labour's Lost*, it was Terence Spencer who pointed out to us that the play was really rather Shavian. Berowne was never pronounced Be-rowne, but he was Brown. The result was a very Shavian, straight-talking character, in the middle of all the oratory. He also pointed out to us a thing we never noticed as theatre practitioners: how remarkably experimental Shakespeare was. At the end of *Love's Labour's Lost*, suddenly one of the actors turns to all the others and the audience and says, "But when all's said and done, this is only a play," and suddenly the actors are actors on the stage. There's Brecht before his time!

I've been very lucky as the director of an all-purpose-built theatre, the sort of theatre in which I believe Shakespeare should be performed. I'm lucky that my life is practically all a kind of scholastic theatrical research and a kind of voyage of discovery into a way of performing Shakespeare that bears a close relationship to the Elizabethan performance. It's one of the great horrors of our time that most Shakespearean productions on which a great deal of money is spent are performed in old operatic theatres. In England, for instance, the National Theatre building, which is a very, very expensive one, has three theatres, and its repertory is based on the works of our greatest dramatists. Not one of those theatres bears the remotest relationship to the Elizabethan theatre. None of them, in fact, is capable of being easily adapted to be like an Elizabethan theatre.[1]

You see, I really cannot stand the idea of Shakespeare continuing to be performed behind a proscenium. From time to time, there is a glorious win over the nineteenth-century theatre form. Peter Brook scored a couple of times with *A Midsummer Night's Dream* and with his marvelous *King Lear*, but, in general, the proscenium places too much dependence on the operatic side of theatre.

Visual splendor is emphasized—not on the actor, but behind and around him. What the director and designer decide on visually becomes the style of the play. Incredibly subtle lighting sets the mood, rather than the use of words, and the proscenium theatre titillates the painterly imaginations of director, designer, and lighting man, rather than exciting the imaginations of the actor and the audience. In the bigger proscenium theatres, it forces the actors to sing, not to speak, and the water of emotion does a color-wash over the reason in the plays. In New York, you Americans are lucky to have a number of theatres which have an Elizabethan flavor. Joe Papp's got at least three of them, but unfortunately, you don't have much Shakespeare being performed in them, which is a pity. In England, we've only got two or three theatres in the whole country in which Shakespeare can be properly performed. The two big national companies still perform in what is essentially a proscenium situation.[2]

Unfortunately, when people do get the right sort of open-stage theatre, they tend to carry on the conventions of the proscenium theatre into that theatre. In the big open-stages, one often sees a complete setting being put onto an open stage bigger than anything you could see in an operatic theatre. Or you find the actors singing away, wallowing in emotion, instead of talking to the audience, as they should be able to do on an open-stage. Also, we're forced into having much bigger open-stages than we should: half because of fire regulations which say that everybody should have 2 square feet around them so they're not crushed together (and so they're not close enough to the stage) and half because of financial considerations, which means that we have to pander to the rich elements in society and give them very comfortable seats at the front, and not be able to have lots and lots of seats close together which are cheaper and allow the more unconventional audience to come in and see our plays. In Elizabethan theatre, the groundlings who paid the least money were closest to the stage. They were the most violent people, too, so that the actors couldn't take risks—or the authors either. That's why they were much more commercially minded then. The majority of the audience actually stood very close to the stage. We understand there were a few people sitting on the stage, very close, but they weren't very many. The stage had to be high because the audience stood up. They didn't provide seats for them. In the seventeenth-century in the Restoration theatres, people sat down, so the stage was a bit lower. They did have to put a railing along the front sometimes, to stop them rioting and attacking the actors. In the eighteenth-century theatre, the groundlings were still the closest to the stage.

At the National Theatre, because we were rather dissatisfied with the current situation, we decided that we wanted to get those groundlings into a theatre where they could be nearest to the stage, where the seats were cheaper, and where they could see the classical plays played something like they were originally. A group of us made a terrific plea that the whole front portion of the audience should be for groundlings; the area should be left without any seats put in; that for sixpence you bought a stool and took it in and sat closest to the stage. The people who wanted to be showy and wear their diamonds could all sit up in the circle around the sides because they weren't as interested as the people who could pay sixpence and take their own stool. We got a group of people together—

designers, directors, and architects—and we all designed our ideal form of theatre in which to perform Shakespeare and the classics. The result was a surprise to all of us. We didn't think we were going to design a Shakespearean-looking theatre; we thought it would be more modern. What we designed was a very simplified version of the Globe or Fortune—the Young Vic Theatre. It cost very little money because it was only a shell, just as the Elizabethan theatres were. It holds about 45 people. They are all within 20 feet of the acting area; they sit on hard wooden benches close together; they're in a great position for listening and watching closely.

Because this theatre was so simple, because we gained an untutored audience who didn't think about previous conventions, we found it also became a kind of center of research. We discovered that as in the Elizabethan theatre, words became dominant. The actor who wanted to make contact with the whole audience was at the front of the stage, in the center of the audience, in a dominant position. Whatever the actor touched and wore set the scene—we couldn't depend on scenery to make a statement first to the audience. Because there was so little setting, and costume and properties, we could make decisions during the rehearsals; we could make decisions a day or two before the play opened, so that we didn't have to commit ourselves until we'd done our research and our discovery-journey into the play. The director wasn't able to make pictures or rotate the scenery during the performance, so he had to depend on the words and movements of the actors in order to get the play over.

We discovered the staging was that of the mobile sculptor, rather than a painter. We had to work within a permanent architecture, so it was rather like doing a Calder sculpture inside a patio, whenever one produced a play. The actor was in three dimensions—not two—and was seen and heard in great detail because of the proximity of the audience. Not only was the audience close, but, because you cannot light the actors specifically, the audience reflected a great deal of light. The first production we ever did in the Young Vic, we'd already done in the Assembly Hall in Edinburgh two years before in nearer-to-normal theatre conditions. When we moved *Scapino* to London, we thought, "We can see the audience in great detail; why shouldn't we just leave the lights on? We want them to join in anyway." Well, we didn't leave the lights on at the beginning of the play, but through the play, gradually the lights got brighter and brighter. We discovered that the audience didn't know the lights were on, if we did it gently, and once the lights were on, they did partake more in the performance. Whenever an actor talked to them, they talked back, or at least nearly did, if they were frightened. When we wanted them to sing and play instruments at the end, which is rather an embarrassing and cheeky thing to do to a normal adult audience, they all did it!

Nobody was worried, because, seeing each other, they all became part of the some group of people doing something. They were all taking part in the same experience. It's a very modern thing, this isolating the actor—with light—from the audience. It's not a thing that happened in any classical theatre. Now, because that audience was as close as they were in an Elizabethan theatre, we found we had to act as presumably Shakespeare wanted; that is, talking to everyone in the audience. We couldn't just talk to the front rows; we couldn't talk to a lot of blackness; we had to talk personally to each person. We could see each person's face; we could see each person's reaction; we could occasionally see each person's contempt; we could hear what they were actually saying to each other. People in the front row would say, "Well, this is a boring bit, isn't it?" in front of us. We had to find a way of talking to those people individually.

Once we got beyond the first sort of worries about scenery, how much scenery we should have, what sort of costumes we should have, what sort of movements we should make, we found that the thing that we really had to think about was how to speak Shakespeare—how to speak the words. That's been the healthiest thing that's happened in the Young Vic. We had to find a way of creating excitement by the words. We discovered that if we used the words properly, they formed a decor; they formed a music; a permanent prod to the audience to stay interested and awake. When we used to play in a proscenium arch, if we did rather soupy lighting, a beautiful decor, and hummed a lot and spoke beautifully, people would go into a sort of serene state of contentment. They were comfortable, and people in that sort of theatre tend to go expecting that sort of contentment. We couldn't continue that style of playing.

The pleasure of the audience in our theatre has been in the story, the characters, and the way the story is told. Their pleasure is in the mastery of the writer. To make sure that the story held, and that every single word held, we found that all our company had to become researchers. That the process of rehearsal wasn't just my arriving and telling everybody, "Well, you move here, and this bit of scenery is here, and this is beautiful, and this is the interpretation of the whole play, and you have to do it like this, and you have to think like this." We found that the final performance would not hold unless every single actor on the stage, even if he stood there holding a spear, understood every word and every thought behind every word in the play. So, our three or four weeks of rehearsal, which are all we can afford, are like a seminar. We spend the minimum of time organizing the actors in and out of doors and doing dances on the final set.

We spend the maximum of time digging for attitudes, meanings, and double-meanings. We question everything, the slightest movement which qualifies a line, the slightest intonation on a line. We discovered as a result of this, lots of jokes that nobody had ever played before. We discovered many meanings that had never been played before. We began to be attacked for adding lines to plays because people thought, "Oh, he can't be as clever and as modern as that—he can't be as funny as that: Shakespeare!" It was because they were hearing things, understanding things for the first time. Only if we're crisply clear about every thought and word, dare we face the audience. And only if every single moment is in the intellectual control of the actor, is the audience held or entertained or fascinated. There's no substitute in the Young Vic, or, I think, in the Shakespearean theatre, for the clear conveying of reason; holding the interest of the audience by understanding every detail of what we're doing ourselves. The great theatrical moments are not enough—the great showy scenes are not enough. What I think we've discovered about Shakespeare in this research into detail is that he didn't depend on the great showy scenes. He didn't depend on the visual moments. He depended on a continual process of discovery with every moment of the play's action.

I'd like to make a final plea for the actor now to be considered an intellectual, an intellectual orator putting over a case to the audience on bchalf of the author, and he is to be helped in this, not directed in this, by the director and designer.

*   *   *

[1]Actually, the Cottesloe Theatre, the National's small experimental theatre-space has the potential to approximate outdoor or indoor Elizabethan stages, as well as later theatre forms.

[2]This was then true. At Stratford, the Royal Shakespeare has, however, tried to overcome this handicap by modifications of stage-audience relationships, effectually "breaking-out" of the proscenium frame. The National Theatre's Olivier and Cottesloe Theatres are free of restrictive proscenia. Its Lyttleton Theatre is not.

A STAGE FOR SHAKESPEARE

C. Walter Hodges
Richard Hosley
Ming Cho Lee
Glynne Wickham
Alois M. Nagler, Moderator

In Odessa, Texas, "The Globe of the Great Southwest" is advertised as the "world's most authentic replica of Shakespeare's Sixteenth Century English Theatre." And there are other "reconstructions" in America which purport to be faithful to the original. In this discussion, Professor Alois Nagler, author of Shakespeare's Stage *and acknowledged expert on Elizabethan theatre, moderates the theories and visions of both theatre scholars and practitioners. It becomes apparent that there are still areas of disagreement—not to mention a paucity of facts— about specific Elizabethan theatres, notably the Globe.*

C. Walter Hodges believes, however, that he has solved the riddle of the Second Globe, which replaced the original, which was destroyed by fire in 1613. But this discussion is not purely scholarly sparring, with leading experts trying to score points off each other. Hodges, for instance, would like to see his conception of the Second Globe made reality, both for historical values and for possible performance discoveries. Others, such as designer Ming Cho Lee, suggest that Elizabethan reconstructions serve antiquarian interests, rather than provide effective modern spaces for staging Shakespeare. A clear line runs the through contributions: whatever the Elizabethan stage may have been, how can knowledge of that prove useful to today's productions?

A British scholar and designer, C. Walter Hodges is well known for his The Globe Restored *(1954) and* Shakespeare's Second Globe: The Missing Monument *(1973). To illustrate this textual version of Hodges' presentation, Oxford University Press has kindly permitted reproduction of a number of the documentary and speculative visuals from the latter book, illustrations used as slides in his talk.*

Also from Great Britain is Dr. Glynne Wickham, Professor of Drama at the University of Bristol. One of his major contributions to theatre scholarship is Early English Stages: 1300 to 1660. *He has also a fund of practical experience acquired as an actor and a director. Professor Wickham is no stranger to America, having taught both at the University of Iowa and at Yale University, replacing Professor Nagler during a sabbatical term.*

Another respected theatre historian is Dr. Richard Hosley, Professor of English at the University of Arizona. He has published many articles, a number of which relate directly to the discussion topic. Aspects of the Elizabethan stage which have claimed his attention are the discovery space, the gallery over the stage, a reconstruction of the Swan Theatre, the origins of the so-called Elizabethan multiple stage, the music room in Shakespeare's Globe, and Shakespearean stage curtains. Ming Cho Lee is a distinguished—and very busy—stage designer whose work is seen on the stages of the Metropolitan Opera and the New York City Opera as often as it is on Shakespeare stages. He has visualized a King Lear *for the Lincoln Center Repertory, but much of his bardic design has been executed for the New York Shakespeare Festival. Illustrations for his contribution are from his own file of production slides. Among those design credits are* Coriolanus, Measure for Measure, Much Ado About Nothing, Richard III, Two Gentlemen of Verona, Comedy of Errors, Titus Andronicus, Henry IV, As You Like It, *and* Antony and Cleopatra. *The moderator, Professor Nagler, retired from his long stint as theatre historian at Yale University, has taught in the same area at the City University of New York Graduate Center.*

*   *   *

NAGLER:

The French, as well as the Spaniards, have excellent reasons to be proud of their dramatic heritage. Yet, I have not heard of any desire on the part of the French to build, as a sort of national shrine, a replica of a tennis-court playhouse such as the Marais where Cornielle triumphed with *Le Cid, Horace, Cinna,* and *Polyeucte,* nor is there any French call for a replica of the Hotel de Bourgogne where Racine reigned supreme. The documentation, especially for the Marais, is complete. We could build this playhouse tomorrow. Is it, perhaps, because there is no need for conjecture, no scholarly challenge, that the idea has not excited the French?

On the other hand, a great deal of guesswork would be required if the Spaniards were to attempt the building of a replica of one of their corral theatres in Madrid where Lope de Vega and Calderon fascinated both the mosqueteros and caballeros. Yet, to my knowledge, no such attempt has been undertaken, while many a precious Spanish courtyard has fallen victim to the bulldozer.

The English-speaking world takes a different attitude when it comes to Shakespeare and his contemporaries. We are intensely, perhaps even obsessively, interested in a stage for Shakespeare. There is a steady undercurrent of desire among scholars as well as practitioners of stagecraft to rebuild the "Glory of the Bank," be it Globe I, which Dr. John Cranford Adams redesigned, or Globe II for which Dr. Hodges has just finished the drawings.

This desire to have another Globe on earth culminated in Vancouver when the First World Shakespeare Congress unanimously passed a resolution "to encourage the hope that a studied effort will soon be made to build a full-scale reconstruction of Shakespeare's Globe Theatre. The Congress considers that such a reconstruction would be of the greatest value to Shakespearean scholarship and to the history of the theatre, as well as of widespread interest to people and to education everywhere in the world."

This was a clarion call for a full-scale authentic replica of the Globe.[1] But it is the authenticity which can hardly be established since Fortune has not favored us with a builder's contract for Globes I or II. Instead, she has given us the Fortune and Hope contracts, and as a special gift, De Witt's impression of the Swan interior. Those are our three most precious period documents[2] from which, however, we can only look only obliquely, as it were, at the two Globes. I get upset when I see the certified dimensions of one building transferred to another—when the magic numbers of the square Fortune (80, 55, 27 1/2, 43, 12, 11, 9) are played rather confidently in the Bankside Bingo. When I look at these ingenious reconstructions which rely heavily on maps and are made without the help of a carpenter's contract and without verifiable measurements, and yet are finished to the last doorknob, my thoughts turn to De Witt's Swan. Here is at least a modest degree of certainty. To be sure, De Witt did not leave us a scale drawing, and, in the absence of actual dimensions, we could not hope to build a replica even of the Swan, though one valiant attempt in this direction has been made. At any rate, it is refreshing to be confronted with one authentic, though crudely drawn, view of the interior of one Bankside playhouse.

In this connection, I would like to let you in on a secret. I have finally solved the mystery of the identities of the eight persons whom De Witt drew in the balcony, when, in 1596, he surprised the Swan actors at a morning rehearsal. The eight persons are, in order of their importance: 1) the author, 2) the author's friend who had just brought the script to the company, 3) the director, 4) the bookholder who had received the okay from the Lord Chamberlain's office for the script, 5) the stage manager, 6) the stage-keeper who had just swept the stage clean, 7) a hired man who had put the bench in place on stage, and 8) an illiterate landlord, Mr. Langley, a goldsmith by profession. If this sounds fantastic, I swear it is not any more so than some of the exotic theories brought forth by other Elizabethan scholars, Mr. Leslie Hotson, for instance.

When this drawing was discovered in Utrecht by Karl Theodor Gaedertz, it changed our entire conception of an Elizabethan public theatre and stage. It was the third great discovery within a century of curiosity. In 1790, Edmond Malone had brought the Fortune contract to light and other relevant Henslowe papers. This was the first important discovery to be used by countless future theatre historians. Then came, in 1831, Collier's publication of the Hope contract, fortunately not one of his forgeries. And in 1888, we had the De Witt disclosure. We might as well realize that since then, we have had no documentary discovery of significance.[3] This is perhaps our dilemma: we have exhausted the available evidence; we have begun to stretch and strain it.

We must not think of Jacobean theatre research as a legitimate branch of archaeology. The classical archaeologist works with foundations, but in Great Britain there are no theatrical foundations left that are younger than the Cornish Rounds,[4] and there are no ground-plans or elevations earlier than the Jones Cockpit-in-Court. Yet, we behave in a sort of pre-Winckelmann spirit, as if a classical archaeologist were permitted to apply the measurements of the theatre of Ephesus to that of Priene. To be sure, both were Hellenistic theatres and as such adhered to a certain period style. They had typical traits in common, but their dimensions differed and are known to us now only because of actual surviving remains. This much under the heading "Replicas."

There is another avenue of approach in providing a stage for Shakespeare. I am referring to various attempts to duplicate the advantages of a Jacobean open-thrust stage in combination with an auditorium which provides modern comfort for the spectators wrapped around three sides of the stage. I mention only the most successful solution in this direction—Stratford, Ontario. This stage reflects Jacobean elements in an arrangement that is both functional in terms of the plays and aesthetically pleasing to present-day audiences. The architectural shell has no relation to any of the towering fortresses which we encounter on the Visscher or Hollar maps. In other words, here is at work what I once called the Idea of an Elizabethan stage—the most we can hope to attain in view of our limited wisdom and restricted documentary resources. The Ontario stage is the closest approximation to the original stage for Shakespeare we can wish for. It showed itself in its full glory in Guthrie's *Richard III* and on many other occasions. At last we have overcome the pseudo-Elizabethan revival pedantry which goes back to Benjamin Webster and his *Taming of the Shrew* at the Haymarket in 1844. Webster, in conjunction with Planche, was the first to search for an appropriate stage for Shakespeare. He was hampered by the proscenium arch and arrived only at a half-baked solution. For the Induction, he still retained a painted set, while the play-within-the-play was enacted with "two screens and a pair of curtains." The production was greeted with mixed reviews. As this is germane to our subject, we might take the time to listen to the opposing critical viewpoints of 1844, as they might still be echoed in the 1970's. *The Times* critic greeted Webster's experiment with enthusiasm:

> It was a suggestion of Tieck that the plays of Shakespeare should be acted on the sort of stage which existed in the time of Elizabeth and James I, and although the revival at the Haymarket does not exactly follow this suggestion, it is in the same spirit, and allows the audience to judge of the effect of the play unaided by scenery. The Induction . . . is played in the ordinary manner before a scene representing an inn, but when he [Sly] is removed into the hall, there is no further change, but the play . . . is acted in the hall, two screens and a pair of curtains being the whole apparatus. By the mere substitution of one curtain for another, change of scene was indicated, and all the entrances and exits are through the centre of the curtain, or round the screens, the place represented being denoted by a printed placard fastened to the curtain. This arrangement, far from being flat and ineffective, tended to give closeness to the action, and by constantly allowing a great deal of stage room, afforded a sort of freedom to all the parties engaged. The audience did not in the least seem to feel the absence of scenery.

The critic of *Oxberry's Weekly Budget* refused to be mesmerized:

> But now, forsooth, we must have Shakespeare as originally acted! in all his primitive beauty! . . . Certain it is, that the exhibition of two blankets suspended from a rod, with written labels announcing the name of each scene is a miserable failure: therefore we say, away with all such pedantic affectation; give us the creations of our great dramatic writer, not as they were represented by the rude machinist of the Elizabethan age, but as the glowing imagination of the poet-

author would have loved to have seen them put upon the stage.

I suppose it's a matter of personal taste. I, for one, would have been quite bored later on by William Poel's pseudo-Elizabethan presentations of *Measure for Measure* or *The Tempest*, simply because, as an ordinary playgoer, I like to forget my academic credentials and bluntly express my preference for Zeffirelli's 1965 stage production of *Romeo and Juliet* (perhaps you might call it *Romeo e Giulietta*), but I was enchanted by it. But then I am quite certain that, in an earlier incarnation, I would have liked the Meiningen *Julius Caesar,* Irving's *Merchant,* and Booth's *Othello.*

Let me now come to the third and last string on which to harp on our theme. Here I am rather comfortable, for I am among colleagues whose primary concerns are the staging methods and techniques employed by Elizabethan and Jacobean directors. The subject in this case is the stage directions of the plays. They are most relevant to our theme: "A Stage for Shakespeare." Let's put the Globe instance behind us. Let us take the Swan elements at their face value: the fluid platform, the two doors, the "above" facility, the "shadow," even the two stage posts, and start operating from there. If any present-day director had the urge to revive Elizabethan staging, he would benefit from the exemplary scholarly work done by George Reynolds on the stage directions for the Red Bull and from the more recent labors of Bernard Beckerman and T. J. King.

I have outlined a few potential approaches to our theme. There are doubtless other options available. So, let us turn now to our panelists, each of whom over the years has paid attention to one or the other aspect of our topic and will now give a brief resume of his thoughts. I will ask Dr. Wickham to start off.

WICKHAM:

As Professor Nagler has observed, our title gives us some latitude. When he asked me to state my position, the first thing I thought I had to do was to ask myself whether I was interpreting "A Stage for Shakespeare" as a stage that Shakespeare himself might have used, or whether as a stage which we in our time ought to be using when presenting Shakespeare's plays. So, in stating my position I shall try, very uneasily I fear, to link these two possible approaches to the topic.

On the first part of the brief, my position is a very simple one—despite finding it necessary to fill three volumes in stating it and taking 15 years about it. I believe that neither Shakespeare himself nor his older and younger contemporaries held any fixed concept of the sort that we envisage when we talk about Elizabethan theatre or the Jacobean stage, with a definite article attached to it. The theatre that they knew was, by contrast, at least as I read the evidence, necessarily pragmatic rather than theoretical or dogmatic. Expediency and opportunism, in other words, were constants in their thinking, if not their vocabulary about stages, stage settings, and about auditoria. If any methodology informed their thinking about the theatre of their own time, then this derived from the simple need to supply an open space in which actors could meet with an audience, together with a convenient changing room. These minimal requirements were essential to their livelihood. Yet, simple as this objective and these requirements appear in themselves, in England between 1560 and 1660, they were never easy to realize and always in danger of being swept away soon as they were realized.

In the first place, acting was not recognized at the start of this period either by the nation at large or by the central government in London as a legitimate profession. Those of you who are interested in the rise of the profession, it changed its nature during this time. Secondly, several sectarian interests, some of which were religious and some of which were commercial, were quite determined that if this situation had to change, then the form of the change should be a total ban on acting of any kind. These interests had to wait until 1642 to be strong enough to get their way. They got it, closing all the theatres and making acting an indictable offence, punishable with fines and imprisonment.

A no less serious obstacle to the formulation of any professional methodology of theatre practice and theatre architecture, was the lack of land and the lack of money to finance the building of theatres on that land, either in London or in provincial cities. Actors seeking either of these commodities had, thus, to fight a constant battle on two fronts: against town councils and against property developers. It sounds very familiar in our own time. Even in the more leisured and sophisticated enclaves of the court, the university, and of the largest schools, acting was persistently regarded as an occasional pastime firmly harnessed to calender holidays and to special festivities of a domestic or occasionally a national character.

In such circumstances and in such conditions, anyone with ambition enough to try to establish himself as the manager of an acting company that earned its living collectively throughout the year by performing plays had no option but to compromise; to compromise with Parliament, to compromise with the law courts—both civil and ecclesiastical, to compromise with financial speculators and with local residents of any given area where the company hoped to build a theatre and present its plays. One further compromise had to be made—a compromise, in my view, of quite critical importance to any consideration of the plays in performance. Companies could not stay permanently based in any one place. Their economy was dependent upon the ability and the need to travel. They had to travel to survive.

Therefore, no company could afford to be very exacting in respect of its architectural, mechanical, and scenic requirements where its theatres were concerned. On the contrary, every company had to adopt a flexible approach and attitude to these requirements, to be ready to adapt its plays or to improvise a solution when these requirements were not exactly forthcoming or suitable to the play in question. They had to be content, in the last resort, with three or four essentials, whether at court in London or in the provinces. These essentials, in my view, were: first, an auditorium to which admission could be controlled and in which the privilege of a place had to be bought in advance, because the actors in question were not amateurs but professionals. Secondly, they required a stage preferably raised on which to act their play and to be the better seen and heard. Thirdly, they required a room or a tent in close enough proximity to the stage to serve as a changing room, or tiring house as they called it. Fourthly, they required a supply of scenic devices, of the kind that we would perhaps describe as large scenic properties, sufficient with these four necessities, the company could, at a pinch, perform any of its plays and thus earn its living.

The physical relationship between the arrangement of these components and the degree of elaboration that was possible in certain circumstances could vary considerably. However, experience taught its own lessons over the years. In the first place, inn and tavern keepers who had been very hospitable in the early part of the period came to be regarded as unreliable hosts. Court patronage, on the other hand, became an absolute essential as a protection against the actors' enemies who were seeking to destroy them and deny them a place in which to perform. It became desirable to be possessed, therefore, of a base of one's own, a home of one's own. To that end it became necessary to find wealthy merchants willing to advance the capital to lease, to buy, or to build that home, and thus to hand over a measure of control of those homes to the speculators who expected a return on their capital.

Provincial touring on muddy roads made it desirable to restrict scenic gear to simple emblems. In these ways, then, there did evolve a style of stage and a style of auditorium which we can recognize today as distinctively Elizabethan or Jacobean. In shape, it could be square; it could be rectangular; it could be circular. That didn't matter to them, nor need it matter to us. What did matter was the convenience of the actors and the comfort, or the relative comfort of audiences. For audiences that had to stand throughout a performance and, indeed, expose themselves to the elements of the English climate, that comfort must have been strictly relative.

But with tenure of the building came security, and with security came alterations and improvements. We know from Ben Jonson that the second Globe was fairer than the first. Londoners regarded the first Globe as an improvement on both the Theatre and the Rose. Others found the Blackfriars superior to both the first and second Globes.

From 1604 onward, companies could have used the proscenium arch stage and perspective settings but they chose not to. They did not wish to be pinned down by the elaborate machinery that was required to operate this kind of theatre, and it is doubted whether they had the funds to pay for it. Their nomadic economy thus effectively controlled the sort of theatre that they required and used.

With that said, and against this backdrop that I have tried to sketch of an evolving organism constantly controlled by the professional character of the acting companies, it's time for me to hand over the filling in of the detail to Walter Hodges and Professor Hosley.

But before I do so, I would like to examine very briefly the relevance, if there is any, of what I have said to the problem of finding a stage for Shakespeare today. I think that there are morals to be drawn from an understanding of the general context of the staging of plays in Elizabethan and Jacobean England. One of them to me is the fact that at the center lay the actor on an open space, an actor who could communicate what he had to say easily to the entire auditory. I think that is perhaps the first requirement. I think the next requirement is to give the eye something to look at as well as the ear something worth hearing.

We find it difficult to know how much to give, being the heirs to a pictorial tradition of staging Shakespeare in the nineteenth century. Half of our concern with the rebuilding of the Globe or any other single Elizabethan or Jacobean stage stems, as it seems to me, from this reaction to the picture stage. We have, perhaps, gone as far as we need to go in determining what kind of stage we need for Shakespeare. Professor Hosley will be talking more about this, I know.

In conclusion, I would like to observe that we have been adventurous in actually building thrust stages and the like. We have been adventurous for the past 50 years in cutting down scenic spectacle and giving the plot and the verse a better chance than maybe it had before. We have been adventurous in letting the actor speak directly to the audience in a way in which he was inhibited from doing within a picture frame stage. But we are still too hesitant in our attitude to the conditions in the auditorium. It is still thought necessary to plunge the auditorium into artificial darkness and to keep the stage highly lit. This vestigial characteristic of the picture stage separates the play from the audience in a way in which Elizabethan actors chose not to separate the play from the audience. The fact that they used contemporary dress as often as not is an indication of their feelings on this point. I think we ought, in other words, to trust the verse, and when the actor says it is night, for us to take it for granted that it is night without having to have an elaborate lighting change to make it so.

The other point: the auditorium. Our auditorium is still a hangover from eighteenth and nineteenth century court theatres. We have fixed seats everywhere and something of the hierarchy of the arrangement of those seats. A theatre auditorium is not an easy place in which to be informal and, yet, I think especially the young today wish to be informal when they are being entertained—when they are deliberately choosing to pay for recreation. I would feel, therefore, a good deal happier were the floor-space not as rigidly laid out in theatres for Shakespeare as they are. I would welcome the sort of situation that prevails at the promenade concerts or at the Roundhouse in London where people can come and go as they please. I think ultimately this presents an exciting and important challenge to the actors, because only if the actors can hold that audience still, quiet, and attentive, can the play work. When this is a responsibility taken off the actors' shoulders by the fixed seating and the inability of the audience easily to come and go, I think we lack something that was important to the staging of plays in Shakespeare's time and which we might, experimentally at least, restore.

With that said, I'm sure Ming Cho Lee, with far more experience of trying to devise a genuine stage for Shakespearean productions, will take that matter further. I hope only to have painted the backdrop for you.

NAGLER:

With this backdrop painted, the pictorial element in the background, we turn to Professor Hosley for filling in.

HOSLEY:

I'd like to make three very simple suggestions, very general suggestions, about the kind of stage which, in my view, we ought to provide for the production of Shakespeare—that is, what a stage for Shakespeare should be.

My first suggestion is that, regardless of whether the stage is to be temporary or permanent, professional or academic or festival, commercial or subsidized or both, it should be an open stage. By open, I mean being surrounded by audience on three sides; a thrust stage if you will, three-quarter-round, an open stage. This is not to denigrate our rich inheritance of proscenium arch stages throughout the world. We have those stages, whether we approve of them or not, and we must use them. One is especially appreciative of the very commendable and, to a degree, successful efforts which directors and designers have made over the past quarter-century not only to develop modes of production that have minimized the more deleterious effects of the proscenium arch, but also physically to adapt the structure of received stages so as to attain some of the advantages of an open stage. But in our sensible, if enforced, willingness to make do with what we have, we should not lose sight of the central proposition that the plays are more effectively performed upon the kind of stage for which they were written—an open stage. When we build new theatres, we should go the route of Stratford, Ontario, rather than of Stratford, Connecticut.

My second suggestion is that we should encourage, wherever possible, the establishment of experimental stages which may be thought of as three-dimensional hypotheses. That is, such experimental stages should have the in-built capacity for structural and decorative modification. Flexibility is the word. Such stages, in general, would embody the essential characteristics which all of us here at least agree belonged to the Elizabethan playhouse.

At this point, I would like to insert a commercial—a message—not from our sponsor. Our attention has been largely devoted to public playhouses like the Globe—those great outdoor amphitheatres which have so fired our imagination. The attention has been well bestowed, nor should it stop. In a moment you will be hearing of the necessity of its continuing. But, suddenly over the past decade, we have come to think we know quite a bit about the private playhouses—those less great but truly as fine indoor boxes which, if resurrected, might also fuel our imagination. The Blackfriars is a possible subject for such resurrection, though the historical remain conjectural.

But there are two other possibilities for reconstruction which would be hardly at all conjectural, which would be fairly factual, because of the survival of architectural designs. Of course, I am referring to the Cockpit-in-Court and to the unnamed playhouse for which drawings in the hand of Inigo Jones[5] survive in the library of Worcester College, Oxford, discovered and published by D. F. Rowan. I would like to interpolate a comment which occurred to me during Professor Nagler's introduction. He made the point that we now have a great trivium of sources: the Fortune contract, the Hope contract, and the Swan drawing. I think it might be argued now that we have a quadrivium, because the four drawings by Inigo Jones of this indoor private playhouse, without a name but dating from the Jacobean period, are a stunning source of information—one that I think is just as important in its own way as any of the first three sources that have been mentioned.

Much information might come from experimental stages. Will a three-door tiring house work? How does a three-door tiring house work? In saying this, I am shocked to realize, and I hope you will be too, even today we do not yet know. We might know, if we had developed proper experimental stages, how even a two-door tiring house works, and Professor Nagler has acknowledged that lack in bemoaning the fact that we have not yet seen the Swan playhouse, as depicted by De Witt, in operation, or anything like it.

My third suggestion relates to what I shall call, in counter-distinction to experimental stages will be, for the most part, academic stages, but the professional theatre requires a design that will be more or less permanent, though, of course, flexibility of decor must be possible. My suggestion is bi-fold; first, such a stage should not be Elizabethan; that is, it should not be be a reconstruction. Various reasons for this will occur to you. Second, a corollary: a fixed-design Shakespearean stage must have an architectural style that we accept simply as a style appropriate to a modern Shakespearean stage, something we can depend on and be comfortable with, both as actors and as spectators. Something we can see simply as a stage, without considering that it represents any particular scene in a pictorial or illusionistic way. Something that will be to us, in the late twentieth century, what the Elizabethan architectural style was to the Elizabethans. Tyrone Guthrie and Tanya Moisiewitsch made a good beginning. Perhaps they have the answer. In any case, other answers are possible and should be proposed. It is up to the designers and the directors.

NAGLER:

We turn now to the pictorial part of our discussion. Dr. Hodges?

HODGES:

My position in this symposium may be very simply stated: I am that proverbial fool who rushes in where angels fear to tread. Perhaps the word rush does not describe my position, but for a long time I have been circling around this circular (or was it polygonal?) building, the Globe playhouse, until it has finally sucked me in like a vortex or perhaps like water emptying out of a bath, and here I now stand, naked at last, to declare openly that we not only can, but in fact should rebuild Shakespeare's Globe playhouse somewhere in the world. The time has come to do it.

The angels, however, do not really agree with me. They are not themselves timid; they are very wise and very learned and responsible people, and they are probably even right! "Beware the Jabberwock, my son," they say. "Beware the hasty decision, and shun the frumious conjecture bird." "There are still too many objections to be overcome." That is true. But I think somebody has got to stand up and take the blame, and since I seem to have gotten myself into that position, very well then, let it be me. So far as objections are concerned, let me offer a quotation from Dr. Johnson's *Rasselas, Prince of Abyssinia* which I rather like. In it one of his characters is made to say, "Nothing will ever be accomplished if all possible objections must first be overcome." Amen to that, say I.

Now let me say why I think we ought to have the Globe rebuilt. But first let me make it clear that it is not a part of my argument that it necessarily provides the best sort of theatre for the staging of Shakespeare. I only think we ought to have it rebuilt, once, somewhere, as an example and as something to experiment with. First, we ought to have it simply because it does not exist. It is the archetypal building of the beginning of the professional public theatre; the first in the world built and managed for and by professional actors. I recently called it the missing monument of theatre history. We do miss it—at least some of us do. Let us have it back!

Secondly, there are things which we still do not know about its structure and appearance and we shall certainly find out a great many of them simply by taking the serious thought and action of setting about its construction. Let me give an example. I was asked several years ago to prepare designs for just such a reconstruction. Because of being asked what I should seriously recommend, instead of dealing with theoretical possibilities, I stumbled upon some very straightforward ideas which had previously been overlooked, I think, by everybody—certainly by me. Some of the ideas, I will be vain enough to say, are almost certainly right, and they are new contributions. If they are all right.

Now let me talk about being wrong. It is nice to talk about that because of its certainty. It is true that if we rebuilt the Globe, as I think we should, we can be quite sure of one thing—that to some extent we must and will be wrong. We have to be brave about that. We need not be very wrong but we must accept a certain degree of wrongness. What we could aim to do is to build a Globe playhouse into which we might imagine the spirit of Burbage and Shakespeare standing in the midst and saying, "That's it! Here we are again. I see they've made a number of changes in the old place since we were last here, and it seems to have been redecorated, but it's very nice. It is a true and proper playhouse."

Now, to do this is not just a cranky and unprofitable idea. If you think so, may I invite you to consider what are today possibly the three most important influences bearing upon our modern stage and its methods. Who have been the modern revolutionaries? Gordon Craig? Adolph Appia? Max Reinhardt? Actually, I think not. I would offer: 1) the Russian experimentalists of the 1920's—Tairov, Meyerhold, Vakhtangov and others; 2) Bertolt Brecht; and 3) Surprise! surprise! Although Dr. Nagler does not agree with me, I think old William Poel and his old Elizabethan Stage Society, with his "notions" about open stages and his proposal—which failed—to rebuild the Globe Theatre in London's Battersea Park in 1899. His theories and his wish to do this inspired and trained a whole school of actors and directors, led notably by Sir Tyrone Guthrie. They have added enormously to the methods and flexibility of modern staging—especially the staging of Shakespeare.

Well, there is more revolution where that came from, I believe. Rebuild the Globe and we shall find the new, if old, music in it. I would again make a comparison which has been made before of the modern revolutionary discovery of the beauties and potentialities of the harpsichord and its music. I hope that is not what is known as being high-falutin'. I actually do not think that any kind of pleasure is any kind of falutin'. I don't want to go into any more general or theoretical discussion at this stage because I have a number of pictures to show you of a building which we actually could erect for Shakespeare's Globe, without too much of that fearful Jabberwocky creature, the conjecture bird, which comes whiffling through the tulgey wood of academic desperation. I must apologize to a number of people in the audience who may have seen some of these pictures before. Most, but not all, of them are taken from a book of mine. But, let us look at them very quickly. I shall just flip through them so that we shall all be on an even footing and then can have a discussion later after Ming Cho Lee has proceeded to a modern area of discussion. Then I shall try, I hope not too unsuccessfully, to defend the nakedness of folly against these kind angels who would try to cover me up.

Now, this we know: Visscher's 1616 Panorama of London (Slide 1). And this: the DeWitt drawing of The Swan (Slide 2). I don't know what the four-fold thing of quadrivium is, but I would suggest that here (Slide 3), Hollar's Long View of London, is the thing that has not been taken seriously, and it is this Globe—the second Globe—the building on the left. I will not go into the business that we have heard so much about the misplacing of the names on these. I must ask you to accept it. The Globe is the one on the left, called the "Beere bayting," and the one on the right, called the Globe, is actually the "Beere bayting." This has been established. Please allow me to take it for granted. Here is a close-up of the Globe (Slide 4). And here is his drawing for it (Slide 5). This was done in full view of the original! This building is drawn by a first-rate artist who was sitting there and looking at it! And it is Shakespeare's Globe. Not the one that he did most of his work for, but the one that he must surely have had a hand in, towards the end of his life. Therefore, it is a Shakespearean type of theatre. And we may take this form reasonably for granted.

Taking it for granted, I have made a number of projections from it, trying to get it as close as possible to the picture that Hollar has given us (Slide 6). I have finally been obliged to accept certain extraordinary dimensions, such as that great roof which you see there. At its base, where it joins the building, it's 64 feet across. You will see that I have left out the pillars on the stage. It gives me great pleasure at this time to apologize to Dr. Nagler who, in his book, *Shakespeare's Stage*, said that he doubted whether there were these two pillars on the stage of the Globe. In point of fact, in the second edition of my own *Globe Restored*, I crossed swords with him about it and said that I could not agree. We were then talking about the first Globe, but when it comes to the second Globe, I have rejected these two pillars. It is interesting that the field of scholarship is beginning, gradually working from different directions, to come together on this. I'm so sorry, Dr. Nagler, about that. Let's accept this.

Those of you who haven't seen this before must be saying, "How on earth can you hold up that huge roof without having

Slide 1. Section of Visscher's 1616 panorama of London.

Slide 2. The Swan Theatre.

Slide 3. Hollar's Long View of London—section showing The Globe and
Beere bayting."

Slide 4. The mislabeled Globe Theatre.

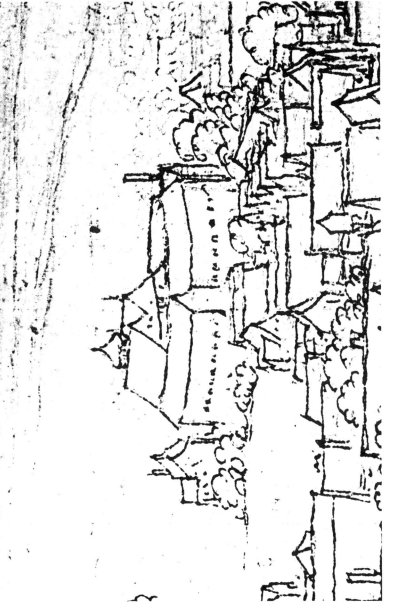

Slide 5. Hollar's sketch for The Globe.

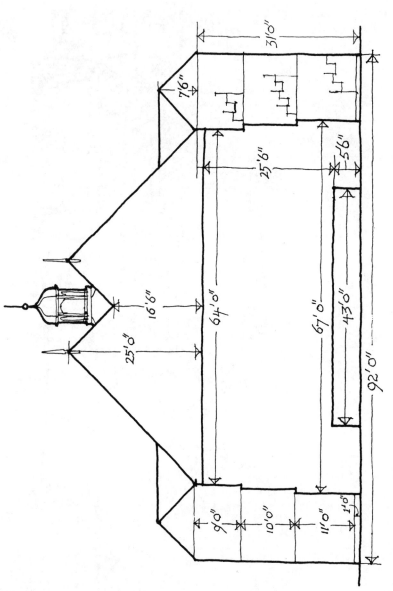

Slide 6. Hodges' projection of the Globe's interior. (Hodges' drawings courtesy of Oxford University

anything to support it from underneath?" This was a problem
that bothered me enormously. The answer that occurred to me
was that the thing that looks like a house up there is not a house
at all. It is a great hollow structure. What you are looking at there
is merely a frontal screen. Inside it there is a structure of
hammer beams. The purpose of that great roof was to be self-
supporting to do away with those posts standing on the stage.

This is a side view (Slide 7), as you see. I want you to notice
that funny little shady portion there at the side. I'm not going to
explain it in great detail, but I was trying to find out exactly how
the big "heavens" roof was connected to the back of the frame
of the surrounding gallery building. It is quite obvious to you
that you couldn't have a great hollow where it is shaded A-C-B
because the rain water would collect in it. You could level it off
at A-C, but the most likely thing to happen would be to bring it
up to A-D merely to take the rafters up and join them to the
back of that building.

Here (Slide 8) is a cut-away, showing the interior of the
previous view. You will see that I have placed above the tiring
house and, in the roof made by that space of the sloped roof at
the back, I have made a position where the flying effects from
the heavens can be arranged.

Here is a drawing (Slide 9) which I made from those
measurements to be as like as possible to Hollar's picture of the
Globe, which I accept as being an accurate representation of
what he saw. This is from the front (Slide 9). Here it is from the
back (Slide 10). You will see that curious peaked-up roof going
up and joining the back of the heavens' superstructure. The
thing I want to put to you very quickly is that if for any reason
one dismantled the superstructure—if it burned down or if it
made the place too dark—or for any reason you didn't want it,
what you would have left would be a thing like that (Slide 11).
Do you see that funny bit where the roof that used to be against
the superstructure sticks up like a little peak? You have to mend
that up somehow, because you've got to replace the thing that
was supporting it. So, I suggested that this was mended just as it
stood, giving that impression from that same point of view.

Come around to the side (Slide 12), and you have that
impression which is recognizable, I think, as that other building

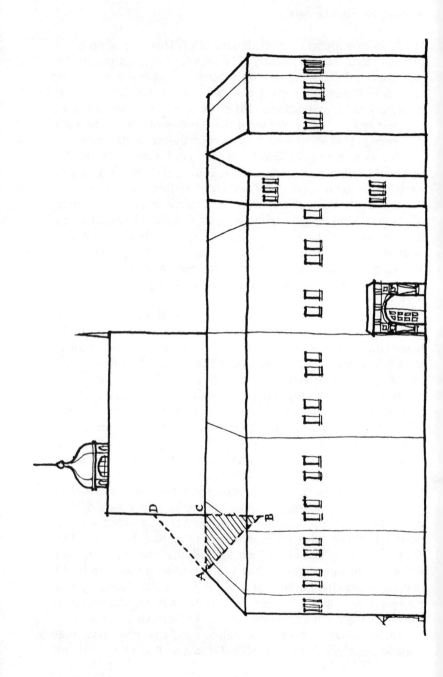

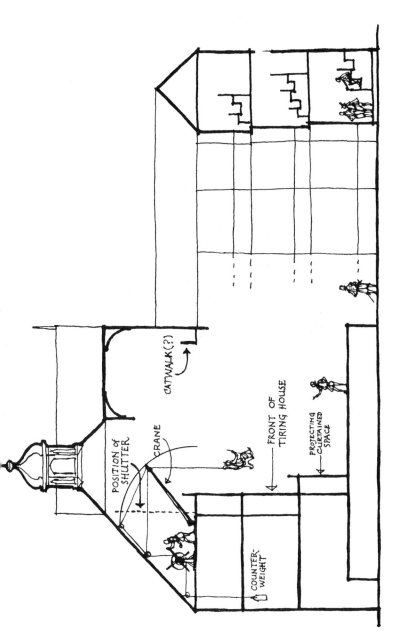

Slide 8. Hodges' sketch of cut-away section of previous view.

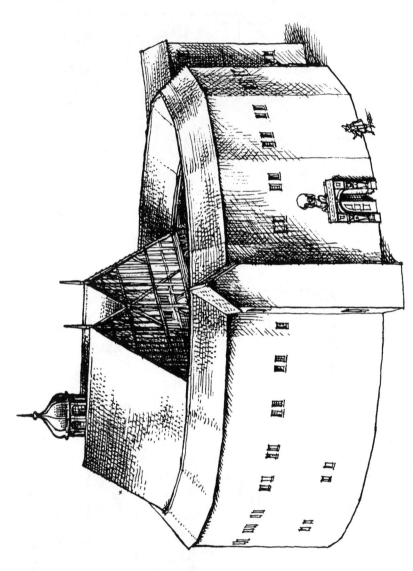

Slide 9. Hodges' sketch of front view of the Second Globe.

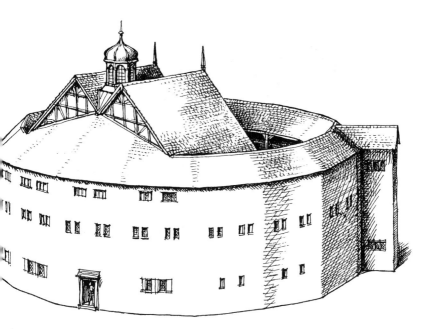

ide 10. Hodges' sketch of rear view.

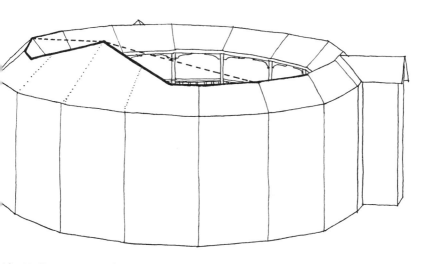

ide 11: Rear view, with superstructure removed.

Slide 12: Side view resembling The Hope Theatre.

Slide 13: Hodges' reconstruction of interior of the Second Globe.

on the right of the Long View picture which is the Hope playhouse. The interesting point about the Hope playhouse is that we know, because we have the contract, that there were no pillars standing on the stage to support so-called "heavens." What I am suggesting is that, in fact, this, as shown here, is a later stage of the building, when they had ceased using it as a theatre and were using it only as an animal baiting arena, and that the heavens made the place too dark, and they dismantled the heavens, leaving only that funny little peaked-up bit at the back.

Here is a cut-away drawing (Slide 13) of the interior, in which you can see the hollow of the roof inside, where the heavens are. You can see, also, how that big, curious onion-shaped cupola on top was a lantern letting in light at the back of the stage. This vast superstructure must have taken away rather more light than it should have done from the stage. They let in more by putting a lantern there between the two gables.

But you've seen enough. My suggestion is that we could rebuild the Globe, and that we should have very great value from doing so—quite apart from the fact that it would be so very interesting!

NAGLER:

It's time for the artist to make an entrance: Ming Cho Lee!

LEE:

I must confess that I have always had difficulty reading Shakespeare. Since English was not my native language, Elizabethan English became just so much gibberish for me. However, I am very fortunate in that I have been the principal designer for Joe Papp for many summers. I have had the opportunity of designing productions for Shakespeare in the Park. Therefore, my contact with Shakespeare has generally been through active production experience. It is only as a practitioner of theatre, as a set-designer, that I will try to talk about how we attempt to deal with this great body of theatre literature.

I think any discussion of the contemporary ways of setting a stage for Shakespeare must begin with Stratford, Ontario. There is definitely a "Before" Stratford and an "After" Stratford. I think it is essential to know the importance of Sir Tyrone Guthrie and Tanya Moiseiwitsch and their association with the Festival Theatre at Stratford, Ontario.

First of all, it is a theatre which captures that essence without *being* the essence of Elizabethan theatre. It captures that essence without being a replica of the Globe. I am not objecting to reconstruction, but that has very little to do with producing a play or setting the stage for a play. In a reconstruction of the Globe, accurate or inaccurate, the interest tends to be historical or architectural. Some of the reconstructions or replicas, also, are not very good. There is one at Hofstra and one at Ashland, Oregon, where earlier attempts at reconstruction resulted in something like high-class Disneyland. You can have every timber in place, all the corner bracing, the roof—everything! But if the stage and the audience are divided, separated, you lose the whole spirit of the Elizabethan theatre.

The theatre at Stratford, Ontario, is not a reconstruction, but it does capture the spirit of Elizabethan playhouses. I saw productions in Stratford before the new Guthrie-Moisiewitsch theatre was built, and they were quite different in staging and feeling from those done after. In the new house, there was an awareness of the spirit of the play. And what is the spirit, the essence that is captured by the Stratford, Ontario, theatre? First, the theatre is non-pictorial, non-literal, and totally non-illusionistic. Secondly, there is immediacy and direct contact. We realize that it grew out of the necessity of having an open place where actors can act and audiences can react. The most important thing is that the performing area and the audience area are under one roof—there is no separation. If there is a stage-frame separating one from the other, no matter how great the acting, the audience is still only looking in. Without the picture-frame, we are all involved in what is happening in the same room. This is one of the important things about the essence of the Elizabethan theatre that the Stratford, Ontario, theatre made clear to us.

Pace is very important to Elizabethan plays. There aren't many long scenes. In grand opera, though, you wait for the great picture to change, and then you wait another forty minutes for another grand scene. But in Shakespeare's plays, you don't have time to rest. One thing piles up on another. You have two people come on; they say something and then go out before a battle occurs. Before the battle is finished, someone comes on and says, "Well, what the heck, I'm just going to die and leave all this nonsense!" It just keeps on going, piling up. But if you're tied down with theatre mechanisms and a lot of scenery and have to wait to change it, then you've lost the spirit of the play—and the theatre!

Another thing that the Stratford theatre made clear is that it is obviously a stage, with all its limitations. You know exactly what the volume is. You are in it; the actors are on it, and you know that if they go out, they are off the stage, outside that space. They no longer concern you. It is that little area, that little stage where things happen. So Stratford, Ontario, has had a great influence in terms of how we direct and design Shakespeare.

I'm not going to talk about the merit of thrust stages versus end-stages—if it manages to capture the spirit of those plays, it is just as good as a thrust stage. So long as it's under one roof, actors can come and go through a variety of entries, and actor-audience contact is immediate.

I think Dr. Nagler is right: that we have gone as far as we can go with neutral architectural stages, with color and excitement coming from the costumes and scenic props. When Tyrone Guthrie and Tanya Moisiewitsch went to Minneapolis to create the Guthrie Theatre, they deliberately did not construct a permanent architectural unit. Thus, it's possible there, when doing Shakespeare, to create a visual statement for the play. This opens up many possibilities.

I want to make a general statement about designing for Shakespeare. First, you should be making an overall statement about the play, separating the general from the specific. Desdemona's bed is a specific, whereas the total visual environment is the overall statement. Lately, designers for Shakespearean plays have been trying to strike a balance between specifics and generalities. If you are designing for *Henry IV, Part 1*, and the statement for the tavern becomes so important, so complete, so detailed that the battle cannot happen within it, then you have designed a tavern, but not *Henry IV, Part 1*. It's the overall statement that you have to make—then only add a specific such as a table or a lamp, to say, "We are in a tavern." Then, the table or the lamp can be removed, and we are someplace else. I hate to reduce designing a play to formulas, but this is a very basic point about designing and staging Shakespeare's multi-scene plays which must be understood.

Now I'd like to show some illustrations which will illustrate what I've been talking about. Gordon Craig and Adolph Appia were innovators in the pictorial proscenium-arch stage tradition. Appia was so concerned with musical drama that he dealt very little with Shakespeare. Craig has designed a complete setting for the sleepwalking scene. God knows what's going to happen for the battle. Actually, the whole play of *Macbeth* happened on the staircase . . . no, that would have been a disaster. Not that this, by itself, is a bad design. It is a marvelous design. Impossible, but marvelous! But it illustrates the difference in the way designers approach Shakespeare. For Gordon Craig, here he wanted to capture the totality of Lady Macbeth's sleepwalking—not being able to wash the blood off, and so forth. And he'd go on, designing scene after scene. But add them all up, and you don't have a production with pace or an overall statement.

There is Robert Edmond Jones' design for *Macbeth*. Jones we call the father of American designers. Jones' approach was usually light, even though this design is rather unique. You see that all those giant inverse teeth can be removed. But it is still a specific, and such a specific becomes a total setting, rather than only a detail within an overall statement for the play. Here (Slide 14) is Douglas Schmidt's Central Park production of *King John*. I would say that this is going pretty far in terms of making a basic statement complete. It is neutral enough. The war-machine structure makes the basic statement about *King John*. This is the general, the essential; then the specifics, the details are brought on and carried off.

Slide 15: *Richard III*, Ming Cho Lee, designer. (Photo courtesy Ming Cho Lee)

This (Slide 15) is my design for *Richard III*. It is a model. This is my overall statement for *Richard III*, which we felt was a pretty nasty play. It is about thrones and crowns and family squabbles. There is a metallic environment for the whole play. The metal has heraldic designs on it, but it is a collage of heraldry in tarnished metal. The throne comes on, and then we have the throne room. We add banners, of course, and then we pitch two tents, it becomes the battlefield. Those are specific things.

By the way, Stratford, Ontario, is marvelous with the specific. The overall is so neutral because it's completely architectural. They spend all their time and effort making props that really crystallize the scene. One set of costumes goes off, and another set of costumed performers come on and change the whole look of the scene.

I am fortunate enough to have designed *Henry IV, Part 1*, twice. This (Slide 16) is the earlier one in Central Park, which Gerry Freedman directed. We felt then that *Henry IV* was a very warm, human, intimate play. That it was less about politics and more about generation gaps, about difficulties between a father and his son. For that reason the structure is wood, not metal, and the crown—the history—is symbolized by the three warriors. Now, I think that was a little heavy-handed on my part.

This (Slide 17) is another *Henry IV*, which I did for Gordon Davidson at the Mark Taper Forum in Los Angeles. The timber is still there. There is an intimate environment, which is that wooden structure, but it is set within a colder environment of stones. This is a collage: pre-Tudor, English Gothic, medieval architecture—but it is not a real building.

Here (Slide 18) is *Comedy of Errors*—a two-dimensional farce, and it was designed two-dimensionally. All the houses pivot for variation. We tried to create a sense of a performance platform. A variety of painted curtains were used to change the scene. Perhaps we carried immediacy too far in *Two Gentleman of Verona*, which became a musical comedy. Still, the approach (Slide 19) is a basic structure, and all the pieces are specifics.

This (Slide 20) is *Much Ado About Nothing*. It was done in the period of 1912. Again, it is a structure making an overall statement about that period and its life and concerns.

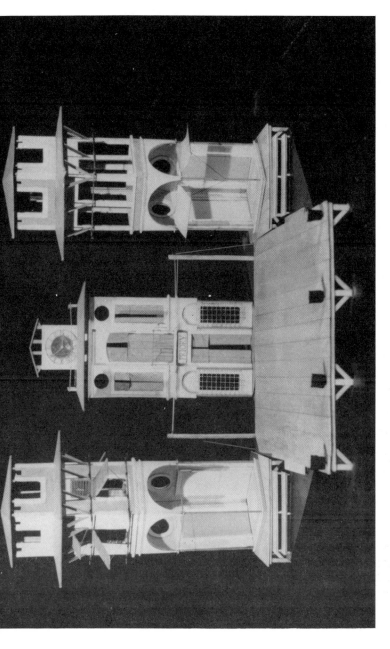

Slide 18: *The Comedy of Errors*, model of set for Central Park, Ming Cho Lee, designer. (Photo courtesy Ming Cho Lee)

Slide 19: *Two Gentleman of Verona*, Ming Cho Lee, designer. (Photo courtesy Ming Cho Lee)

Slide 20: *Much Ado About Nothing,* model of set for Central park, Ming Cho Lee, designer. (Photo courtesy Ming Cho Lee)

NAGLER:

Thank you very much, Mr. Lee. Now let's open the floor to any questions you might have.

* * *

QUESTION:

The pictures of the Globe that Mr. Hodges showed us pose a question raised many years ago by Alfred Harbage. If you have people standing around the stage, those on the sides aren't going to be able to see the inner stage are they?

HODGES:

This question of the inner stage is one of those problems that we might find out more about if we had a reconstructed Globe with an adaptable tiring-house facade. The difficulty is that it would appear that in certain theatres at certain times, the most privileged spectators would sit not only at the side of the stage, but in the lord's room over the stage, whatever that might be. It might have been that upper stage into which Professor Nagler put the stage manager and all those other persons he spoke about. We simply don't know what they expected to see or how much they expected to see into the inner stage. For this reason, I have tended to support the idea that there might have been a little curtained booth thrust out onto the stage, which could be seen very much better from all around. There is, in fact, a quotation—which I cannot give the exact reference for at this time—a fairly late quotation about the audience peeping into the "discovery." So it would appear that some of the audience in the auditorium were able to see behind the curtains used for discovery scenes.

HOSLEY:

I'd like to add one or two points about the inner stage. The first one is that there was no such thing as an inner stage. There was no inner stage, and I'm quite convinced of that. That position, which may seem to you very iconoclastic and perhaps even unduly captious, is emphasized for us by the fact that we do have three illustrations of Elizabethan or Jacobean stages or Caroline stages which have utterly no ambiguity about them. The Swan drawing is one; the Cockpit-in-Court drawing by John Webb is another, and Inigo Jones's drawings for the unnamed Jacobean playhouse which I have referred to is a third. In each of these illustrations, we see a tiring house facade simply with doors in it; two in the one, five in the second, and three in the third, but no hint of an inner stage. Discovery was fairly simple. You put up curtains in front of the doors and you had a space which you could use occasionally, if you wanted to discover Falstaff or hide Polonius and that was it. The stage directions really make very little demand for such use of curtains. Another proof of this pudding is in the professional theatre approach to the problem. You don't find inner stages in the professional theatre. Why is that? Because when you need to have a curtain to discover Ferdinand and Miranda, for example, you fit it up wherever it's convenient in the set you provided.

LEE:

There is a misconception in usage for the "above" and "below." There is an above and below, but many designers feel that since it is there, you had better put a lot of money into constructing it and play a scene there. Even Stratford, Ontario, which has one of the greatest aboves, never plays a long scene up there because the sightlines are so terrible. You take four steps back and the whole bottom half of your body is lost. It is there because, aside from an obvious thing like Juliet on the balcony, it gives tremendous possibilities for relationships and movement—you can start a scene up there; you can finish the scene downstairs and suddenly have people coming through underneath. It is that kind of relationship, the fluidity, the potential for movement, that the above and below provide. I am certain that's what happened on the Elizabethan stage.

WICKHAM:

I wish to strongly support both of these two statements. In respect for the Cockpit-in-Court, where we have the actual dimensions, anybody can simply draw the sightlines for himself on the ground plan and find that there is no space in which to act a substantial scene. As far as the point that I was making earlier about the essentials of the Elizabethan stage, I think it can be further refined to mean a stage for the actors, a tiring house or changing room, and a frame, as they called it. These are three separate and independent items which can be put together as you like. The whole question of the upper stage has arisen. We have failed to see that it is part of the auditorium and not part of the stage.

QUESTION:

You talk about the sightlines. If you have columns on stage, they would obstruct sightlines for a lot of people.

LEE:

You are right. I don't think sightlines are that important, in that sense. The whole horseshoe opera house, with people sitting three-deep, has bad sight lines. If something special happened, everyone would stand up and peep around. I think it's the whole ambiance of the theatre that's very different from fixed-seating, where people can't move their seats and then you have to worry about sightlines. It's a different kind of theatre, so worrying about sightlines for the inner stage, in a way, is going against the spirit of the whole theatre.

HODGES:

It is obvious from nearly everything that is said about the the Elizabethan theatre that the emphasis was upon hearing rather than seeing. There was plenty to see, but as I think Professor Wickham said earlier, the audience was auditory. People were listening—you went to hear a play. In this respect, what Ming Cho Lee has to say about opera houses is relevant because you go to hear an opera. So opera houses were built in order that people could sit and hear. I don't think the sightlines were very bad, but they were not perfect. But the acoustics were excellent.

WICKHAM:

The auditorium was mobile; people had standings, not seats. That is important here. Anybody who has sat behind a pillar in a London or New York theatre of a certain vintage and got frightfully irritated tends to think of Elizabethan sightlines in those terms of reference. The Elizabethan was not pinned down in the seat that he was sitting in. He could simply move a little to the left, move a little to the right, if he wanted to see.

QUESTION:

Professor Wickham has just made a decisive statement about seating on the stage. Isn't there a lot of controversy about that?

WICKHAM:

Seating on the stage was de rigeur up to 1631, subject to correction from Professor Nagler, because of the vulgar matter of money. I suppose it is a built-in characteristic that goes with snobbery; there are many people who like to be seen and who, given the opportunity, like to be part of the show. This is something that you could be made to pay for, and Elizabethans and Jacobeans made them pay for it. They paid a shilling for their seat on the stage in the public playhouses—much more for seats on the stage in the private houses. They were the most expensive seats of all. Charles I, on the other hand, banned sitting on the stage at the Salisbury Court. I don't think that the ban extended to the public theatres.

NAGLER:

You mentioned a controversy about it. There isn't really. We are all in agreement that sitting on the stage started in Blackfriars, a private playhouse, and from thence, custom spilled into the public theatres. By 1599, when the Globe was built, we assume, though we have no proof, that spectators were admitted onto the stage. Of course, by the time Dekker's pamphlet appeared, *The Gull's Hornbook*, which is 1609, we have a satirical comment on the gull who pays his shilling and gets onto the stage with his tripod, creeping out from the hangings, "as if he were a piece of property." There we have the strong proof that a curtain was in the back from which this gull made his entrance at the last moment. If he had come in earlier, the audience would not recognize him. So, by 1609, the custom was established. There is no controversy about it.

HOSLEY:

When Dekker talks about this in *The Gull's Hornbook*—how a gallant should behave himself in the playhouse in 1609—he's referring to both the private and public playhouses. It just seems as though he's referring to the custom—at least as it may refer to the public playhouse—as a new thing—something that may have spilled over, as has been said, from the private playhouses to the public; presumably through the King's Men playing alternately in winter and summer in both kinds of playhouses. I think that is a good way to look at it. In 1604, at the time of Marston's *Malcontent*, which was played first at the Blackfriars and then at the Globe, we have, in the Induction by John Webster, a categorical statement on the question. The character Sly, who has come on stage, wishes to sit on the stage, but he is not permitted to by the actors who have come on stage to play this Induction. He is shown to a room, to one of the boxes, presumably where he will be comfortable—a lord's room or a gentleman's room.

NAGLER:

By 1609, the lord's or gentleman's room had become out-of-fashion. It's known for the hirelings or whoever were sitting there—the mechanicals, the citizens. But I would say the reference in *The Gull's Hornbook* is clearly to the public playhouse because the way the groundlings behave towards the gull, they couldn't be in a private playhouse.

HOSLEY:

Another advantage of sitting on the stage is that you come in through the tiring house, so you're going backstage, not only after the show in order to have champagne in the star's dressing room, but also you're going backstage before the show begins, hobnobbing with the actors.

QUESTION:

Where on the stage were they sitting?

HOSLEY:

At the sides.

NAGLER:

There's nothing wrong with spectators seated on the stage. Molière, throughout his entire career, had spectators on the stage. He didn't mind them. The only time Moliere minded spectators on stage was when they were ill-behaved; some marquis tried to show off his clothes or that kind of thing. Otherwise, it was an accepted convention, just as we accept now that the actor steps almost into our laps.

*   *   *

[1]The call has been heard at Wayne State University and in London, where actor-producer Sam Wanamaker plans a "reconstruction" of the Globe near its original site.

[2]This changed with the 1989 discovery of the foundations of the Rose Theatre (ca. 1587) near the original Globe site, where excavations were also under way, revealing some Globe remains as well.

[3]101 years later, new evidence appears. But Professor Nagler was speaking well over a decade before the discovery of Rose and Globe Foundations.

[4]See above.

[5]A replica of Inigo Jones' Cockpit is to be included in the Wanamaker Bankside Globe project.

*   *   *

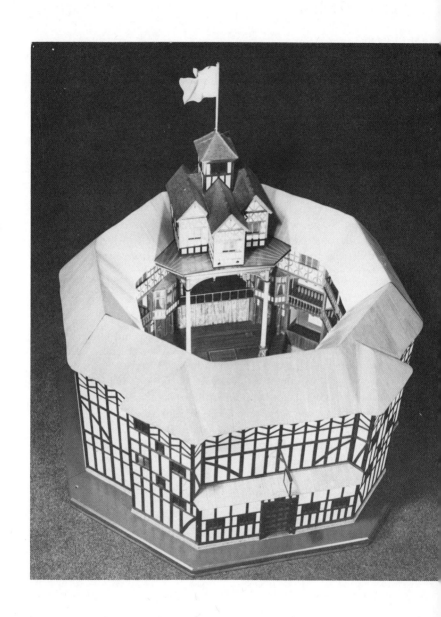

Figs. 14 and 15: John Cranford Adams' Conception of the Globe Theatre: Model now in the Folger Library, Washington, D.C. (Photos: Hofstra University)

MUSIC AND SHAKESPEARE

Suzanne Bloch
Richmond Crinkley
Richard Peaslee
Virgil Thomson
Stoddard Lincoln, Moderator

Too often there seems to be an almost schizoid split between theatre scholars and theatre practitioners. Some of the former affect to despise virtually any contemporary production, especially if it is "commercial." And some of the latter insist that their own "feelings" about Shakespeare and other master playwrights are the only guides they need for effective acting, directing, or designing. This discussion, however, shows how research and practice can cooperate for exciting results on the Shakespeare stage. The participants demonstrate ways in which a knowledge of the music and lyrics of Shakespeare and his contemporaries may prove useful in modern production. But they also explore the possibilities of new music for old lyrics, of new ways of using music to heighten the effect of the Bard's dramas on stage. Unfortunately, although the lyrics used as examples can be reproduced here in print, the accompanying music cannot.

Suzanne Bloch, on the faculty of music at the Juilliard School, is an accomplished lutanist, well versed in the musical literature of the Renaissance, including Shakespeare's England. She is a writer, composer, and performer, skilled on the recorder and virginals, as well as the lute. She has concertized in the United States, Canada, and Europe. Her "Lachrymae" was performed in 1946 by the New York Philharmonic.

The late Richmond Crinkley first won attention in the theatre world as Artistic Director of the fledgling Folger Theatre Group, working in the Folger Library's attractive, intimate prototype Elizabethan theatre. His skill earned him a production post under Roger Stevens at the Kennedy Center in Washington. From the JFK Center, he moved in 1976 to the ANTA Theatre in New York, still under Stevens' watchful eye, where as Executive Director, he began planning an ensemble for production of the classics. Later, he produced Elephant Man *on Broadway and moved to Lincoln Center. Crinkley functioned as a critic—for the* National Review—*and he is the author of* Walter Pater: Humanist *(1970).*

Peter Brook helped focus attention on composer Richard Peaslee. His elemental and forceful score for Brook's 1965 RSC Marat/Sade *production was an achievement recognized alike by critics and the public. In 1966, Peaslee provided Brook with another score; this time it was for the RSC's US. And then, in 1970, came the memorable Brook* Midsummer Night's Dream, *with its charming Peaslee music. Peaslee has also composed music for* The Merchant of Venice *and* Troilus and Cressida, *as well as* A Cry of Players, *a play about William Shakespeare. His scores have illuminated productions of* Indians *and* Endicott and the Red Cross.

Virgil Thomson was, of course, a legend in his own time. Composer, critic, teacher, patron, sage, and prophet: all those roles belonged to Thomson. He taught at Harvard and Carnegie Tech. He conducted America's major symphony orchestras, in New York, Boston, Philadelphia, among other places. His books include Music Right and Left *(1951),* American Music Since 1910 *(1971), and* Virgil Thomson *by Virgil Thomson. He composed important works in a variety of forms, but perhaps the best known are the two operas he composed to texts by Gertrude Stein:* Four Saints in Three Acts *and* The Mother of Us All.

Stoddard Lincoln, the moderator, is not only a Professor of Music at Brooklyn College, City University of New York, but a distinguished harpsichordist, scholar, and music critic as well. He has concertized widely.

*   *   *

BLOCH:

I have done so much work on early music and, of course, have gone into Shakespeare. From Shakespeare, I learned a great deal about the music of the time. We have all this music in lute tablature. In some places, we have the songs written out in the texts of Shakespeare's plays and we have the instruments. Now, how did they play? We don't know; we have no recordings. We have to use our imagination, and frankly, while you can read books of musicology, the only way really to know the essence of how they felt about the music and how they played it is by reading Shakespeare. Though he doesn't use much music in his plays, he talks about music. He uses music to moralize sometimes. You can see that he knew very well what the hit tunes of the time were.

When Shakespeare uses music, he weaves it into the play so that nothing stops for the music, and yet it is of great importance. There are many, many examples of that. You have to realize, too, that the music he used was known by the people. It was part of their lives. It was not so professional; there were just a few groups who played. But people lived with music; they didn't have television, movies, radios, and record players. They made music at home when they could. They had these instruments, and it was a tradition. Since they knew music as part of their lives, it was not something new when Shakespeare introduced it in his plays. In *Twelfth Night*, there is a scene in which Shakespeare has his drunken people and Sir Toby Belch sing shreds of a song which everybody knew, "Farewell, Dear Love," by Robert Jones. He changed it—he was careless—they sing "Farewell, Dear Heart," two lines of that. They bawl it out, and the maid says, "Stop your caterwauling."

In *Hamlet*, there is the wonderful scene with the recorders. That whole speech is so extraordinary as a study of form because, among other things, it talks about breathing and talking. Hamlet asks his friends, who are trying to psychoanalyze him, if they can play the recorder. They say no. He insists and says it's as easy as lying. "Trying these ventages with your finger and thumb; give it breath with your mouth." Then he says with great indignation, "You try to play upon the stops of my soul, and you can't even play on the stops of that little pipe." That's a wonderful speech, using the recorder which everybody knew was very easy to play. We know that lutes were very cheap at that time—in *The Taming of the Shrew*, Kate bashes a lute on the head of her teacher. We wouldn't do that anymore in our times. They're too expensive. Also in one of the plays, Bardolph runs off with a lute case and sells it for two ha'pennies. Well, no more now.

There are many extraordinary speeches about how they sang. If you think they took it too seriously, they didn't most of the time. Shakespeare's speech covers so many things: " . . . to jig off a tune at the tongue's end, canary to it with your feet" (canary was like a tap dance), "humor it with turning up your eyelids, sigh a note and sing a note, sometime through the throat, as if you swallowed love by singing love, sometime through the nose, as if you snuffed up love by smelling love; with your hat pent-house-like o'er the shop of your eyes; with your arms crossed on your thin belly-doublet like a rabbit on a spit; your hands in your pocket like a man after the old painting; and deep not too long in one tune, but a snip and away. . . ." It covers so many different things about this approach to singing and the carefreeness and making a few steps. That was from *Love's Labour's Lost* (Act III, Scene 1).

There are three ballads written on Shakespeare's plays—we don't know whether before or after. There's *The Merchant of Venice*. There's one on *King Lear*, with the stupidest tune you ever heard. Droning with that tragedy, it must have been horrible. There is a marvelous one of *Titus Andronicus*, which is based on "Fortune, My Foe," which is called the hanging song. It is a marvelous lute piece, and they sang it when they saw people being led to the gallows. The ballad is absolutely hilarious; it is so gory. Everything is described. How they died—they cut the boys' throats. The daughter of Titus holds the pan, with the blood running into it. Then out of the bones, they made powder and made a pie. They took the meat of the sons' own flesh and served it to the mother. All that is in this wonderful ballad. It is so gory; it is just great! At the very end everybody gets killed, and Titus kills himself. The only person I'm sorry for is the Moor. It is very racial, you see. The Moor is always the villain, and they put him in the desert where he dies of thirst. Years ago

I made a very good accompaniment on the lute. I even had dripping blood. At the end when I came to this, my heart goes out to the Moor. I couldn't help it.

Then there is the great speech in *Richard II:* ". . . how sour sweet music is/ When time is broke and no proportion kept!/ And here have I the daintiness of ear/ To check time broke in a disorder'd string;/ But for the concord of my state and time/ Had not an ear to hear my true time broke." This is very profound. When he says, " how sour sweet music is," meaning sweet dynamics, when no proportions are kept. He meant rhythm, because in all this early music we don't have much dynamics on our instruments. They are too delicate, and the whole expression, the whole bone-structure is for the rhythm—only rhythm. If you learn this music, you have to understand how they did rhythms, and what is written is not played that way. The whole thing comes alive.

Then in the musical expression, especially in the music for virginals, you have sad pieces. You know in music we have our twelve notes and maybe more now, with sounds and noises. We are supposed to express feelings. It's not just mathematical music; it's a language. It affects emotion. The great miracle of music is that, through all the different ages, with these twelve notes, they've had different ways of expressing emotion. In Elizabethan music, there is a piece called "Why Ask You?" on the virginals. It's sad, but I'll always think of one of the heroines of Shakespeare who in the greatest sorrow had a certain angularity, a certain spirit. Elizabethan woman had this sort of thing in music. When I play these pieces, I think of that and I do it. You don't think of that when you do Chopin and Debussy, where it is all curves; this is angular. All of this helps us to understand the music.

Shakespeare wove music into the play. In one of his plays he uses a song to tell that everybody is unhinged. It has a horrible feeling of jealousy. There is terrible weather outside; Desdemona has lost her memory, and she will be murdered, and she sings the willow song in the last act before she's murdered.

My mother had a maid call'd Barbara;
She was in love, and he she lov'd prov'd mad
And did forsake her; she had a song of 'willow';
An old thing 'twas, but it express'd her fortune,
And she died singing it; that song to-night
Will not go from my mind; I have much to do
But to go hang my head all at one side,
And sing it like poor Barbara.

(Act IV, Scene 3)

Now, that is genius. By saying "hang my had all at one side," it is not breast-beating, as in a Verdi opera. She hangs her head on one side, and she sings a song. That, in itself, sets the stage. Then she begins to sing this song and suddenly she stops. She says, "Ha! What's that?" And the maid says "'Tis the wind." You don't need wind-machines and lighting and stage effects for that. You have it all there. She starts again and then she stops on the stanza dealing with jealousy, which shows you don't need Freud. It shows how she's obsessed by it. She says, "Oh, I sang it wrong." The she continues. Now, its quite extraordinary that the whole thing is said by that. It was a song everybody knew. Again, Shakespeare took liberties; the original song is about a man sitting by a sycamore tree, but he changes the text, and it's a woman. The song is for the lute, and I will sing it to you with a very small voice, with the original accompaniment so that you can see what it was. And think of her sitting with her head on one side:

The poor soul sat sighing by a sycamore tree,
    Sing willow, willow, willow.
Her hand on her bosom, her head upon her knee,
    Sing willow, willow, willow, willow.
Ah, willow, willow, willow, willow shall be my garland.
    Sing ah green willow, willow, willow, willow.
I think the green willow shall be my garland,
The cool stream ran by her and murmured her moans,
    Sing willow, willow, willow.
Her hot tears fell from her and softened the stones,
    Sing willow, willow, willow, willow.
Ah, willow, willow, willow, willow shall be my garland.
    Sing ah green willow, willow, willow, willow.

Ay me, the green willow shall be my garland
I called my love false love, but what said he then?
    Sing willow, willow, willow.
If I court more women, you'd couch with more men,
    Sing willow, willow, willow, willow
Ah, willow, willow, willow, willow shall be my garland
    Sing o'er the green willow, willow, willow, willow.
Ay me the green will shall be my garland.

So this is a song that they knew. You know what's beautiful? Listen how the lute sighs [she plays]. That's all you need—just a few chords to give that feeling, the sighing. That's the original accompaniment. There is a question: in some versions it says, "My garland shall be," which is better prosody. There's another version: "which shall be my garland" but is not the prosody. Nobody knows which is the real version, but I like to use that one because it shows how they "unhinged."

Musicologists are always arguing about things. There is a wonderful sonnet by Shakespeare about someone playing the virginals. It talks about the jacks kissing the inward of her hand. The jacks are where you tune, up behind the keys. How do you play the virginals, and have the jacks kissing the inward of your hand? So, these people ask me how you can make it work by tuning. I twisted myself inside out. It doesn't work. I decided that Shakespeare had been very careless about certain things. Having genius, he thought saying the keys kissing the inward of her hand was ugly, but that jacks kissing is more musical. It's a great idea. But then a person specializing in the poetry of Shakespeare said no. In those days the young swains were called "jacks," and he made a pun on the young swains and the jacks that pluck the virginals.

You see, Shakespeare is like the Bible. You can take any speech and tear it apart and argue about the meaning of it. A hundred years from now, a thousand years from now, they still will be discussing Shakespeare. "O Mistress Mine" is a problem because it's mentioned in *Twelfth Night*, and is a tune which was found in the Morley consort lesson. Thomas Morley knew Shakespeare. They don't know though if he composed the music. There is a matter of dates about the performance and the publication of the consort lessons. Consort means ensemble music. If it's a consort of one type of instrument, it's all lutes—a consort of lutes. If you say "broken consort," that's a variety of instruments. In one of Shakespeare's plays, he talks about broken music. It means a consort.

So, the consort lessons had all the hit tunes. In fact, the music in Shakespeare is closer to our pop music than any other time, because any hit tune could be taken by a composer who made his own arrangements. You find "Go From My Window" for lutes or virginals—everybody doing their own variations or arrangements. There were no problems of copyrights and money. You could copy as you wished. The first person to object was John Dowland, who complained that they played his music and didn't even give credit to his name. That started it. Protection.

There are two versions of "O Mistress Mine," and I'll give you the first with a song and text. This is one of the harmonizations which is not as authentic, because I had to transpose it:

> O mistress mine, where are you roaming?
> O mistress mine, where are you roaming?
> O stay and hear your true love's coming
> That can sing both high and low.
> Trip no further, pretty sweeting.
> Journey's end in lover's meeting
> Every wise man's son doth know.

The Morley version, which may be more authentic, is this, and I'm playing it, not singing it. It's too high. [Music played.] That is the most authentic version of "O Mistress Mine" that we know of.

LINCOLN:

You seem to have led us into *Twelfth Night*. We'd better go on to *Twelfth Night* and Richmond Crinkley's experience with it.

CRINKLEY:

I would like to state what my principle has been in working with music in Shakespeare and other Elizabethan drama: rampant eclecticism. I thought for a long time that one of the problems of Shakespearean production in our own century was that the theory enunciated for the production was in many instances so wonderful that the production couldn't live up to it. On the other hand, the production was never consistent with the theory. I thought that it was best to start out with the theory which was almost not a theory, and hence, rampant eclecticism became something of a basis for productions of the Folger Theatre Group.

When I did *Twelfth Night*, I was working on a principle which was that the production should, as I think almost every Shakespeare production should, disappoint the audience's expectations in every conventional way and surprise the audience in every possible way. So that when they come to the work, the work seems a new play. Therefore, for the Folger's fakey Elizabethan theatre, which is a timbered stucco affair stuck in a rectangular building, Reynolds Aluminum donated a geodesic dome. The production doubled Sebastian and Viola, the implication being that there was only one of them all the time. Feste was played by a woman as a sort of aging diseuse, an Edith Piaf type.

The composers, Bill Danoff and Taffy Nivert, had done a show earlier for me, a musical adaptation of *The Bacchae*. With their Starland Vocal Band, they've had several hits: "Afternoon Delight" and "Take Me Home, Country Roads." They're soft-rock- country composers, and they came to the *Twelfth Night* project with a great deal of trepidation. Ms. Bloch mentioned how Shakespeare's music was very much the popular music of its time. Our endeavor was very much a play about performance and a play in which performance was such an integral part for the production— performance as performance, as opposed to the performance of a production—we brought into it a number of other Elizabethan lyrics. The Marlowe and Raleigh exchange, the "Passionate Shepherd," some Dekker poems, and others— we ended up with about fifteen songs. We were running against a number of things; for instance, a musical called *Your Own Thing*, which basically junks Shakespeare, and I think did nobody any great honor because it became an entirely different work. It was not a Shakespearean work transformed or translated.

It was a new work that had a life which perhaps depends on Shakespeare in the mind, but not in any real way.

Our two composers, who had not had any experience working with such eminent lyricists, didn't know how it was going to work. When they began to use the words and to work in the rhythms that the words dictated, they found some wonderful richness. They composed chiefly on a guitar. When Ms. Bloch was speaking of the breaking of a lute over someone's head in a play being unthinkable now, because the lute is a valuable artifact, that was funny. There is nothing strange in plays and films about breaking a guitar over someone's head. It happens all the time, and it may be that the whirligig of time may bring us to the point where the guitar becomes an artifact, too, and a thousand years from now, it could be a matter of breaking a Moog synthesizer over somebody's head, with all the attendant chaos that would dictate.

I want to play this song, with all the usual apologies about how this was recorded under utterly miserable conditions, with everybody sick and on terrible equipment, and that what you are about to hear is beneath human contempt and cannot in any way reflect the true wonder of the original occasion. And so with that caveat, I will . . . [tape-recording of soft-rock version of "O Mistress Mine"]:

> O mistress mine! where are you roaming?
> O stay and hear; your true love's coming,
>   That can sing both high and low.
> Trip no further, pretty sweeting;
> Journey's end in lovers meeting,
>   Every wise man's son doth know.
> What is love? 'tis not hereafter;
> Present mirth hath present laughter;
>   What's to come is still unsure;
> In delay there lies no plenty;
> Then come kiss me, sweet and twenty,
>   Youth's a stuff will not endure.
>
> (Act II, Scene 3)

I suppose that what we were doing might have been what happened in an Elizabethan context, to the extent that the people singing the songs, the people performing the music, were the ones that the music was written for. We had a peculiar way of working. I tend to be an activist producer and interfere all along. I also was directing the show. We had an appointment every Tuesday afternoon to hear two or three new songs, and of course they were never ready, so it was ritualistic that it was always put off until Wednesday. The score that emerged was one of considerable richness.

We had such situations as having a song that was written, but we finally didn't have people to sing it. We had one cast change, and so a rather big wedding song for the end got junked. On the other hand, we had a strong sense of involvement of the audience with the music, and, interestingly, the music was performed without electric amplification, which is very unusual for a rock score.

In doing a show like this the next time around, I would want a little bit more preparation time, but I think the thing that would be most important to me would be feeling for the contemporary idiom, a feeling for the sounds that are familiar to the people hearing them. The peculiar effect that Shakespeare has as a lyricist and as a playwright is that Shakespeare gives a certain form to ideas which are always current. Shaping and form are constantly changing, yet there is a constant in the rhythms of the language. That constant must of necessity communicate itself to that part of the music which is vocal, to that part of the music which has lyrics.

The eclecticism that one finds in a number of rock scores, chiefly in soft-rock scores—I think that soft-rock is much more receptive to the Shakespearean line—is something that does reflect a basis of the play, not only in Shakespeare text, but also in the life of our own times. I think this is essential.

PEASLEE:

I wanted to pick up on that idea of rampant eclecticism—which is the story of composing in the theatre, because it gives you the opportunity to do all those things you aren't allowed to do in music school, and also to be inspired by some of the best and some of the worst composers.

Suzanne Bloch's comment on the way Shakespeare's music

is woven into the text and action: there isn't this business of everything stopping while we have a number, as you have in so many Broadway musicals. This has its disadvantages for the composer. For instance, I just worked on a Shakespeare show, and I went into the office of the business manager who was leafing through all his bills on his desk, and he said, "Look Peaslee, I can't understand how we spent all this money on that little bit of music you did for the show." This didn't go down too well with me, because I had been spending the last couple of months working very hard, and I had all this tape to show for it. At any rate, that is the story of working on Shakespeare. I can't imagine the business manager saying that to Felix Mendelssohn or Tchaikovsky after he did a score for *Hamlet*. But today at least the music becomes an integral part of things, and things don't stop so that the audience can turn their attention to the music.

Also, one thing you learn about theatre audiences is that they're usually deaf to all sorts of music except for the most flagrant types, such as songs. When there is a real song they can say, "Aha! Somebody wrote some music." But all that other stuff, all that does is in some way, we hope, help the play along.

My experience on the Peter Brook *Midsummer Night's Dream* production was really interesting for me because it opened up a couple of new areas, thanks to the director. Usually there are two traditional types of incidental music: one is the stuff that Shakespeare calls for in the text, whether it be fanfares or songs or alarums, and the other is what the director puts in himself, which you could call "music to move scenery by" or "music to get them set for the next scene." But Brook turned those concepts upsidedown. First of all, there was no scenery to move. Instead of that kind of music which you had in the nineteenth century, massive bits of music to cover the big scenery changes, what Brook uses is sort of "goosing" music— music that "gooses" the play along. It's like the Kabuki concept: percussive jabs, things that propel the action along. That was one type of music.

The other type was the songs. There are a lot of songs in *Midsummer Night's Dream*. However, I was looking back through the score, and seven of the ones we did were not called for by the playwright. In other words, Brook would find a passage in the text that he thought made a good lyric and he'd say, "Well, let's write a song—this is a good place for a song." Or else the action was heightened to the point where it seemed natural to burst into song.

Conversely, there were a couple of places where there traditionally was music. For instance, there's a dance that Titania calls for near the end of the play. Brook scrapped that idea and just had silence—which is a form of music and which, in that particular instance, seemed much more effective to me. Those new approaches really opened my eyes to a lot of possibilities in composing for Shakespeare, which often is a labor of love for the text and the poet. You certainly usually don't do it for either the money of some other musical satisfaction, because often it's overlooked. Being able to work with a genius like Shakespeare is really helpful, because a lot of principles and ideas carry over into your own craft.

LINCOLN:

Virgil Thomson, you've done a Shakespeare score, for John Houseman's *Measure for Measure.*

THOMSON:

It has been particularly successful, that production of John Houseman's, and so he has reproduced it on a number of occasions. The original production was done in Stratford, Connecticut, in 1956 or 1957. I did a whole series of Shakespeare plays with him during those two years. Later, he reproduced this one in Los Angeles. On that occasion, he very wisely recorded everything but one song, and, when he later did it at the University in Kansas City, I think he used the recorded trumpet-and-horn cues, and also the whorehouse music. Interest in *Midsummer Night's Dream* reminds me that that particular play is one in Shakespeare's repertory that one can pin on, so to speak, about as much music as one can on any of them. Partly because it's not a play anyway; it's a masque within a masque. The masque was essentially a musical form, and although Shakespeare himself didn't write any other masques, he did it on this occasion, because with the plague going on, the thing was produced in a private house, and private houses were where you did masques. So, he made a masque, with which you always have music, instrumental music as well as songs here and there. Then the Pyramus and Thisbe affair is a masque within a masque. It's not a play within a play, as in *Hamlet.*

You can have here music laid on music which is, in general, far from Shakespeare's preference or certainly from his practice. Of all the Elizabethan playwrights, Shakespeare used music the least. As Suzanne Bloch points out, he talks about it all the time, but he's pretty careful to keep it out of the show, except just enough to make the audience think there is some and to keep the Establishment quiet. You must remember that in Shakespeare's time, the big, rich, powerful establishment was music, not the stage. The poetic theatre, which played in a slum quarter on the other side of the river, was a novelty beginning to bloom, but it was a novelty about like films in 1910. Films didn't pay high wages in 1910, but the theatre did.

Music had been going like mad in England for about a century. There had been a lot of music in England even before the sixteenth century, chiefly in the monastic establishments. But under Henry VII in the early sixteenth century, there burst out a great deal of lute music and virginal music, instrumental imagination and practice. Henry VIII was himself a composer and wrote quite presentable music. With the disestablishment of the Roman church, two things of interest happened for music. One was that the English government took over the monasteries, which had been a possession of Rome, paying tribute to Rome. So now they owned the property and whatever income that was produced by the agricultural lands on the property. And the monastic and cathedral establishments had money to spend on their own thing, which was highly ornamented religion.

The new services were ecumenical, as we would say, because they went into English—Latin was abandoned. The Latin chant, the plainsong, was abandoned, and until a repertory could be composed for the big set-pieces, a form of chanting suitable to the English language, which loves patter, was perfected at that time and still survives in the Anglican church. "Oh, come let us sing unto the Lord; let us heartily rejoice in the strength of our salvation."

This is very different from the Latin melismatic dwelling on vowels. But the combination of consonants and vowels with rhythmic snaps is as characteristic of the Anglican chant as it is of our language, and this is the glory of the Gilbert and Sullivan operettas three centuries later. Between the time of the disestablishment, about 1538, to the publication of the Edward VI Prayerbook in English, which was about another twelve years, the English language got established for chanting use. Then, with the texts of the psalms, the canticles, and the big set-pieces of the liturgy available in English, composers were commissioned, and for pay started writing highly reputable music for the church services.

Masques were given in the rich country houses, and these involved lots of dancing. And in these same country houses, on nights when they didn't have a masque, the gentlemen would sit around the table after dinner, singing glees and other contrapuntal music. They would play things with flutes. A gentleman should be able to hold his own with a flute or in a glee, just as he was supposed to be able to ride a horse.

I'm just giving you a picture of the breadth of the English musical repertory, and if I cited famous names, from Tallis in the middle of the sixteenth century, on down through Byrd and Morley, you have a list of world-famous, first-class English composers.

They were not working in the theatre. They did better outside the theatre, made more money, and kept more distinction. On the other hand, some of the younger ones coming up would have liked to get an elbow or foot into the new business, which was the poetic theatre. Actually, Marlowe allows for ballet-like accompanied scenes to an extent that Shakespeare does not. Ben Jonson, who wrote lots of comedies, left plenty of places for songs to be interpolated and for comic instrumental effects. A little younger than Shakespeare, Webster let music in a way that was perhaps dramatically inadvisable. *The White Devil* contains one whole act which is nothing but music; it's the coronation of the Cardinal. The play stops, and you have this great spectacular. *The Duchess of Malfi* contains an extended ballet all about madmen, which the brother stages to scare the hell out of his sister. There is another ballet-like sequence, which requires instrumental composition. Shakespeare would have none of that. The music in Shakespeare, in spite of all his talking about it, is always clearly dramatically motivated.

What does it serve? There are two kinds of Shakespeare. There are the tragedies and the comedies, and it is possible to separate them not merely as literary genres, but as performance styles. I've worked on fifteen or more of the tragedies. (You only really find out what's in a play when you start producing it or functioning in terms of what it can and cannot do.) The tragedies invite a few offstage trumpet calls, sometimes with drums, and certain amounts of weather, which you do on thunder drums and thunder sheets. It might be possible occasionally for a soft or sentimental scene to have offstage lutes and recorders, but they're not nowadays indicated. In his own time, I doubt if that practice existed too much. Today, of course, with Shakespeare safely dead, music again elbows in, and we stick in as much music as possible to cover up the Shakespeare.

Shakespeare has only two tragic heroines who sing at all. They are Ophelia and Desdemona. In *Hamlet*, there are Ophelia's predominantly dirty songs, which she sings as a madwoman. There is also an ironically tragi-comic song for the grave digger, for *Hamlet* is, as a play, almost a comedy-tragedy. It's the richest of all Shakespeare's plays in genre; it hasn't the grim seriousness of *Macbeth*, or the constant edge of violence which is present throughout *Romeo and Juliet*. You get in *Hamlet* two song-numbers, counting Ophelia's mad-scene as one.

Now when you get to the comedies, you're not going to get much more than two. He just wasn't letting music take over from his precious text. The comedies have some instruments and a little bit of dance, of course, but dancing is a stage prop—a situation. And there is no weather in the comedies. They talk about the weather but they don't represent it. You really do have weather in *Macbeth* and *King Lear*—oh, my, those awful storms with offstage instruments. But sound-effects would upset the charm of the comedies. If you want to create an ambiance, you do it with offstage lutes and recorders, or once in a while even on stage you can add these without injuring the sentiment of the play too much and without interrupting its forward march. But, when it comes to real music, then you have in the comedies rarely more than two songs. Outside of *Midsummer Night's Dream*, is there a comedy with more than two songs?

CRINKLEY:

Twelfth Night has at least five. It depends on how you count.

THOMSON:

And they are very short. *As You Like It* doesn't have many either, but they are very famous ones. Anyway, as you have more offstage trumpet calls in the tragedies, in the comedies you have virtually no offstage anything that really functions. You do have a few more songs, but they are limited. The comedies are not "musicals" in the modern sense. Shakespeare was firm about this in his built-in arrangements. Of course, a comedy is a looser structure than a tragedy, and the Shakespearean comedies are not heavily timed like modern comedies—not tightly timed. They are very loose in timing and structure, and you can always take time out to sing a song, if it has some reasonable function.

After all, Shakespeare's contemporaries were not just foolishly sticking in interpolated numbers without dramatic purpose, but Shakespeare was by far the strictest of them in economizing music and limiting it, to prevent the Establishment from moving in on his theatre, which they could have done easily when the theatre troupe gave royal performances. They wouldn't have had to move over to Southwark to do it. They could just say, "Well, Queen Elizabeth, now what about us? We've had lovely ideas for this production you're going to have at the house."

Shakespeare pretended a great love for music. I sometimes think he didn't even like it, because he called it dirty names all the time: "The food of love." You play music to rats—they stay awake for days and do nothing but make love. The food of love is what rats consume, as music. On another occasion, he referred to it as "a concourse of sweet sounds." I don't know

how much Establishment anger that brought down, but if
anybody had referred in Shakespeare's hearing to poetry as a
concatenation of lovely words, I think they would have heard
from papa. Music is constantly considered as a thing valued for
its sentiment, and chiefly its softness as sentiment, you see, in
Shakespearean accounts of it.

At the same time, whether or not he liked the stuff, he
certainly wrote words very beautifully for music. He knew the
difference between a text for reading and text for singing. A
great many composers have written operas to plays by
Shakespeare. Those who have used the English text, however cut
it may be, have practically all fallen on their faces, because
Shakespeare's verse is much too strong as image. Blank verse, in
any case, does not lend itself to music; it does not ask for music;
it does not like music. The successful operas that have been
written to Shakespeare's plays have all been written in French,
German, or Italian, in which case, they tightened up the play a
little bit, and got rid of the Shakespeare. You acquire verses or a
text of some kind in the language you're going to use, and
you're not stuck with the sacred liturgy of the Shakespeare lines
in *Hamlet, Othello, Falstaff.* And you get any number of
successful operas in the continental languages.

Now, Shakespeare knew what to do if he had to deal with
music. This is a little book that I brought along called *Words for
Music,* by V. C. Clinton Baddeley, published in Cambridge in
1941. He actually put his finger on piece of text which proves
that there were in Shakespeare's time, or very close to it, two
styles of writing poetry: one for reciting, and another for
singing. This is a poem by John Donne called "Love's
Infiniteness." Unfortunately, the other example is not by Donne,
but it's from a poet of his time and is a translation of Donne's
poem into singable verses. The Donne goes—and imagine
singing this:

> Thou cans't not every day give me thy heart,
> If thou cans't give it, then thou never gavest it:
> Love's riddles are, that though they heart depart,
> It stays at home, and thou with losing savest it:
> But we will have a way more liberal
> Than changing hearts, to join them, so we shall

Be one and one another's All.

You see, it moves in jumps. You have to stop and think about the grammar all the time, and there are means which explode in the middle of it. The version for singing goes:

> You cannot every day give mee your hart
>> For merit;
>>> Yet if you will, when yours doth goe
>>> You shall have still one to bestow,
> For you shall mine, when yours doth part,
>> Inherit.
> Yet if you please, weele find a better way
>> Then change them,
>>> For so alone (dearest) wee shall
>>> Bee one and one another all;
> Let us so joyne our harts, that nothing may
>> Estrange them.

There's a predominance of long vowels and virtually a complete absence of pictorial symbols—all the specifications that are suited to music, plus irregular line lengths. Musicians don't like four-by-four, you know. The author of this book says, "In these two arrangements of language, the same ideas and even the same words have been framed in two separate designs; the one is a poem: the other is words for music." Then he brings up—and I would have brought it up, if he hadn't—the supreme lyric for music in the entire English-language repertory, which is out of *Measure for Measure*. You can't say it without taking off into song. Shakespeare knew exactly what he was doing there, and he didn't do it for the actors:

> Take, O take those lips away:
>> That so sweetly were forsworn;
> And those eyes, the break of day,
>> Lights that do mislead the morn:
> But my kisses bring again,
>>> bring again,
> Seals of love, but seal'd in vain,
>>> seal'd in vain.

You can't do anything with it but sing it. It's a beaut.

LINCOLN:

One of the ironic things about *Measure for Measure* is that
during the Restoration period, Congreve, Dryden, the great
poets, found Shakespeare very crude and barbaric. He was
always rewritten. Music as "show-stopper" was introduced. Henry
Purcell at this time wrote a very fine little opera called *Dido
and Aeneas*, which was given at a ladies' boarding school. It
never hit the London stage. In 1700 after Purcell was dead and
after Shakespeare was dead, Charles Gildon rewrote *Measure for
Measure* and he inserted, as entertainment, *Dido and Aeneas*,
broken up into three acts. That is the ultimate.

THOMSON:

The ultimate starts really in the masque, which is a complete
break-up of drama into poetry, music, dancing, and singing. And
the masque itself comes to a dramatic apotheosis again in
Purcell's *King Arthur*, with its text by Dryden. But in the
Mendelssohn version of *Midsummer Night's Dream*, produced
in one of those state or municipal theatres in Germany where
they had on call a full symphony orchestra and a public which
didn't mind at all sitting in the house for four to five hours . . . .
Mendelssohn, at the age of sixteen, produced a vast, very
beautiful symphonic score which practically left the play
behind. It has its own life now.

CRINKLEY:

Genius should breed genius. I think this is a basic thing about
music and Shakespeare and acting and directing. A very basic
thing from a producer's point of view, and one that you achieve
only a few times in your life and then incompletely, is that you
want Shakespeare to not only be a genius in and of himself, but
the cause of genius in others. When you get music that does
respond to the impetus of Shakespeare, the challenge is
absolutely phenomenal. When you say the Mendelssohn work
takes on a life of its own, that's a remarkable instance in the
history of music where there has been a response to

Shakespeare that continues. As in the ending of the first act of the Brook *Dream*, with a few bars of Mendelssohn's *Dream* was one of the most exciting moments of theatre any of us had ever seen. When you have a deluge of paper plates coming down, Titania going off with Bottom, with an obscene gesture, and thunder of the Wedding March. . . . The Mendelssohn March is one of those things that is like much of Shakespeare: it's trite enough but also so much the matter of genius that the two become indistinguishable.

BLOCH:

Whatever music Shakespeare used already existed. He didn't commission anybody to write. All the tunes are tunes that were well-known before. This is why the music came before the play. You say Shakespeare's plays inspire other music. You're right there. He probably didn't care to commission anybody to write music for him.

THOMSON:

Fred Sternfeld, of Oxford University, found a whole batch of them in Ireland in a library some years ago. They are in his book, *Music in the Tragedies of Shakespeare*. It's a little bit like the case of *The Beggars' Opera*. The familiar ones are of a folklorish nature, like your willow song, so they could be quite ancient. They have that kind of authenticity, but the composed ones from the period are never as strong in music as the text of Shakespeare is in words. It wouldn't make too much difference whether he used something else—anything to jolly it up, because the music of the period tends to let the show down.

BLOCH:

He uses music when he sees fit, for a purpose. When he does, it's damn well used, whether you like it or not. When it comes in, it may not be terrific, but it fits! You are right that his great text should not be taken over by music. It doesn't need it; that I've always said. The poetry of the text is great. it is its own music. His genius in using the willow song makes it very important. It doesn't need gimmicks or sound effects.

THOMSON:

But do you know any music of the period for "Take, O Take Those Lips Away?"

BLOCH:

There is, you know . . .[she hums].

THOMSON:

That's awfully silly.

BLOCH:

Oh, I don't like it.

THOMSON:

It isn't nearly as good as mine.

PEASLEE:

A problem arises if the music upstages the actor. If you write some underscoring that suddenly is very striking, the actor can get very uptight because he doesn't feel people are paying attention to him. Or else the volume is too loud on the sound system. Then you have a problem. You become aware, when you're doing a job on a Shakespeare play, that you have to know your place. You can't write what you've always wanted to write or get in to this self-expression bag, upstaging what's going on out front. I think this was less of a problem in the nineteenth century, wasn't it—when there was a lot of time between scenes?

THOMSON:

They didn't have time between scenes either. It's the twentieth century that needs scene-change music.

LINCOLN:

They used to watch the scenes being changed. That was part of the show even in the eighteenth century and earlier. If they had drawn a curtain and would not let the audience watch, the audience would have walked out. They would want their money back. That was part of the show. They didn't need the music to change scenes.

THOMSON:

But your nineteenth century audiences, particularly in Germany, where they had such a big theatrical establishment, were very music-conscious. As in Elizabethan times, music was their big affair, and they could take quite a lot of it.

PEASLEE:

That's the big difference today. The theatre audience is here, and the music audience is over there.

CRINKLEY:

Today, when the set change is non-existent, the function of the music is to propel the action. It doesn't exist as an entity; it becomes more a part of the fabric.

QUESTION:

You talked about using the soft-rock-country. That's not so unusual; in a way, going full circle. The people who came over from England into part of the South once spoke an Elizabethan form of English. When I listened to Ms. Bloch's tunes, I sensed an awfully close relationship.

CRINKLEY:

I would hope so. I always felt one of the peculiar things about being at a Shakespeare library, and being in production and performance, is that there are time when you feel you are closer to whatever the essential truths are than the scholars. One of the reasons was that there were so many textual students working and squirreling away at the Folger, trying to find a definitive text from amongst many variants.

One of the things that you realize, if you work in the theatre, is that you are in a situation of constant flux in producing a play. And this was certainly true in Shakespeare's time. I have a feeling that for many dramatists, at the moment in which a play is in composition, it is futile to talk of definitive text. The text is constantly changing. You feel closer in spirit to what Shakespeare was doing than scholars are, in hunting for the definitive text.

The point you make with the music is well taken. Our composers took volumes of Elizabethan tunes away with them and learned to play them. None of them surfaced in *Twelfth Night*, as such, but I'm sure that somehow there was an effect there. It's an effect that also is true in terms of the way the music communicates itself to the audience: that score of *Twelfth Night*. Each production is in and of its own moment in time.

QUESTION:

I was interested in what happens to Shakespeare's words when they are set to music. There is a great deal of logical and syntactical complexity which seems to get distorted when it is put to music.

THOMSON:

Let me interrupt you right there. The finest English poetry for music is that by Burns and by Thomas Moore, and they were both made to music. Burns would memorize a tune and then write lovely words for it or around it, and they would sing. He worked very much as George Gerswhin and his brother did. George would write a tune, and then Ira would put some words in.

QUESTION:

It seems to me then, as you pointed out, that the words have a different nature!

THOMSON:

It is not known whether or not Shakespeare wrote his songs to existing tunes, except in a few cases of folklore ones or classical ones. It is known with regard to Goethe, for instance, that all his famous lyrics were made to tunes. Goethe had no sense of music at all. He fancied himself as a universal intelligence, and in order to keep up this image, he had to have lessons in music appreciation from Zelter, who was Mendelssohn's teacher, so he wouldn't make boners when writing about music. He did have a great lyrical gift for words—and just enough musical ear to be able to remember a tune. Again, it was Fred Sternfeld who raked up the Goethe tunes. It's in one of the publications of the Renaissance Society.

You do beautifully, if you write to a tune. This occurs in all languages. The French standard diction for tragedy is rhymed hexameters, alexandrines. They don't set very well to music, but if a song is desired, as it often was in the comedies of Moliere, then a song is made to other meters and other kinds of words. The ultra-visual doesn't set well to music. Poetry which is all about visual images, flopping at you, exploding, doesn't set well. The kind of thing that sings is "My love is like a red, red rose"— straightforward like that. After all, music expresses sentiment better than ideas, and if you give us songs that express a feeling and do it in reasonable longs and shorts—particularly plenty of longs for melisma: "Way down upon the Swanee River, far, far away. . . ." That sings!

BLOCH:

May I say something right now? To me the greatest marriage of music and words in English are the spirituals because they must have grown together completely. The Negro spirituals—take any one of them and there's not one skip going up or down: "Nobody knows the trouble. . . ."

THOMSON:

But you know what they are? They're Scottish tunes and Scottish words. They've all been found.

BLOCH:

"Joshua fit the battle of Jericho" is a Scottish tune? That's extraordinary. And "Nobody knows?"

THOMSON:

It's right out of the *Southern Harmony!*

BLOCH:

Are the spirituals exactly the same as these Scottish hymns?

THOMSON:

Of course not.

BLOCH:

Then this still proves my point. From the hymn material, a transformation was made—changes of rhythm and melodic configuration, expressing the natural feelings of the Negroes in their own vernacular. This certainly created a new prosody, very different from the original forms.

*   *   *

SHAKESPEARE IN OPERA AND BALLET

Clive Barnes
Edward Downes
Károly Köpe
Siegmund Levarie, Moderator

Adaptations have long been a staple of the theatre repertoire. Popular novels are translated to the legitimate stage as dramas. Popular plays are transformed for the lyric stage into musicals, operas, and ballets. Shakespeare's major works are obviously popular enough to make them attractive targets for adaptors. As is discussed elsewhere in this book, both the comedies and the tragedies have been adapted, reworked, improved, altered, or even distinguished beyond recognition as plays. They have been digested or reduced as musicals. And they have served as the inspiration for some important operas and ballets, as this discussion emphasizes. There are, however, problems about turning the poetry of Shakespeare into the lyrics of opera. These and other related concerns are reviewed by men who are experts.

Clive Barnes may need no introduction, but his credits—in addition to his powerful positions as both dance and drama critic for The New York Times *and later for* The New York Post—*are considerable and not widely known. He wrote on dance, films, music, and theatre for* The London Daily Express *from 1955-65. From 1959-65, he was dance critic for* The Spectator. *From 1961-65, he was editor of* Plays and Players *and* Music and Musicians, *having been editor of* Dance and Dancers

202 Staging Shakespeare

since 1955. His books include Ballet in Britain Since the War *(1953) and* Dance Scene U.S.A. *(1967).*

Edward Downes is an opera expert, a well-known critic, but he is also Emeritus Professor of Music both at Queens College and at the Graduate Center of the City University of New York. Since 1958, he has become known to millions as the quizmaster of the Opera Forum Quiz, a regular intermission feature of the Metropolitan Opera Broadcasts. He has given seminars in opera production and interpretation during the Bayreuth Festival. Professor Downes is the author of Adventures in Symphonic Music *(1943), among other musicological and critical writings.*

Károly Köpe is both a theoretician and a practitioner of opera production. An organist and conductor, he has worked in opera at both Hunter College and Brooklyn College, where he is now Emeritus Professor of Music. At Brooklyn, he has staged and conducted two world premieres of operas, plus some classics. He has conducted at the Lake George Opera Festival. Among his contributions to opera literature are critical writings and translations, including a version of Hofmannstahl's Ariadne auf Naxos.

Like Köpe, Siegmund Levarie is also an Emeritus Professor of Music at Brooklyn College, City University of New York. Educated in Vienna, Professor Levarie is expert in both German and Italian opera. His books include Fundamentals of Harmony *(1954),* Guillaume de Machaut *(1959), and, with Ernst Levy,* Tone: A Study in Musical Acoustics *(1968).*

* * *

DOWNES:

To me the topic of Shakespeare and Music, which is often broached in articles and discussion, is a very strange topic for the reason that one would expect an enormous number of works since Shakespeare to be based on or at least stimulated by his dramas and his poetry. Yet, considering the magnitude of what he offers both in quantity and quality, it seems to me that it is very strikingly small. The specific topic that I would like to bring up is one opera of Verdi, namely his *Macbeth*. As you know, Verdi is probably the most successful of the composers who have used Shakespearean operas.

Verdi's relationship to Shakespeare was a rather strange one, in the sense that I think it was a relationship that was full of tensions. He was enormously, passionately interested in and fascinated by Shakespeare. The three Shakespeare operas that he did do all represent peaks in what, as you know, was an enormously brilliant and successful career. Yet, there is a great deal of evidence that Verdi never fulfilled to his own satisfaction the goals that he had very much in mind. I don't mean to imply that the three operas are not very great works. I think they are. The reason that I chose *Macbeth* is that, quite simply, it is the one that I am extremely fond of. I think it is a very remarkable work. I am not pretending that it is as great as *Othello*, but it has a lot that I think is very interesting to speculate about, in addition to its innate quality.

The first of the three Shakespearean operas is *Macbeth*, which he wrote when he was thirty-three—it was produced in 1847, in Florence. He later revised it for Paris in the 1860s, partly because he was very attached to the subject and felt that he could do better with it than he had the first time. It had not been an enormous success, except at its initial production in Florence. Then a very interesting episode comes along which not everybody except Verdi fans are apt to know about. He did not just toy with the idea of a *King Lear* opera; he worked at it very actively for a period of well over two years, which is quite a time, because Verdi was accustomed to producing operas, at that time in his career, rather fast. It was not at all rare for him to produce two operas a year for over a considerable span of years. This was two years during which his correspondence with the librettist whom he had chosen, Cammarano, is copious. He decided to try, although at first he said, "I don't know how we can ever manage to squeeze a work of this cosmic significance into a mere opera libretto." Eventually the libretto was finished, and there seem to be sketches somewhere, although the whole problem of getting Verdi material is complicated by the fact that the heirs sit on the material and don't like to let anybody look at it.

The two most famous Verdi Shakespeare operas are the *Otello*, which came when he was seventy-three years old, and the *Falstaff*, his final opera, when he was seventy-nine years old—rather extraordinary. There are many people who feel that the *Otello* is the greatest Italian opera ever written. Verdi tells several people in his correspondence that he had been fascinated by Shakespeare from his earliest youth. This came out apropos of some criticisms of the Paris *Macbeth*, where they said that he didn't know Shakespeare very well, which enraged him. He didn't mind it if people thought the music was poor. He said, "I may not have written a good opera, but to say that I don't know Shakespeare—that I don't understand him . . . I have carried Shakespeare around with me ever since I was a boy and I reread him continually." Probably he had some claims to a good understanding, limited perhaps by whatever his background was, but nevertheless he was very familiar with Shakespeare. We do know that to this very day in his villa, next to his bed on a little bookcase there are two different Italian translations of the complete works of Shakespeare—and very well thumbed indeed. They obviously got a great deal of use. So he was not posing when he talked about this.

When he undertook *Macbeth*, he had a feeling that he must make a very special effort. I think that part of the tension that we sense, and it had some very good results as well as negative ones, is that he had a feeling that he must do something really extraordinary. He wrote to his librettist, Piave, in this case, and said, "If we can't produce a really great work of art, let us at least produce an extraordinary work. I beg of you do your absolute utmost. I go down on my knees to you . . . you must outdo yourself in this." He was so involved that he did something that he had not done before, to my knowledge, and I don't think he ever did afterward. He wrote out the complete libretto as he wanted it in prose and sent it scene by scene to Piave and left him the job of putting it into Italian verse. The whole scenario, down to the details of the dialogue and so on, was Verdi's, which brings him interestingly in the neighborhood of Richard Wagner. I'd like to come back to that in a moment.

There is another point that I would like to raise here apropos of the Italian text. I don't know whether you have had the same experience that I have had listening to great works of literature which have been used particularly for opera or cantatas or oratorios. I was speaking to Professor Levarie the other day about having listened to a performance of Schumann's *Scenes from Faust* that was performed at the Philharmonic. Indeed, it is little bits taken here and there, except for the final apotheosis and the salvation of Faust. But I had the feeling that although Schumann obviously was a very great composer, his music was simply overwhelmed by the greatness of the poetry; that the music never had a chance, so to speak. Absolutely crushing. I think that this has happened sometimes with Shakespeare, when music has been composed for the verse in original English. It may have been a blessing that Verdi composed it in translation. I won't say the original verse crushes vitality, but it is something so tremendous that it simply might have dwarfed even Verdi's talent. He was a very great artist, but I wouldn't necessarily put him on a par with Shakespeare.

The opera was a very innovative opera, and Verdi was well aware of this. He used the orchestra to an extent and with an originality of imagination and technique which are quite extraordinary for the time in Italian opera. For instance, the sleep-walking scene in *Macbeth* gives a very considerable role to the orchestra, not only in a long prelude which sets a quite eerie mood for the scene, but also in the accompaniment of the—I hesitate to call it an aria; actually Verdi called it "grande scene del somnambulismo," which I think is rather nice. It is a "grand" scene in the best sense. I believe it is one of the greatest scenes that Verdi ever wrote. I don't think he ever surpassed it. He equalled it perhaps in different ways in other moments of other operas, but I don't think he ever wrote anything that was more imaginative or more stirring with the multiple, conflicting emotions that one almost necessarily has about Lady Macbeth when she's portrayed by a very fine actress. Verdi gets a great deal of these conflicting and many-levelled feelings into his music.

Also in the vocal writing, he does something which is not at all the conventional Italian: tuneful, balanced phrases that one expects from Donizetti, Bellini, and most of all, Verdi. He writes something that's semi-declamatory and that moves from declamation into a more melodious style in and out, and is strikingly flexible and responsive to each individual word and idea that the text contains. It is an extraordinary thing, and it is really on a par with the most advanced vocal style that Wagner had evolved by this time. As you perhaps know, Wagner and Verdi were born in the same year, and there were tensions involved there, although they never met each other. Each was rather conscious of the other and of a certain rivalry. We don't need to go further into that, but I've always been struck by the feeling that, at this point in their respective careers, they were really neck-and-neck. I think *Macbeth* is perhaps a more uneven opera, and *Lohengrin* is perhaps more balanced in certain ways. Somehow to me, it is less interesting than the *Macbeth*, although I am an admirer of Wagner.

There is another thing which shows how very seriously and imaginatively Verdi went about *Macbeth*. There is a letter that he wrote apropos of the second or third production—one where he was not going to be present in Naples. He learned of the prima donna who had been chosen for Lady Macbeth, and he wrote, in some perturbation, to the theatre and said, "I understand you have taken Madame Tadolini for the role of Lady Macbeth . . . I must tell you frankly I think she has far too fine qualities for this role. You may think that sounds strange, but Tadolini, first of all, has a marvelous, pure voice, and I don't want Lady Macbeth to have a marvelous, pure voice. I want her to croak. I want a harsh, ugly sound for Lady Macbeth. Tadolini has a beautiful figure and she exudes goodness. I want Lady Macbeth to have a twisted, ugly figure and I want her to be really evil." He went on in these descriptions of a style of voice and a style of acting.

If Richard Wagner had said this, everybody would have said, "Well, there you are! Germans have no concept of what opera is about—no concept of bel canto—of beautiful singing. Obviously, that's the basis of opera. Wouldn't it be just like a German to say, 'just sing ugly; that's what I want!'" But Verdi was not kidding. I think he was being somewhat diplomatic and was saying, in effect, that this woman—and we know this from other reports—did have a beautiful voice, was a handsome woman but was a trifle cool and inclined more toward the nightingale type than toward the dramatic. Verdi rightly knew that this was not what he wanted. I don't think that he meant that you could singly badly and survive many performances of Lady Macbeth, which is terribly demanding, just technically and vocally. In any case, he describes this style of acting and vocalism that he wants from Lady Macbeth; indeed, he wants this from Macbeth also. He goes into great detail, and there is a marvelous account of the rehearsals by the lady who sang Lady Macbeth in the original production. She tells about the other main number in Verdi's mind, the duet in the first act between Lady Macbeth and Macbeth, just after he has murdered Duncan, up to the point where she goes in and smears the grooms with blood. Apparently they had one-hundred-and-fifty rehearsals on this duet alone. She said, "He wanted us really almost to talk, not really to sing. Verdi himself says this in a letter. He says, "This must not be sung; this must be mimed. It must be declaimed, but it must all be done in a dark, suppressed, semi-whisper, full of horror." He simply did not want any part of the traditional bel canto.

There is lots of other evidence of how seriously he took this. In scenic details, he insisted on supervising everything and sending copious letters to various theatres that were performing it. When he got through with it, after the first performance, he dedicated the opera to the father of his first wife whom he adored and worshipped like a father. He said, "This is, of all my operas, the one which I value the most . . . that's why I am dedicating it to you." To another friend he said, "This is the opera of all my operas which interests me most, and therefore, you must forgive me if I write you a few things about how it should be done."

In spite of this, it never made a big success anywhere after this first performance. That may have been due to the fact that Verdi couldn't go and supervise performances everywhere. In any case, he later revised it, as I mentioned, for Paris. It still was not a success. It went around a little bit outside of Italy. I was astonished, when I heard *Macbeth* in 1938 in Glyndebourne, to learn that this was the first performance in England of Verdi's *Macbeth*. Perhaps this is explainable by the fact that the

Englishman, who is apt to know his Shakespeare somewhat better than we do, just found the whole idea of making an Italian opera out of *Macbeth* too grotesque, and impresarios perhaps felt that it would be wasted on an English public. Here in New York, *Macbeth* was performed in 1850. Verdi apparently decided, by the time he had revised *Macbeth* and it was not a success, that this was the verdict of time, and that he had been on the wrong path. But he only half-accepted it, because he wouldn't have gone on with this tremendous preoccupation with *Lear*, which he never quite had the courage to finish. When he regarded his career as finished—we know from his letters he felt his career was finished and he had a tremendous achievement behind him—he'd written all the popular operas we know; he'd finished *Aida*; he said now he was going to compose for himself. It was at this time that he was persuaded with great diplomacy to undertake the *Otello*. It was a tremendous success, and *Falstaff* was even more a success. In his correspondence, he said, "I'm writing this for myself . . . maybe I'll never have it performed . . . I'm going to take my time."

At that point, after he was the great man of opera in Italy, I think he may have had the courage to do what he had obviously been longing to do for much of his career. There is an interesting passage that occurs in old Gatti-Cazazza's memoirs. He was the manager of the Metropolitan for many years and before that had been manager of La Scala. When he was a young man and first took this job as an impresario, he talked to Verdi. According to him, Verdi said, "You must keep a very watchful eye on the box-office; that is the court of last appeal. A theatre is there to be full, and it is your job to fill the theatre."

I've always wondered, assuming that Gatti was accurate in his memory, whether Verdi really took the box-office that seriously at an age when he no longer needed to. He died a rich man, and he had all the adulation that any artist could ask for. It had occurred to me that perhaps it is a great tragedy that he did not have sufficient conviction of his own rightness when he wrote *Macbeth*. Most people feel that the great parts of *Macbeth* do rank enormously high. What if he had been able to say to himself, "I'm right, and this whole stupid public is wrong—one day they will come and listen to this." If he had this kind of—I won't say inflated—ego that Wagner had . . . . Whatever it was, it made Wagner objectionable in many ways. However, it gave him the conviction to say to himself, "You are all wrong. I know that I am on the right path." The result was, I think, that he achieved a fuller self-realization than Verdi did.

I always have a melancholy feeling that if Verdi had been able to go ahead rough-shod and continue on the path of *Macbeth* and *Lear*, he might have done things that we can't even imagine. This brings me back to what I think is a fact: there was a tremendous tension in his relation with Shakespeare, and it was, on the whole, enormously fruitful, because these three operas really are the peaks of Verdi's career. I'd be interested to know whether anybody else finds an explanation or agrees or disagrees with me about that.

LEVARIE:

I don't want Professor Downes to remain melancholy one more minute. Schopenhauer once said that a great man inevitably knows that he is great. He says that it is impossible for a great man, and we all stipulate that Verdi was one, not to realize his own value. Listening to your Gatti-Cazazza story, I'm quite sure that Verdi knew what he had done in *Falstaff* and *Otello*, and that he probably didn't care too much about the box-office. The story sounds exactly like that of a director of the Metropolitan Opera. I'm sorry our colleague, Sir Rudolf Bing, isn't here right now to confirm my suspicions, but I do know that in his twenty-some years at the Met, he did have an eye on the box-office. He had to, but he's not a composer; he's a manager. May we turn from opera to ballet and hear from Clive Barnes?

BARNES:

I wouldn't dare talk about opera in the face of all these specialists. But there are two remarks I would like to make on Edward Downes' comments. The first is, I never realized how fortunate I had been in hearing Lady Macbeth ideally cast on quite a number of occasions. [Laughter] The other point is that there is a certain advantage to Shakespeare in translation. You can do so much more with it. You can modernize it. One of the great advantages the Germans have in their Shakespeare productions is that they don't have to worry about Shakespeare. It was Brecht who first really understood that when you translate a play, you can do much more with it than if you have the solid, all too solid, solid text. So, I think that, to an extent, in opera this would be true.

But there are a couple of instances where English composers have done some rather interesting work. Of course, one is Vaughan Williams' *Sir John in Love*. I certainly wouldn't compare this with *Falstaff*, but I would say that it was a far better work than the more popular *Merry Wives of Windsor*—the Nicolai, and there some of the libretto is actually taken from Shakespeare. Of course, a much better example is the Peter Pears' libretto for Benjamin Britten's *Midsummer Night's Dream*, which is, in fact, adapted from the Shakespeare original, and it sounds absolutely marvelous. I think it's one of Britten's finest operas. Of course, Britten is not a major composer in the way that Shakespeare is a poet, but somehow the two do enhance one another. I've even heard it in Moscow. Perhaps it sounds better there, but still . . .

I'm going to talk about Shakespeare and dance. There are two aspects of this, and the first we don't know much about: there is dance in Shakespeare, and then there is Shakespeare in dance. To take the first one, we really don't know. We do know that the Elizabethans were a pretty dancey kind of people. There is a great deal of Elizabethan dance that we have some idea of. I am not at all an authority on historic dance, but quite a lot of work has been done on the Elizabethan dance, and a lot of it does appear in Shakespeare.

You find Sir Andrew Aguecheek who boasts about his ability to dance the corranto and things like that. Obviously, dance was a part of Shakespeare. The Shakespearean fool, or clown, to a large extent would have been a dancing role. He would dance and do acrobatics and gambol around, sometimes much to the distress of his fellow actors, as you will recall from Hamlet's address to the players. But, we really don't know too much about dance in Shakespeare. Certainly dance was less important in Shakespeare than it was in some of the other Elizabethan and Jacobean plays. Ben Jonson, for example, created a number of masques which some people regard as the English equivalent and even the precursor of the great court ballets. Jonson was very concerned with masques, and, in fact, he collaborated with Henry Purcell on them. Quite obviously, to Shakespeare the play was the thing, and dancing, like music, was something incidental and extraneous.

On the other hand, Shakespeare has provided a considerable source of inspiration to choreographers, and the reason for this is very simple to understand. It could all be summed up by Balanchine's famous law of narrative ballet. Balanchine's law of narrative ballet says: "There are no mothers-in-law in ballet." This is why Shakespeare is so popular. The difficulty of ballet is to be specific in narrative. If you have a man and two women come on stage, it is extremely difficult, unless you are going to provide people with copious program notes, to explain that this one is the mistress and this one is the wife; or this one is the mistress and this one is the sister; or even, this one is the mother and this one is the aunt. As Balanchine said, "There are no mothers-in-law in ballet."

As a result, choreographers have tried to find themes that are readily recognizable—emblematically recognizable—by the mass audience, and there are not too many kinds of themes that everyone knows. There are the fairy tales that people know, and there are biblical tales that people used to know—I don't know whether they do now. There are certain famous stories of classic literature such as *Don Quixote*—I suppose most people have some idea of *Don Quixote*—and, of course, this is true of Shakespeare, or at least the major Shakespearean themes.

It is interesting that ballet took Shakespeare up fairly late. As far as I know, the first Shakespearean ballet was by Vincenzo Galliotti, which was created in Copenhagen in 1811, and that was a ballet to *Romeo and Juliet.* 1811 is fairly late. I don't know when the first Shakespearean opera was, but what is interesting is that in the years following Shakespeare's death, Shakespeare's repute went into something of a decline; his works on the stage were often produced in rather curious ways. His work was not exactly simpatico to the prevailing emotional and cultural currents of the eighteenth century. It really wasn't until the Romantic movement in the first part of the nineteenth century that people began to reassess Shakespeare. Artists started bouncing off Shakespeare—composers like Berlioz, and painters also. They all began to take an enormous interest. The large Shakespearean themes seemed to have something special to say to the romantic spirit. Curiously, this did not affect ballet very much. I've said in 1811 came the first Shakespearean ballet, but I would be hard pressed to tell you when the second came. I'm not at all sure that it wasn't until the twentieth century. I'm sure someone must have done a *Hamlet* in a blue spotlight and tights somewhere. Certainly Shakespeare was not very popular.

The reason that Shakespeare was not popular in ballet, whereas he was popular in the sister art of opera, is really simple. It's because romanticism in ballet took a very peculiar and very specific form. It took the form of the sylphs and the fairies.

It went almost overnight from the court spectacles to the romantic ballets of *Les Sylphides* and *Giselle* where young men run in anguish and despair after young ladies in the woods. This really became the archetypal romantic ballet, and ballet wasn't taken all that seriously. That was in France, of course, from about 1820 until 1860 or so.

When it moved to Russia, more and more people turned to fairy tales: *Sleeping Beauty, Swan Lake*, which was not a fairy tale but had some of those elements in it. These were popular ballets. Of course, *Cinderella* was popular, not the version we know, but an earlier version. These themes seemed to provide the narrative framework. People really weren't too particular about a narrative framework; for example, one of the most popular ballets of the late nineteenth century was called *Don Quixote*, which really has nothing to do with *Don Quixote*, except that he wanders on rather forlorn during the course of the ballet. It's hardly a ballet about *Don Quixote*. So you see, people were not really that interested in Shakespeare in dance. I think that people took ballet very lightly and thought that Shakespeare was perhaps too heavy for dance.

It was in the twentieth century that people started to look at Shakespeare seriously as thematic material, and even then it took some time. At the beginning of this century, Michael Fokine tried to make more serious the whole art of ballet. He tried to devise more serious subjects, tried to make it much more expressive than it had been in the past. It was from that time on that people started to think in terms of Shakespeare. Even in this century there have been surprisingly few Shakespearean ballets. Professor Downes mentioned the paucity of Shakespearean operas, considering the impact Shakespeare has made on the world. The same seems to be true in dance. I think the reason for this is fairly apparent: Shakespeare's stories are not always particularly easy to follow when the people talk. When they don't talk, they are much more difficult. As a result, it's only the enormous, emblematic subject matters that can really make much impact in dance.

Sometimes the thing is too enormous for dance, it would seem. For example, *Lear*. . . . Can one imagine a danced *Lear?* As a matter of fact, Martha Graham did do a ballet to *Lear* called *Eye of Anguish*, but it didn't stay long in her repertory. Mind you, I can't imagine anything having stayed long in Martha's repertory where she couldn't play the lead, and no one else has had the courage.

Let's look at the comedies first. There has been a ballet to *The Merry Wives of Windsor*, done by a number of hacks in Russia. It is a fairly popular ballet, done by local ballet masters in Russia. It is absolutely deplorable. I've only seen it done by the Stanislavski company, the Moscow second company, but it is an absolutely terrible ballet. Then there has been John Cranko's remarkable ballet, *The Taming of the Shrew*. I say remarkable, because it tells the story extraordinarily well. I don't like it very much as a ballet, partly because I don't like the music and partly because it's not a particularly good ballet. But it does tell the story very well, and it has proved extremely popular. There have also been one or two attempts to do a ballet to *Twelfth Night*. Fredrick Ashton toyed for years with the idea of doing a ballet of *The Tempest*, because Margot Fonteyn wanted to dance Miranda. He contemplated it, but finally used for his ballet *Ondine*. No one has ever done *Pericles*, or any of the Roman plays. I think it would be difficult to imagine a *Julius Caesar* ballet or a *Coriolanus*. No one has ever attempted those. The histories are, again, verboten. I can't imagine a *Richard III*. Can a dancer act out: "A horse, a horse, my kingdom for a horse?" I don't think that the histories have been very productive.

The one comedy that has been extremely useful to ballet has been *A Midsummer Night's Dream*, and you can see why. It does have many of the romantic elements that people associate with ballet. There is a lot of dancing in most productions of it. There have been two major productions of the *Dream*, both using Mendelssohn's music. The Fredrick Ashton version, a one-act ballet, is in the repertory of the Joffrey Ballet. The George Balanchine version is a full-evening ballet and is in the repertory of the New York City Ballet. Balanchine has added to the incidental music by adding the symphony and one or two other pieces to spread it out into a full score. What is interesting about both of these ballets is how extraordinarily well they tell the subplot of the lovers. One of the difficulties in Shakespeare is the subplot. But in both these ballets, you find this interchange between the lovers—everyone getting gloriously mixed up—is sometimes clearer than it is in the theatre. I don't quite know why, but it is certainly a testament to their skill.

Of course the major work has been done with the tragedies. The best known: *Hamlet, Othello,* and *Romeo and Juliet.* There has been a production of *Hamlet* in Russia by Nikolai Serguieff, which was premiered with the Jewish dancer Valery Panov. The creation of that role was his last act on stage that was well regarded there. Also, there was a Freudian, Dover Wilson-style *Hamlet,* done by Rob Helpmann to the Tchaikovsky *Fantasy Overture* in 1941. *Hamlet* has not been quite so popular as others—*Othello* for example. There have been many *Othello*s. The Tiflis Company has done a most elaborate Soviet-style production, where they act out the plan in grim detail, but it still looks a bit silly to have *Othello* jumping in the air and twirling around twice before he strangles Desdemona. Perhaps that is something we should discuss—the various conventions of opera and ballet, and their impact on the differing conventions of Shakespeare.

I think the most successful of all the *Othello* ballets has been a very, very simple one by José Limon called *The Moor's Pavanne,* which takes just four characters. You have to know *Othello* to really know what's happening. But even if you don't know *Othello* and you don't understand what's happening, it doesn't matter, because the dance itself is of enormous beauty. The four people are called the Moor; the Moor's friend, who is Iago; his wife, who is Desdemona, and the friend's wife, who is Emilia. These four dance a series of dances in a very formal manner to Purcell, but through their dancing runs this thread of the entire tragedy. It's absolutely brilliant. It's one of the most brilliant and succinct of modern ballets, in my opinion, and it's found in repertory all over the world.

Then, of course, there is the most famous Shakespearean ballet of them all, *Romeo and Juliet*. I don't know how many ballets have been created to *Romeo and Juliet*—hundreds and hundreds I should say. The essence of so much of ballet and dance is the duet, and almost always this is a love duet. If you put a man and woman on stage and start them dancing, they are almost essentially making love. Therefore, *Romeo and Juliet* is a natural for ballet. The story is well enough known for people not to have to worry about the details.

The most important version musically of *Romeo and Juliet* is that written by Sergei Prokofiev. It took a great part of Prokofiev's creative energy and is one of his major works. It is certainly his most important ballet score, exceeding both *Cinderella* and *The Stone Flower*. Prokofiev put a great amount of time into it and he had great difficulty in getting it staged. Curiously, it was nearly staged in England before it was staged anywhere else. Anthony Tudor, who wanted to do a ballet to *Romeo and Juliet*, went to a concert to hear this music. He didn't like it and decided to get a score selected from Delius; that's the Delius score that the American Ballet Theatre does for *Romeo and Juliet* today—they started in 1942.

The Prokofiev ballet was first done in Czechoslovakia, in Brno, in 1938, just before the German invasion. It wasn't done in Russia until 1940, when it was produced in Leningrad, danced by Ulanova and Serguieff—the same Serguieff who later choreographed the *Hamlet*. This was a major breakthrough in Soviet dance and, to an extent, in world dance. The Leonid Lavrovski version, which can still be seen in Russia, remains very important. What Lavrovski did was to try to equate in expressive dance some of the poetry. For example, the death of Mercutio in the ballet, the "plague on both your houses," is very graphically described in dance. The "Queen Mab" speech is also very graphically described. With some of it, you actually hear the lines in your head and you say, "My god, how clever—fancy being able to describe that!" In a sense, that is art of recognition rather than beauty. Everyone who sees the allusion gives himself a little congratulatory pat on the head. On the other hand, it is a very successful thing.

However, it is a static ballet, and certain Western choreographers—Fredrick Ashton for the Danish Ballet, Kenneth MacMillan for Britain's Royal Ballet, John Cranko for the Stuttgart Ballet—have taken a more dance-way with *Romeo and Juliet*, still using a cut-down version of the Prokofiev music, and they have created a rather more modern version. The Lavrovski version with its very impressive dramatics I still think is the best. It looks as though *Romeo and Juliet* is here to stay, and Shakespeare always will have that to say in dance.

I do think that Shakespearean themes will continue to emerge in dance. For the Shakespearean quadracentenary, Kenneth MacMillan did a ballet on the Sonnets called *Images of Love*, so you can see they can choreograph with almost anything. As long as choreographers need stories which are readily identifiable, I think that Shakespeare will continue to have a fairly large part in ballet dramaturgy.

LEVARIE:

Let us return to opera and to Károly Köpe.

KÖPE:

When I tried to organize my thoughts as to what I might say here, I saw them going in so many directions that I gave up in despair. I simply asked myself the question: what influence did Shakespeare have on opera, if any? The answer lies in so many different areas that I prefer to touch on only a few subjects. As an opera conductor, even as a stage director, I must confess that I find myself always a servant of the score—of the composer's intentions. I don't think there's any other way of doing it properly. An opera is a play already ninety percent staged by the composer. The director doesn't have all the choices he can have in a play—the inflections, the pacing, the mood have all been already set down by the composer, so that the conductor must really be a faithful interpreter of those things. He must be able to understand the composer, the author, and read their minds. I don't think any serious conductor would want to conduct *Otello* only knowing Boito's libretto; he would want to know Shakespeare's *Othello*. That is really a very roundabout way in which Shakespeare exercises his influence on the actual performance. When it comes to staging, a Shakespearean subject requires very fine acting—the performer has to create a character, but that is true of all good operas. Shakespeare is not an exception.

I find great difficulty with translations. Now, it is a fact that some of the great masterpieces on Shakespearean subjects are not in the English language, but in Italian, French, and so on. I firmly believe opera should be done in the audience's language. Although I have translated a number of operas into English— some with success—I have despaired of ever succeeding in translating a Shakespearean subject. To give you an example, in *Falstaff*, "Bardolfo and Pistola." Those are the words that Verdi set music to. In translating those words back into English for an English audience, you are already stuck with a musical line that requires three syllables: "Pi-sto-la." I would find it ludicrous to sing "Pistola," when everybody knows it's "Pistol." I would find it equally uncomfortable for myself to adjust the musical line to fit a two-syllable word. But these are some of the problems that I encounter. To me they don't matter so much, for these are problems of my craft, things that go on in the kitchen.

There is another question which fascinates me more: if we answer the question, "Did Shakespeare influence opera?", we tend to say, "Yes, indeed, look at *Otello*." Then we go further and say, "All right, and then what?" *Falstaff* and *Otello* and *Romeo and Juliet*—these three are the best known in operatic repertoires. In view of the number of plays, both tragedies and comedies, that Shakespeare has left us, why so few adaptations and why so late?

Rounding the figures, we can say practically three-hundred years had to elapse: if we take 1600 as Shakespeare at the height of his powers and 1900, which is a very few years after Verdi's *Falstaff*, that's three hundred years. When Shakespeare died, Palestrina had just died, and Bach was almost a century yet to come. Those three hundred years bring up very little. Now, the answer to that is: you have to look at what happened in history to theatre in general.

Are Shakespearean plays difficult to put into music? That could apply to all great poetry; it is not only true in Shakespeare's case. In opera, the most popular topic is love, pretty much like the run-of-the-mill Hollywood "opera." There has to be love: boy meets girl, boy is about to lose girl, or boy loses girl—that's a tragedy; or boy gets girl back. The lovers unite despite all odds, through their wits, in comedy, and in tragedy usually they don't unite. If you look at the great block of Shakespeare's works, many of them are really historical works. Love is not the central subject. The one in which it is—*Romeo and Juliet*—has been made into opera. Also comedy, yes, his *Merry Wives of Windsor*.

In turning to other great masterpieces, it is my impression that operatic composers seem to want to extract the love motif. Look at *Faust*, which the Germans to this day refuse to call *Faust*, but call *Margarethe*, because it concentrates only on one episode from the tragedy of *Faust*.

The reason why Shakespeare's influence was not felt for so long is purely historical. If we keep in mind that Palestrina had just died, and Bach was still a long time to come, and we look at the state of theatre on the continent, we realize that the continent was under the domination of French Neo-Classicism. Even Venetian opera, which bore a resemblance to Shakespearean comedy, after the reform of Apostolo Zeno and Metastasio, turned classical.

It wasn't until Romanticism, through Germany I believe, that Shakespeare conquered the continent. In the Romantic period, we see him emerge as the great inspirer. While I say that his direct influence has been minimal, his indirect influence has been enormous, not only through his fertilization of the romantic spirit but since then, also through his omnipresence. So, to the question of whether or not Shakespeare inspired or influenced music, the answer is absolutely, Yes! The arts, theatre, poetry, and through that, the poet in sound—the composer. In a way, I might say that the answer to the question becomes as obvious as if we asked the question: did the sun's rays influence music or its development? The answer is, indeed it did. Shakespeare is as all-pervasive as the sun. He touches on all aspects of the arts, because he was one of the greatest poets and one of the greatest knowers of the human heart.

LEVARIE:

When I was asked to participate, I remembered a passage from an essay that I had read some years ago, and I'd like to share that passage with you. It has direct bearing, I think, on everything my colleagues have said, and I hope you will respond to it. In order to put it in its proper relief, let me say a few words about the author. The essay is by Hans Pfitzner, a man known to musicians, though not particularly popular in the United States these days. He was a German composer who died shortly after the Second World War. He wrote a number of operas which are still quite popular in Germany. His major work, an opera named *Palestrina*, has been recorded and is now available here. The composer Palestrina is the hero of that opera.

Pfitzner belongs to that category of romantic composers like Schumann, Wagner, Berlioz, who wrote a great many essays besides writing music. That means that he knew a great deal about literature. For instance, he wrote the libretti to all his operas. He knew exactly the pitfalls of libretti and the relationship of the libretto to music. He was a very intelligent man—I have to say this because you are likely to disagree with many things that you will hear. He was a conductor, a pianist, and he had practical experience. He was a good musical thinker. When Busoni wrote a theory of music aesthetics that Pfitzner didn't like, Pfitzner retaliated with a book of his own, developing his own concept of music aesthetics. In short, he deserves to be taken seriously. This is from an essay that he wrote in 1915, when *Falstaff* and *Otello* were relatively modern operas. Certainly they were less old than, let's say, Berg's *Lulu* is today. They were rather recent in the repertory, particularly outside Italy. The essay is rather long, over 100 pages. I have just a few paragraphs that I would like to share with you. The title of the essay is "On the Basic Question of Opera Libretto":

I want to speak about the widespread popular and apparently indestructible mischief of arranging literary masterworks, particularly dramas, as operas. Wagner said, "Two items signify the descent of the German theatre into abomination, they are called *Tell* and *Faust.*" He was referring to the very famous operas by Rossini and Gounod. Now, a generation later one can state that it has continued this road to the abominable. To *Tell* and *Faust* have been added, to name only the best known examples: *Mignon, The Merry Wives of Windsor, Hamlet, Otello, Falstaff, Beatrice and Benedict, The Taming of the Shrew, Romeo and Juliet, Werther, Goetz von Berlichingen,* and *The Winter's Tale.* No dead and no living poet is protected from being operated on in the most terrible manner. There is no more scandalous symptom of not having understood a piece of poetic literature; there is no more indecent and disgraceful concept of the nature of poetic literature than the opinion one could transcribe a Shakespeare play into an opera. Whoever arranges the masterwork of a great playwright as an opera sees in those dramas only the plot and not the poetry—in *Otello,* for instance, only a piece in which a Moor named Othello out of jealousy kills his wife, named Desdemona. This is the crudest possible attitude toward a poetic literature; for the higher and finer the literary product, the more closely it has grown together with its form, the less it is possible to separate content and form. Shakespeare is the superior master of drama, and drama is the most difficult and highest of all poetic forms. The popular use of Shakespeare's dramas for operatic material is no accident—it leads to sad considerations also morally. When such an arranger comes and makes an opera out of a Shakespeare drama or of the Goethe novel, like a vest out of an old pair of pants, he sees in those dramas only what also the tailor sees in the old pants—the material. The alternative would be for the arranger to stand as far above Shakespeare as Shakespeare above the storyteller of *Capitano Moro,* a most unlikely feat which the libretto of Mr. Boito could not demonstrate either. I wish to make one more distinction among operatic arrangements of dramatic masterworks: those which are merely stupid and those which are impudent. To the first kind belong in unselfconscious freshness, operas like *Faust* and *Mignon.* The second are represented in product by Verdi's *Otello* and *Falstaff* which doubtless want to improve Shakespeare. These last two operas are highly respected by the upper 10,000 of our public in musical life. They are called "masterful" and not just in regard to the music alone. *Falstaff*, in particular, is talked about in one breath with *Die Meistersinger* and, according to a questionnaire, is judged to be the opera since Wagner. This is a paralyzing thought for anybody who truly responds to the magic of every moment in *Die Meistersinger*. I can praise Verdi's masterly musical technique, but even if God instead of Verdi had written the music to *Falstaff*, the result would still be just an opera belonging in the category of *Faust* and *Mignon*. In short, to a kind in which Wagner saw the disgrace of artistic standards.

Let me add personally that I share the admiration of my colleagues for Verdi's three Shakespearean operas, and I would like to reconcile my admiration and yours with a fairly similar admiration I have for Pfitzner as a person.

BARNES:

I don't know about him as a person, but I do know about him as a composer. I think the *Palestrina* is really one of the most boring operas I have ever heard in my life. It's deadly! I can well understand him not being recorded until now. I think the answer to this is really very simple, isn't it? After all, *Othello* was taken from a play by Cinthio. Shakespeare himself used other material and transformed it. Merely to look at the libretto of a Shakespearean opera and say that it's not as good as Shakespeare is entirely to miss the purpose of opera. In actual fact, a very good dramaturgical point could be made that the Boito libretto for *Falstaff* is infinitely superior to *The Merry Wives of Windsor*. The changes that Boito has introduced have all been dramaturgical improvements. I would not say that is entirely true of *Otello*, but, in any case, he keeps much closer to *Othello* than he does to *Merry Wives*. I disagree with the idea that you cannot use a Shakespearean play or, indeed, any play or part of a play as a jumping-off ground. . . . I mean, where did the themes of Pfitzner operas come from? Perhaps one could object that *Palestrina* is not exactly an accurate biography of the composer. It's rather a romanticized view, isn't it?

Romanticized and boring. I would say that this is just a stupid, pedantic, and completely worthless argument.

DOWNES:

I agree one hundred percent with everything you said. I might also add one thing: in the case of Boito, we are dealing with a superior talent. His Italian libretto is inspired. Not only for the Shakespeare story, but also for the very subtle psychological insights of Shakespeare, it is also quite a masterpiece of the Italian language. I wonder if Pfitzner's Italian was adequate to judge that? It is a very sophisticated Italian, and I don't think that a superficial knowledge of Italian would suffice to appreciate the beauty of that libretto as a poetic work.

BARNES:

I want to add that while I know that the second act of *Palestrina* is a dreadful bore—the Council of Trent scene—there is a great deal in it that I find very beautiful. It is static and conservative, not to say reactionary for its day, but perhaps only in productions that I have seen.

LEVARIE:

I was very careful and polite not to contradict you. I think it is a very beautiful opera.

BARNES:

I think it probably does depend on the production, because it's one of those things that has to be very beautifully done. As you are aware, this is a kind of a lament for the whole romantic culture. You know the Mahler story about the last wave? He was also a very late romantic, obviously, and felt himself part of the tradition of Berlioz, Wagner, Liszt, and so on. A friend was lamenting that with Mahler practically all music now was going to end. They were mountain-climbing alongside a brook, and Mahler suddenly cried, "Oooooooo!" And his friend said, "What is it? What is it?" "The last wave!"

LEVARIE:

That friend was Brahms, I seem to remember.

DOWNES:

I wouldn't have thought they would have been good friends.

LEVARIE:

I would like to answer Mr. Barnes who, I think made it a little easy for himself by pitting his opinion against somebody else's opinion. I am trying to get the reasons that lie behind Pfitzner's very strong statements. I repeat, he was an intelligent man. The answer that I am trying to work out for myself was almost suggested by Professor Downes in his opening statement, though he didn't know it at the moment. It has something to do with language.

Permit me to draw on a personal experience. I grew up on opera in German—all operas in German. That means my *Faust*, or *Margarethe*, as it's called in Germany, was sung in German, not in French. I thought it was dreadful because the German translator found it necessary to use as many literal quotations from Goethe's *Faust* as he could squeeze into the libretto. The vicinity of that music to Goethe's *Faust* was simply painful to anybody who knew *Faust*, in the same way in which you apparently were pained by Schumann. Now, that pain disappeared completely when I began to hear *Faust* in New York in French. It doesn't bother me one bit, because the relationship to Goethe has just about disappeared.

Probably in Verdi's *Otello* and *Falstaff*, we have a very similar situation. You remember Othello's last words in Shakespeare:

. . . No way but this,
Killing myself, to die upon a kiss.

I dare anybody to set this to music and improve upon it. Well, Boito's last words are simply Otello saying, "un' alto baccio"—another kiss, finished. He knew what he was doing because this is a phrase one really can set to music without being pained by it. I don't think it's an accident. I don't even think it's a characteristic of English music or composers that they haven't really tackled Shakespeare—Britten is the one exception—just as German composers, at least of first rank, have really not tackled Goethe. *Mignon, Faust, Werther.* You realize those are all French composers? By the time you have translated that masterwork into a different culture, into a different language, I think it ceases to suffer from the vicinity of the masterwork.

BARNES:

Isn't it perhaps Pfitzner's mistake that he really thinks that Verdi, or whoever it may be, is trying to improve on Shakespeare? This is really a total misconception. Verdi was not that conceited. He simply thought that this was a marvelous subject for an opera, and he was right.

*   *   *

QUESTION:

In my minimal readings of criticism on Shakespeare ballet and opera, I think two things happen; 1) the criticisms suffer from Shakespeare idolatry, so that what you get is: "It's not Shakespeare." Of course, you're defeated immediately. And, 2), very often when I see a Shakespeare ballet, it occurs to me to wonder why they call it Shakespeare? In other words, they are trying to capitalize on this genius, and it backfires on them. If I remember correctly, Shakespeare's *Othello* has about 4,100 lines and Verdi's *Otello* has less than 900. What happened to 3,200 lines? I looked up several thousand articles, and there are only two on this subject. Incidentally, when I was in Birmingham at the Shakespeare Library, I came across a catalog that lists 700 Shakespeare operas. Where are we getting this sense that there are so few operas—and all of these within 150 years?

DOWNES:

But none of them in the permanent repertory. I wonder how many Goethe operas have been written if one really looked at it? Quite a lot, I would say.

LEVARIE:

You remember the list of operas that Pfitzner mentioned? I know opera literature reasonably well—so does my colleague Professor Köpe. But we had to look up the composers of *Goetz von Berlichingen* and *The Winter's Tale*. There were three settings for *The Winter's Tale* in the nineteenth century—none of them in the repertory, none of them ever heard. That probably accounts partly for your number.

KÖPE:

Your question, referring to the 3,200 lines left out: You will find that any time a known work—a drama—is turned into a libretto. It has to be that way for very obvious reasons: it takes longer to sing a text than to recite. Therefore, if an opera is to remain within acceptable proportions, you have to shorten the text. But that's only one reason. The other important reason—I think artistically even more important—is that in dramas there are many passages pertaining to the action, the situation, or the characters that must be achieved through words. It is not all action. Long soliloquies, poetry, words, must create that characterization or create that dramatic mood or tension. The moment there is music, much of that becomes superfluous because the music instantly creates this. A very primitive example: you can put a tremolo in the violins—this means fear. You can do it in two seconds.

QUESTION:

You just lost 150 lines . . .

KÖPE:

We have just saved 150 lines. These are the two reasons I see.

BARNES:

Could I just say about ballet that very often people like stories? They like readily identifiable stories, and there aren't too many that the entire audience will know. Stories like *Romeo and Juliet* are so universal that you can guarantee that even with a fairly unsophisticated audience, something like eighty percent of that audience will actually know the story.

QUESTION:

Then why don't you say Cinthio's ballet?

BARNES:

Do you know that the last *Othello* ballet done in this country was done by Jacques D'Amboise, and they did say Cinthio's ballet? It seemed extremely affected.

QUESTION:

Mr. Barnes, I think you sounded rueful over the fact that there aren't many Shakespeare ballets. Why should there be? I don't think it's a matter to be deplored, if anyone deplores it. Why isn't there a ballet to Milton's *Paradise Lost*, or Boccaccio's *Decameron* for that matter? Part of Balanchine's genius is that he can create ballets on entirely original ideas, so let's forget ballets on Shakespeare.

QUESTION:

I wonder what you people thought could be achieved in adaptations into dance and ballet and opera that cannot be achieved in a dramatic production . . . or what has been achieved?

BARNES:

It's completely different. It's rather like saying, what can be achieved by a steak that can't be achieved by roast turkey? You are dealing with quite different things. There are people who like opera; there are people who like ballet, and there are people who like plays. There are people who like all three of them.

LEVARIE:

There are people who don't like *Palestrina*!

BARNES:

But still the pleasures and conventions of each art form are quite different from one another.

*   *   *

Fig. 16. Catherine Malfitano, as Juliet, prepares to join Romeo in death in Gounod's *Romeo et Juliette* (Act III, Scene 2) in the Metropolitan Opera production. (Photo: Metropolitan Opera)

SHAKESPEARE IMPROVED

M. C. Bradbrook

Not only is Professor Muriel Bradbrook of Cambridge University an internationally respected Shakespeare scholar, but she has been Mistress of Girton College, Cambridge. That means that administration has made some claims on her time, but it certainly hasn't distracted her from continuing investigations in the world of Elizabethan theatre or from working closely with her students to help them achieve the same mastery of material and research techniques which distinguish her numerous essays, critiques, and books. The latter include: Elizabethan Stage Conventions *(1932),* The School of Night *(1936),* Shakespeare and Elizabethan Poetry *(1951),* English Dramatic Form *(1965), and* Shakespeare and the Craftsmen *(1969).*

This talk, wide-ranging in its considerations of "improvements" on Shakespeare, combines Professor Bradbrook's formidable scholarship with her attractive gift for critical speculation. It offers an interesting amalgam of insight and information.

* * *

To improve Shakespeare is more than a duty: to those who can meet the challenge it becomes a pleasure. This means, of course, not to surpass him, but to "improve the occasion," to bring him forward, project him in the present. Theatre people—

for whom each performance marries the word to the deed—
must continually keep this marriage in repair; they cannot live
happily ever after with the Shakespeare of Irving or Gielgud.
Bernard Beckerman has remarked that "when one speaks of the
history of the nineteenth century, one speaks of actors. To speak
of twentieth century Shakespeare, one must speak of directors,
whose first allegiance is to the life of the play. . . ." He quoted
Peter Brook: "This form of intensity makes all questions of the
play's past unimportant. It's happening now."

Imposing a "frame"—Beckerman borrowed the film
language—entails coordinating costume, setting, and acting style
with "the world view which the action unfolds." Attention is
concentrated, response channelled, interpretation imposed.
This may bring out latencies implicit in the original design, or
may challenge it.

When the frame was traditional and changed only slowly, it
could take a hundred years to set up Macready's historic
reconstructions and replace them after World War I by modern
dress. Now, total theatre and total eclecticism range from the
magnificent Zulu *Umabatha* to Kozintsev's *King Lear*. In the very
home of tradition, the Comedie Française, Trevor Nunn evolved
a new *Richard III*:

> Eh bien, l'hiver de nos chagrins
> Devient l'été par cet astre de York.

By putting the language into a strong and consistent non-
verbal context, every modern director becomes a translator. In
John Barton's *Richard II* production, a strong frame revives
social and ethical assumptions latent in the text. It derives from
those lines of Richard:

> Within the hollow crown
> That rounds the mortal temples of a king
> Keeps death his court; and there the antic sits
> Scoffing his state and grinning at his pomp.

An antic is a silent actor—the term is theatrically precise—
and this Icon of Death comes straight from Holbein's "Danse
Macabre." The frame, however, is reinforced by Tudor political

doctrine of The King's Two Bodies recovered and set out by Ernst Kantorowicz. Like that of every other man, Richard's Body Natural "travails with a skeleton." A skeleton emerges too from the Body Politic as power slips away. Here the story of Aumerle is crucial, though I do not think John Barton is justified in intruding from *2 Henry IV* the sufferings of Bolingbroke, or in making him appear as the groom. At the end, all is concentrated in Richard, man and icon, as his abdication of self peoples his Pomfret dungeon with figures of Remorse, doubly imprisoning flesh that is already half of death's other kingdom. In his own idiom of abdication and alienation, a modern writer has caught the implications of self-imprisonment:

> God give those drunkards who wake at dawn.
> Gibbering on Beelzebub's bosom, all outworn,
> As once more through the windows they espy,
> Looming, the dreadful Pontefract of day.

In Tudor times, the beast fable was a powerful political weapon, as Spenser learnt to his cost. The flesh is given its separate representation as the tiny gaily colored hobby-horses of the list give way to the great black war steeds, and finally to gigantic Northumberland, brooding like a raven over the captive king, whose final pathos is intensified by the little toy horse proffered in humble consolation by his groom.

Alternative perspectives are kept open by the Elizabethan practice of doubling, so that the chief of Richard's favorites is identified with his murderer; the main part, given, handy-dandy, now to Ian Richardson, now to Richard Pasco, ensures that this shall work for the "chameleon players" also. As Richard hangs suspended in his death throes, will he offer to the audience an Icon of Christ, or Marlowe's Governor of Babylon; the Archetypal Albatross or Billy Budd? The choice is ours; any of them will work. It's happening now.

The visible chorus of identically clad nobles—groups of three men meeting to plot, to part—becomes symbolic when the three gardeners appear as monks. Against this choric background, the royal group plays out its contrasts and pairings. The same grave opens for Gloucester, Gaunt, and Richard. Here the frame, which has developed from the RSC Theatre-Go-Round's rapidly paced production, grows dense as history itself.

To set against *Richard II*'s tragic frame the comedy of Peter Brook's *Midsummer Night's Dream* illustrates even less direct methods of "improving the occasion." Its technique is Expressionist—that is to say, for physical representation of objects, it substitutes commedia dell'arte revels, that Tudor midsummer gaiety denounced in 1573 by the Puritan Philip Stubbes. Bottom's exit to the strains of Mendelssohn's Wedding March recreates the Morris Dance:

> Then march that heathen company towards the church and churchyard, their pipers piping, their drummer thundering, their stumps dancing, their bells jangling, their handkerchiefs swinging about their heads like madmen, their hobbyhorses and other monsters skirmishing through the crowd.

Brook transmutes the festivity of Midsummer by decreation, or the removal of the conventional expected response that woodland sets and gauzy fairies supply. Instead, with a tingling electric shock, he exposes the beautifully spoken words in a pure energy of muscle and light.

The art of performance is essentially ephemeral as that of African mud sculpture or Japanese flower arrangement, but it demands a hidden skill and knowledge. The director himself may not be fully conscious of his own craft skills, and his audience will feel only its effects. Long ago, the founder of classical Japanese art for the Noh plays remarked on this hidden strength, the control that expressed itself in an actor's absence of movement. Such art does not conceal art, but allows it to re-emerge as a second nature, the spontaneity which is the last reward of discipline.

Shakespeare and he alone seems to tolerate these constant acts of decreation and recreation. Ben Jonson, as I've tried to show, is much less amenable. The contemporary trend, being to black comedy, imposes dark frames, to which the problem plays lend themselves very readily; whereas sinister versions of festive comedy are often designed solely to shock.

Some frames, of course, merely familiarized, like setting *Hamlet* or *Othello* in the mid-nineteenth century, or *Romeo and Juliet* in New York's West Side. There has been sufficient denunciation—Gareth Evans, John Russell Brown, and Bernard Beckerman among the chorus—of the gimmicks that play against the lines only to shock, "insulting" the text to see how much it can take. The positive world, harnessed in the service of reduction, then endorses a frame designed by Thersites or Apemantus.

In New York, when celebrating the fourth Shakespeare centennial, Frank Kermode spoke of the "patience" of Shakespeare, meaning his capacity to absorb and reflect whatever image his "improvers" project. The adaptations of those who resist the original are no less a tribute than those of the idolators, and here again the form reflects the age. In the nineteenth century, the Divine Shakespeare was venerated for his text; the sacred quality of the Work, projected by the terms "Canon" and "Apocrypha," entailed all the traditional apparatus for the transmission of Holy Writ. The present mood sets up Shakespeare as the source of all mythology; his performances in color, procession, gesture, icons, all belong to an older faith. The mode may be Catholic, but the dogma is often Freudian or Marxist; our dark gods emerge in his bright mirror. Adaptations of Shakespeare have dealt with the death of an American President; the alienation of the little men, Rosencrantz and Guildernstern; Edmund has been deprived of his repentance, and Desdemona of her virtue.

Such adaptations have not been customary since the late seventeenth century, the Age of Newton that enthroned Reason and Symmetry, in Dryden's *Troilus and Cressida* or Tate's *King Lear.* "God said, 'Let Newton be,' and all was light"; a rosy color was then diffused over the darkest plays. Our own attempts to insult the lines get out of our system something which perhaps could not otherwise be projected at all. When composing *Brand*, Ibsen is said to have kept on his desk a beer glass holding a scorpion. "From time to time the creature became sickly; then I used to throw a piece of soft fruit to it, which it would furiously attack and empty into it its poison; it then grew well again. Is there not something akin to that about us poets?" he asked Peter Hansen.

So, Shakespeare is still "the medicine of the sickly weal," and the impotent gesticulation of four-letter words in Marowitz's *An Othello* offers an indirect tribute to the eloquence of the food of a godless world.

In Shakespeare's own day, I would suggest, the pattern or decreation and recreation lay nearer to that of the Restoration. Conservative scholars have even seen something of the process in Shakespeare himself. Has it not been suggested that *The Merry Wives of Windsor* is a series of comic revenge actions, and the finale a parody of a murder in a masque? Here Auden must come to my aid, for comment:

> Listener, you have heard
> What Hibbard says occurred.
> Well, it may be so.
> Is it likely? No.

However, Shakespeare had discovered his own comic structure largely by parody in *A Midsummer Night's Dream* and *Love's Labour's Lost*. He was to refashion the memories of obsolete romances in his last plays, and these initiated a process of recreation in his contemporaries even more widely than his *Richard III* or his *Hamlet* had done. If parody is the tribute of the new to the old, burlesque is the most mutually elevating form of homage. ("See, your reputation is so unassailable it can be joked about.")

I should like to end with a Jacobean burlesque, an example of Shakespeare Improved, which happens also to be topical. A while ago, at Melbourne Hall in Derbyshire, the manuscript of a hitherto unknown Jacobean play was discovered. Sotheby's sold it in November 1973, and on 11 January 1974, Lord Perth, John Ehrman, Sir Anthony Blunt and Basil Gray—who sound like a conspiracy out of *Richard II*, but who are in fact the British Export License Reviewing Committee—sat to decide whether it could leave England's shores. It has been attributed confidently, but I think mistakenly, to Thomas Heywood.

Its story of Tom a Lincoln, the Red Rose Knight, found in the romance of Richard Johnson (1599), is the sort of tale that Shakespeare perhaps began to act in—Sir Clyamon and Sir Clamydes is recalled in *Cymbeline*—the sort of play Francis

Flute asks for, when he hopes Thisbe is "a wandering knight." Johnson's hero in this drama echoes several popular successes of 1611, especially Heywood's *Golden Age* and *The Winter's Tale*. It can be dated round the Christmas season of that year or the next.

King Arthur—caught in a situation closely resembling that of his descendant Edward III, in a play attributed to Shakespeare—behaves with much less restraint; approaching the lovely Angelica, daughter of the Earl of London, as she sits in a summer bower, he lays passionate siege to her and after twelve days wooing wins her. Conveniently removing herself from her father's eye by being professed a nun at Lincoln, Angelica there gives birth to a son who, exposed on the King's orders, is found and fostered by a poor shepherd. Overjoyed by the rich purse of gold tied round the infant's neck, Antonio takes him as his own and names him Tom a Lincoln.

The birth is displayed by Time as Chorus in a dumb show, with words not unfamiliar:

> I that have been ere since the world began
> I that was since this orbed ball's creation,
> I that have seen huge kingdom's devastations,
> Do here present myself for your still view—
> Old, ancient, changing, ever running Time,
> First clad in gold; then silver; next that, brass;
> And now in iron, inferior to the rest,
> And yet more hard than all

Having shewn the removal of the babe, Time concludes this speech:

> . . . thus in short time
> Time briefly hath declared what chance befell
> This hopeful infant at his happy birth—
> Be your imagination, kind spectators,
> More quick than thought, run with me, think the babe
> Hath fully passed sixteen years of age. . . .

Beginning his career at a summer feast as the Red Rose Knight, Tom achieves fame and fortune as a highwayman. After delivering a highly moral denunciation, his aged foster father dies of grief, but King Arthur, recognizing the seed of royalty, summons Tom by no less an emissary than Lancelot du Lake, promotes him to the Round Table and to military leadership of a punitive expedition to Portugal. Tom displays unusual military virtues, imposing strict discipline and regular pay issues to his troops; he sacks Lisbon and returns in triumph with the captive king.

Setting out as adventurer with a hundred knights, including Lancelot, his next triumphs culminate in slaying the dragon of the Hesperides. On the way he has been determinedly wooed by the Fairy Queen, whom he leaves with child, a son, the Fairy Knight. Prester John who had offered his daughter, Anglitora, as prize for the dragon-slaying, withholds her from a mere wandering night, but the two elope, encountering on the way home the drowned corpse of the Fairy Queen who has cast herself into the sea, having first tied on her crown and affixed a lamenting letter to Tom. Arriving in England, Tom marries the Princess and buries the Queen. Throughout he has been accompanied in the play by a clown named Rustican, who indulges in fond reminiscence of his native Lincoln.

Tom combines aspects of Shakespeare's lost princelings with the instincts of a Cloten, the predations of a Autolycus, and the unsinkable resources of a Stephano. His adventures make Pyramus and Thisbe seem like an exercise in classic restraint. He also recalls Heywood's Four Prentices, and some of Heywood's more peculiar coinages appear in the text. When the Fairy Queen is about to raid Tom's bedchamber, she compares herself to "lust-spotted Tarquin," thus combining Shakespeare and Heywood in one lurid image.

The play, which came to Melbourne Hall with the papers of the great lawyer, Sir John Coke, originated at Gray's Inn, and its principal scribe or improvisor—there are three—signs himself Morganus Evans. The colophon runs:

Finis Deo Soli Gloria.
[Quae] Quam perfecta manent, strenno perfecta labore,
Metra quid exornat? Lima, litura, labor
Morganus: Evans:

The MS was his and includes some memoranda; he was a student at Gray's Inn, admitted 12 June 1605. This was two years before Francis Beaumont of the Inner Temple had put on the stage at Blackfriars *The Knight of the Burning Pestle.*

The sophisticated young lawyers of Gray's Inn were expected to put on a play at Christmas, when everything, down to the kind of food provided, followed custom. Such plays often dealt with Times and Seasons, being part of the festive calendar, and frequently they united the near and far, grandeur and burlesque. A twin play to *Tom a Lincoln* can be found in the anonymous *Comedy of Timon* (MS Dyce 52, V. and A.). It also burlesques Shakespeare, also contains a clown who goes on adventures to the Antipodes. This MS, which like the Melbourne Hall MS is in several hands, as I attempted to show some years ago, belongs probably to the Inner Temple, since one of the leading characters is Pegasus, the arms of that Inn. Gray's Inn had an alliance with the Inner Temple, and the two plays may be dated within a year or two of each other. The griffon or dragon who provides the climax of *Tom a Lincoln*, constitutes not only the arms of the Principality of Wales, but those of Gray's Inn also. Heraldry always played an important part in the revels of the mock Court.

A comparison of this new play with *Gesta Gravorum* (1594), with the Oxford *Christmas Prince*, but above all with the anonymous *Timon*, suggest that *Tom a Lincoln* included in its banter some hits at the courtly success of 1611, *The Winter's Tale*—which Glynne Wickham would see as a celebratory play for the true Prince of Wales, Henry. That was in turn a subtle reshaping of the romance of Shakespeare's old enemy and detractor, Greene, *The Triumph of Time.*

It is possible that Heywood may have written a play on Tom a Lincoln. The adventures of Tom a Lincoln's son, *The Fairy Knight*, were to be treated in 1624 in a lost play by Dekker and Ford. But that the present text is actually by Heywood must remain open to question, although it was confidently attributed to him in the notice of the sale. The use of his more outrageous words may be compared with Jonson's use of Marston's vocabulary in *Poetaster*. Heywood's theatre, the Red Bull, was in Clerkenwell, closely adjoining Gray's Inn, the most northerly placed of the four Inns of Court, but it was a popular, rowdy place. The nearest legal neighbors were Lincoln's Inn. It seems to me more likely that Rusticano's fond recollections of his native Lincoln and indeed the name of the hero are aimed at the other lawyers, rather than embodying—as was suggested in the sale notice—memories of Heywood's native county. What would the lawyers care about Heywood's origins? Topical and local "hits" were what counted, and Rusticano's recollections of the dung-carts of the City of Lincoln could have pointed a local quarrel about the disposal of Gray's Inn refuse in Lincoln's Inn Fields. As other surviving texts show, the familiar jokes of a great household at Christmas included the sort of mockery that all jesters practiced, and parallels can be found in Feste and Lavache.

There was not one but several Jacobean theatres; the lawyers were acutely aware of social gradations and in joining a play of the King's Men to a product for the plebeian Red Bull Theatre, they were able to project a playful dream of success in love and war before their critical audience of "severe Areopagites with their contracted eyebrows." The Prince of Poets and his royal success was a necessary ingredient in the humbler revels of their own Christmas Prince.

*   *   *

FILMING SHAKESPEARE

Franco Zeffirelli

One of the most memorable of the National Theatre's productions under Lord Olivier at the Old Vic was Much Ado About Nothing. *Franco Zeffirelli took his cue from Shakespeare, who indicated Messina as the locale of the comedy. It was a thoroughly and delightfully Italianate production. But Zeffirelli has other Shakespeare credits in other performance media as well.*

Under Sir Rudolf Bing's regime at the Metropolitan Opera, Zeffirelli staged four operas—three of them based on Shakespeare's plays: Falstaff, Antony and Cleopatra—*which opened the new house, but not without difficulty, and* Otello *were the three. Can it be coincidence that two of those three were by the same Italian composer, Verdi?*

This talk, however, concentrates on concepts and problems involved in filming Shakespeare's work, especially the Zeffirelli Romeo and Juliet, *which he had already staged with great success. His Elizabeth Taylor-Richard Burton version of* The Taming of the Shrew *is given some attention, as are related problems of staging the Bard's plays as plays and as operas. In introducing Zeffirelli and his topic, Sir Rudolf Bing commented: "He is one of these strange directors who knows what he wants and also knows how to get it. He has asked me to say particularly that he is not a lecturer. He has no prepared speech, and he looks to you for questions—any questions—indiscreet questions.*

I think it was Oscar Wilde who said, 'Questions are never indiscreet; answers sometimes are.'"

* * *

ZEFFIRELLI:

I am not a good lecturer—even in Italian, my natural language, let alone English which is for me a border language. But my history with the English language is quite simple. Actually, I was brought to understand the beauty of this language when I was a student in Florence where I studied my first years of art. The war brought me the pleasure of knowing more deeply your language—but that doesn't mean that I am expert in this salty language that you have.

The fact that they called me, when I was still exclusively an opera director, to direct a Shakespearean production in London really surprised me. I thought it was a bad joke of some friends I had in London. They called me when I was in Milano and said, "Would you like to do for us a production at the Old Vic of *Romeo and Juliet?*" I said, "Yes, certainly, provided the Queen is there." At the other end, they thought the answer was a bit odd. They said, "Well, we'd better write you." So they did. They wrote once. An energy crisis. They finally wrote to me, and I understood what kind of enterprise I was going to face—I mean, directing Shakespeare at the Old Vic. Can you imagine what it meant for anybody of my age and my position, especially being a foreigner? An exciting privilege and great honor. I said, "My God. I have to do Shakespeare! I don't know anything about it."

Actually, then one goes back to one's own roots—what you studied, what you learned from years that really mattered—between the years of 16 and 20, when you face the great masterpieces in our culture and civilization and you somehow put them in yourself, in your spirit, in your brain. So, I had to think back to these treasures that I had covered up, and it came back—loud. I had just read the plays of Shakespeare in Italian and the Sonnets in English. Suddenly, what I had learned many years before came back to me, and I didn't see any difference between having studied these pieces in Italian or French or whatever language, and doing them in English. That was something that really taught me a lot.

This man Shakespeare—apart from the beauty of his poetry, his language—has got something else which applies to every human being on earth, no matter what cultural background, what language he comes from. To me and to all Italians, to all French, to all Chinese, to all Germans, Shakespeare is the greatest playwright who ever lived. No matter if you cannot have the beauty of the original language, even in a translation there is something that this man is able to project. Something like the great Michelangelo. No matter what civilization one belongs to—take somebody from the center of Africa, and he comes to the David—he understands. It goes beyond the values of a particular civilization. So I approached Shakespeare with this great belief in my heart that even if I was Italian, I was able to deliver the love, the understanding for this great genius. It went very well.

Actually, I must confess to you that at the first rehearsal I had studied the piece in Italian, so I said, "Let's do the painting first, and then we'll put on the frame." The frame was the language. The original poetry was an additional beauty to the painting, but the painting was there, apart from the beauty of the poetry. That was one of the reasons why many of the critics attacked me, because I didn't start from the poetry, going down to the dramatic values of the piece.

Anyway, it worked very well. I had great fun. We put on the play in four weeks, which is short. There was an issue: they grew their hair long which, at the time, was quite a surprise to the people of London, to see these young people with long hair. The Beatles had not appeared yet. Actually, I don't think it is my credit to have started this as a fashion. It started this way, I remember: the actor who played Romeo originally was a bit square in his manners. "Shouldn't we wear wigs? I hate to go around and see my parents, my relatives in that long hair. They say, 'Whoo, look at him!'" All the men in the cast went about together—they never dared to go alone.

But there was something explosive in this new approach to Shakespeare, which was actually my ignorance of the poetry of Shakespeare. Or really my strength to revise it, my lack of understanding. But concerning the questions, "How do we approach this matter?" or "How do we do that?", the pragmatic function of this kind of meeting between people who have achieved certain desires and others who want to achieve is to talk about practical ways to make things happen. I have always been practical; I have always believed in the core of things. You must have one basic value to hold in your fist. Never let it go—otherwise you lose the whole operation. You have to be able to grasp that value and hold it near your heart, in your mind, for the length of the operation. This thing—build around it, like a spider-web. Build around it and finally create whatever it is you are able to create, given the conditions you are working under or the possibilities you are offered. But it's important to go to the core for these things.

We are talking about *Romeo and Juliet* because apparently I am branded with it. I did it. Actually, this is unfortunate because there are many other things that I consider equally interesting. It could be as interesting for you to know that I've done a *Hamlet* in Italian which was the Italian contribution to the Shakespeare Centennial '64. We brought it to London in Italian, which was something which never happened before. There again, something extraordinary happened: most of the English audience was familiar with Shakespeare. They followed it beautifully—they didn't have any need of a translation because we brought out the heart of what Shakespeare meant, apart from the words. Of course, "To be or not to be" was "Esse o non esse," but it happened; we communicated. The point: if you stick to the essence of the work of a great creator, you travel with it like good wine travels throughout the world—it is good. A good Chianti, or a good champagne you can drink in Tokyo or Dallas—it works. If we really believe in the great values, we communicate one way or another, despite the difference in language, civilization, background, and age. People who are eighty communicate easily with people who are eighteen.

If we go into an elaboration of intellectual values or fashions and fads, then we are in trouble. But if we stick to the essence of the classical background. . . . That's why always to young people who come to me for advice I say, "What is your classical knowledge? What do you know of the classical novels of the past? Have you ever read *La Princesse de Cleves* or *War and Peace* or *Les Liaisons Dangereuses?* You will create your own uses. No matter what practical application life offers you, you have a very healthy and rich ground in which your roots will develop and absorb values. In other words, if you want to be a Shakespearean director, I don't think it's necessary to bog down for three years and exclusively study that. You might get a bit confused. What matters is to create for yourself a platform of knowledge and culture that might be extremely nourishing for occasionally—as in my case—doing Shakespeare.

So, you want some practical answers. And I'd like to hear your practical questions. I'd like very much to be of use to you, because I feel we have to communicate a lot—especially with young people—and pass on whatever we have found out or done with our hands or spirits. Not to brag because I have done these things—1964 that I was at the Met is not the point. I consider these glorious achievements that my life and career have given me to be episodes of practical experience. The glory of them? You know very well today you are on top of the hill, and tomorrow you are in the bottom of the abyss. That's how life is. But for us, any experience means something. I personally cherish more the memory of certain flops I had than the big successes. Thinking back, there were certain things which were not fully achieved but were great, good ideas which, for various reasons, couldn't come to life.

As I have said, I am a very practical man. To my company, I never try to articulate, to tell them with words what they have to do. I say, "Well, let's stop this. I'll show you how it happens, and you show the thing, even if you don't know the words, but the feeling is there." Actors are very visual and they have antennas and they absorb the idea which is offered. Actually, I am very disturbed by complications of the mind applied to practical problems. Practical problems have to be solved practically. I have learned what I know only by working with other people first, for many years, and then working on my own, making my own mistakes. It worked out better before, when I worked with others. Then they made the mistakes, and it was a lot easier. But you have the moment when you have to take on your own responsibilities and make your own mistakes. At the same time, you make your achievements.

So whoever aims to work for theatre or cinema has to keep practicality in mind. Of course, you prepare your cultural background and have it in the back of your mind as a platform for operation, but then you come out with the practical and do. Let's do. Let's read a scene. Let's try to make a speech. Let's stage something. Let's paint ourselves a piece of scenery. That is how it started for me and that's the way I want to keep young for my work for the future. [Sighs.]

QUESTION:

How did you decide what to cut in *Romeo and Juliet*—since the things that you cut are things that people wait for, like Juliet's potion speech?

ZEFFIRELLI:

I know. I know I did a terrible thing with that—the potion, and the apothecary scene, that's all. I shot it actually. I couldn't put it in. With the cinema, you have to make up your mind whether you do a film for a small number of people who know it all— and it's not very exciting to work for them—or really make some sacrifices and compromises but bring culture to a mass audience. This was what I was trying to do; sometimes I also succeeded. What I wanted to do with *Romeo and Juliet* was to keep the attention of the movie audience—normal movie-goers—alive, as if they were looking at a film of Carol Burnett. Something that they could really identify with. There were areas where we were terribly in danger of parting company with the audience and asking them to contribute the kind of attention which comes through the brain and culture. It is a beautiful piece of poetry, but they knew it all dramatically. In that moment, Juliet could not go into this beautiful piece of poetry. Really, my heart bled when I had to cut it.

Also, you know why the apothecary scene is wrong? Because the suicide of Romeo can be accepted on the wave of emotion—he makes that long speech and then he poisons himself and dies. But if you begin to question, "Where did he get the poison? Why did he choose the dagger?" then you can part company with the audience right there. You lose the beauty and the emotion is dead because they arrive at that point with a lot of questions in their heads.

I think the cuts were sound. We had a good show. We had to cut the killing of Paris, which I shot. You don't want that. I mean young people wanted us to have the romantic meeting between the dead girl—who was not dead—and Romeo who had threatened to kill himself. If he was a murderer—"Ugly boy, ugly boy!" It wouldn't have worked. And besides, the thing was already long enough.

QUESTION:

You did a lot of transposition in the lines when they were on their way to the banquet. Romeo's speech about a fate hanging in the stars occurs after they've moved off, and his line, "On, lusty gentlemen," which to me seems crucial to be his, I think you gave to Benvolio. He doesn't say, "On, lusty gentlemen" in your movie, but he does in the play. What was the reason?

ZEFFIRELLI:

The reason was that the mental syndrome of Mercutio was he had to have his own area on the way to the party and give an atmosphere of anguished Verona. Romeo had a premonition about what was going to happen. As soon as Mercutio goes away with the gang of other kids, Romeo sits and he sees the moonlight and looks at something bigger and infinite. He looks at the stars and sees his own destiny, and that's why he had that premonition.

QUESTION:

I see that. Perhaps you can tell me what Mercutio is supposed to mean in that particular sequence. I've seen the film four times, and Mercutio has confused me in different ways each time.

ZEFFIRELLI:

Mercutio is a confusing, an unclear character. Mercutio and the Nurse are the only two characters that Shakespeare introduced in his adaptation—you know there was an Italian novel of which the tragedy is practically an adaptation. But Shakespeare felt there was something missing, something he couldn't fully identify, in this story of two ill-fated lovers. He had to choose some characters who were somewhat closer to him.

He picked up this Mercutio—Mercutsio—who in the story is nothing, just nothing. It is beautiful the way the story mentions Mercutsio. Juliet is dancing a famous, fashionable dance at the moment; one gentleman-one lady-one gentleman hold hands and dance. And the girl masquer feels with the left hand an immensely warm hand; that was Romeo's hand. On the other, she felt an icy cold, wet hand; she turned, and it was Mercutsio. That's the only time it's mentioned. When Shakespeare read it he must have been fascinated by his hand. He said, "I bet this Mercutsio must have been an interesting character."

So he wrote this character which is repeated through practically all his plays and tragedies—which is himself—a kind of evil, witty, funny, pessimistic, cynical, and existentialist character—which is his portrait in a way. This is Iago, Jacques, his Mercutio, and so on. Shakespeare invented the dramatic function of Mercutio. The character of Mercutio is above the class, above the plane of his people. He is a kind of chorus who lashes back at their sighs or cries at whatever happens and shouts at them. He is a bitter, very modern character. He's like Hamlet, you know.

It's a big problem to put it on the screen unless you have a Barrymore who does all this hamming about. But to make him that kind of logical angry friend, very contemporary . . . which I think the actor did very well. You don't expect that kind of character to be integrated in logical, dramatic terms—just the flash of intelligence, genius and pessimism, black and white there in the tragic. So we tried. I tried several ways to handle Mercutio. I thought I couldn't do it any better.

"Queen Mab" is a good piece in the film. It helps understanding the moods of Romeo after; also how much he is looking for a hopeful solution to the problems. I mean, while

Fig. 17. Olivia Hussey and Leonard Whiting as the young lovers in the Franco Zeffirelli film of Shakespeare's *Romeo and Juliet*. (Photo: Paramount Pictures)

Fig. 18. Leonard Whiting (right) as Romeo duels Michael York to avenge Mercutio's death in the internationally acclaimed Franco Zeffirelli film, *Romeo and Juliet*. (Photo: Paramount Pictures)

Mercutio constantly thinks of the black answer to life, Romeo wants a hopeful answer. That's what you find perhaps a bit disturbing, jarring in the attitude of Mercutio. But I think it enhances so much the color which we want to see in Romeo, hoping to find love and to live—and yet to die for love.

QUESTION:

An actor prepares his part and then he plays his performance on the stage from moment to moment. He knows where he was in the rehearsal and where he's going. In dealing with your actors in the film, how much did you rehearse them in the total characters as they moved through the story?

ZEFFIRELLI:

The film we didn't rehearse much. Actually, we couldn't, because the two leads were not experienced, and I had to instruct whatever I could, day-by-day, night-by-night. I did a lot of scenes all over again. I saw them in the projection room, and they weren't good enough. I brought the actors to see what they had done. I said, "Look, we can improve this. Let's do it all over again."

In the history of film there hasn't been a film that used more stock than mine. It cost us a fortune in film stock. It was worth it. So it was impossible with them to follow a regular scheme of preparation, rehearsals discussing characters, and so forth. I had to talk with them like a nurse talks to the children. I had to say, "Now when you hit your head, oh, your mother does this and you do that." Very, very simple. I kept to the simplest with the two children. Of course, with Michael York who played Tybalt or John McEnery who played Mercutio, we could go much more deep. Analysis of the part and dissection of the characters.

QUESTION:

Had either of them played those parts before?

ZEFFIRELLI:

No. None of them had ever played the roles. That was an advantage because it brought great inner discovering of the emotions, which was fresh. That is an advantage of the cinema, you see. In the theatre, as you say, an actor arrives and he feels that he knows it all in experience, and he has to dig back to the original freshness, the first emotion that he had when he read the play or saw it for the first time. But in between is sandwiched so much work and travail and destroying and finding. Then, at the last moment, there is the audience. In cinema, generally I don't have that. At least in my films I never like to do that, because really cinema is a day-by-day discovery, and fresh is best. When it's fresh, you have to eat it, you know. You can't let it get stale and heat it up again. It's quite a different operation.

QUESTION:

Did you shoot sequentially?

ZEFFIRELLI:

As much as I could, yes. It was very important for them to follow their own line of thinking. But sometimes we couldn't, because we shot in the studios.

QUESTION:

You mentioned before why you cut the killing of Paris, and yet in the Prince's speech, the Prince still says "I have lost a brace of kinsmen." Did you assume that your general cinema audience would not pick up the phrasing, "brace of kinsmen?"

ZEFFIRELLI:

I think nobody picked it up except people like you who are very knowledgeable and who know the play. I think the fact that there has been a slaughter going on—like a Mafia fight—for years in the town sufficiently explains or justifies the use of "brace of kinsmen." Nobody really objected. Also, because Mercutio was one of his kinsmen, and he was dead.

QUESTION:

I have a question about Mercutio's death. Why did you choose to make the whole sword fight scene a comedy until Tybalt actually stabs him? I find that indefensible from the text of the play. I think that they are very deliberately disliking each other, and Mercutio eggs him on to a genuine fight.

ZEFFIRELLI:

I don't know. It's a choice. Many people like it, and I preferred that kind of handling of the scene. It is true that they hate one another, but it works this way: despite the fact that Mercutio hates him, he teases him and he laughs at him and he jeers. The words, "I'm dying," are very applicable to this kind of solution. It justifies saying, "Call me tomorrow and you'll find a dead man," or "not as big as a church door." He makes a big joke about his own dying, and only at the end is he devilish and begins to curse the families. I practically improvised this with the actors. I don't like this dying of Mercutio to be so serious, because later we have the other duel which has to be very serious; there must be no fun in it—to the bitter end, the last drop of blood. It is also too long to have two serious duels one after the other, and the first one is much more exciting, is much more in the portrait of Mercutio. He wouldn't die dramatically like a tenor. He has this high intelligence on stage. He would make fun of his own death, wouldn't he?

QUESTION:

But you have that after he's been stabbed; you have that in his death scene. You don't need to give five minutes of comedy sword fight, but you do it.

ZEFFIRELLI:

That's all right. I don't agree. I like it very much this way. I quite understand your point that it is not quite what Shakespeare meant, but I think he would have liked it.

QUESTION:

Could you explain how you arrived at the whole balcony section? I'm always used to seeing Romeo and Juliet never actually get together and touch in the balcony scene. It seems to me to provide a tension in that scene, a beauty. And yet in yours, they touch quite a bit.

ZEFFIRELLI:

Well, one has to approach the classics, giving them a chance to progress with the times. Take a play that was written at the end of the sixteenth century where the conditions of the stage and the theatre and the audience were quite different. To begin with, the casts were entirely of men—Juliet was a boy. As you know, in no Shakespeare tragedy of play is there a love-scene—I mean love in terms or kissing and hugging—because we couldn't see two boys doing that.

Anyway, one thinks now that the conditions are different, that the times have changed. Two boys cannot kiss, but perhaps a girl and a boy can do that. Also they can do it more freely—I mean every year more freely. If Shakespeare was given the possibility of writing for today's humanity, today's audience, would he handle that love scene that way? Everything suggests that there is a physical contact. There is a need of holding one another in one another's arms and kissing and hugging. He wouldn't deprive his actors of that great possibility.

Especially the audience of today would demand it; otherwise, of course, you're going to have to hire Norma Shearer. The whole point of this approach of ours was to make the thing really happen for the audience of today—to make the audience understand that the classics are living flesh. That we can identify with things that were written three centuries-and-a-half ago. And I'm sure again in my presumption that Shakespeare would not have disapproved.

QUESTION:

When she later says, "I have bought a mansion but not yet possessed it," doesn't that seem to say that they've pawed each other a lot? It seems to me that the beauty of the scene is the anticipatory element which she finally gets after the "gallop apace" speech. It would be nice to get that element of wanting Romeo.

ZEFFIRELLI:

You think that Juliet, being the character she is, really means hugging and kissing? I think kissing is not enough for her; she wants something more and she gets it later. That's exactly what she means: "Oh, it is not enough, it's not enough. You kiss me; I hold you, but I must have more; I must have all; I must have it." Really, Juliet is such a modern character. My love scenes in cinema are played by girls between 15 and 20 because they identify fully with Juliet. It is not over-romantic nonsense. She's very practical—she gets it.

Then, we had an escalation. The next scene which is again in Shakespeare, the balcony scene, the second balcony scene, they did in the nuptial chamber. They were naked, and we really gave the feeling to the audience that they had fully fulfilled their union. There's nothing wrong with that. I'm ready to admire anybody else who does it in a different way. I like the way I have done it. Every time I see it I am moved. There are areas where I am not pleased, but I won't tell you.

QUESTION:

Mr. Zeffirelli, when you said you begin with the painting and work toward the frame, is that just with Shakespeare, or with drama in general? Could you elaborate on what you mean by that?

ZEFFIRELLI:

Shakespeare was a very practical man. He made his living by writing plays for a certain medium which was the theatre of his time. He had to serve the audience who wanted to see stories happen on the stage. Of course, he couldn't use anything else, being a poet, but his beautiful poetry. But if he weren't a poet, he would have written just the same kind of plays. For him, the point was to create a repertory for his theatre. Given the culture of the moment, the fact that plays had to be written in poetry, he supplied marvelous poetry. But I insist adamantly that this was an additional beauty in it, an additional jewel to his crown. That's why I say. . . .

QUESTION:

Well, in other words, you start with the story, then dramatize that, theatricalize that?

ZEFFIRELLI:

The point is to tell the story, to get people involved with a kind of fairy tale, to make the fantasy of the audience come to life and run together with the actors. That is the point of theatre. Then, in addition, Shakespeare had to express himself in poetry like Verdi, who had to express himself with music. If you look at the musical theatre medium, which is opera, you see the drama was essential for Verdi. He had to get involved with the libretto, the story, before he could write a bar of music. The music served the dramatic action of the play.

There again, music is more overwhelming and more intruding than poetry, but it has a certain kind of function which is the medium he had to use to express this rite of the theatre, which is telling a story, getting people involved with what you want to say, expressing your own field of fantasy, making them follow this path with you. And then either use the camera, as I sometimes do, or the stage or opera or poetry. Do you see what I mean? Poetry is a medium, and he had to use it. I'm glad he did it.

QUESTION:

You mentioned opera. Do you find any difference between your approaches in staging opera and staging drama? I'm thinking particularly of your staging of *Otello*, which I've seen at the Met, and also your staging of *Romeo and Juliet*. Do you take a different approach, even in the matters of production like opulence and literality, as opposed to non-illusionistic staging and so on?

ZEFFIRELLI:

Well, in music, the author already supplies you with a great part of what you need . . . I mean the author of the score—in emotions and drama. Even if you go against the music, as many of my colleagues do often, you cannot cripple or deprive the author of what he intended to say. It's already there, so you simply have to add something, and, of course, what you can add in the opera is not written, because there is a music conductor in control. What you have to do is all visual. The contribution that the director has to make is, of course, to make the singers play and sing as well as possible—and not be too fat—so they look natural. Of course, that is the new style. But it's all visual, the contribution of the opera director or designer. That's why we have a tendency of creating the visual opulence that you are mentioning, because that's a field in which we can move.

The rest, the emotions are all in the score, ending in the performance. So, you can heighten the performance working with the singers and surrounding them with a kind of frame that enhances the values of the music, which already gives the audience, let's say 85 percent of what the opera then is. It would be a crime to over-do a production without music, but to illustrate richly a production with music is important, because music requires a visual equivalent which has to be as rich as what your ears receive. You can't have *Otello* without scenery. I think it would be a mistake. It wouldn't serve the music.

QUESTION:

The musical medium in particular intrigues me. In relation to the songs, I'm wondering how the actors worked with the music.

ZEFFIRELLI:

We put it in later, when they were busy doing another picture. No, no, except for *Romeo and Juliet*, the last song; it helped them tremendously. It gave them a vivid feeling that in that particular context was very important. It was not background music; we had music there. They knew they were saying those words while somebody else was singing just next to them. But otherwise, the incidental music was put in later.

QUESTION:

You mentioned you had a problem of working with Olivia Hussey and Leonard Whiting in *Romeo and Juliet* because they were so inexperienced. When you did *The Taming of the Shrew*, with Taylor and Burton, how did you direct someone like Burton who had done so much Shakespeare? Do you really have to tell them what to do as you would in the case of Whiting?

ZEFFIRELLI:

No, any actor—I do not consider them generally—there is not a collective of actors; every actor is a human being—is an artist. It's like every actor is a different lock, and every lock has a different key. So you must use different ideas with every person you work with, and sometimes the lock of an actor like Burton is very complicated. You have to know it very well, or else it doesn't open. In fact, I am not fully satisfied with the collaboration we had with Burton in *Taming of the Shrew*. I was a bit inexperienced—it was my first film, and I had a great reverence for him. I shouldn't have had it; perhaps I don't have it anymore. But the fact that I was admiring him so much deprived him of my breaking certain of his patterns in his performance. Certain of his patterns are a bit stale, though I think he gave a marvelous portrait of Petruchio. It was easier with Elizabeth Taylor, because she was fresh, like me. She was new and very insecure, and so we worked on a lot of new ideas, and she burst out in a much more unexpected way than her husband.

QUESTION:

When you made the comment that you had to work with the actors in *Romeo and Juliet* who had been so inexperienced, I remembered a little comment I had read that you had interviewed 200 people to play Romeo. I now know that you just saw this face and said, "This is he!"

ZEFFIRELLI:

That's what I thought, yes. That was absolutely the core. The main thing that made the film successful was that I took literally the indication of Shakespeare that Juliet must be fourteen and the boy a little older. It worked on stage because Judi Dench and John Stride, although they were much older in their day, they really played fourteen and eighteen. That was the thing that I held in my head, no matter what happened. In every scene I said, "Don't forget she is fourteen. She's fourteen, and that holds the structure of the play together." That's what Shakespeare wanted—I defy anyone to say it's wrong. I'd like very much to see a boy of fourteen even in the age of Shakespeare do justice to those verses. I don't think they did any justice, but Shakespeare could care less. He wanted a young kid to play the part. So, that was the idea that I held in my fist very jealously and firmly up to the last moment.

QUESTION:

When you are starting production of a work that is a classic, and so many people have read it—it has lasted so long—where do you start?

ZEFFIRELLI:

Every generation likes to look at the classics with different eyes and make them a mirror of themselves, in which they can reflect their image; it's their classic. That applies to all kinds of classics. Every generation has done *Hamlet* in a different way; at least 20 different approaches through the centuries. If you really count, it becomes some kind of contest. We say, "Let's try to do this because our generation has not done it yet—let's do it for ourselves. Let's see what values we want to bring out in ourselves and how they can apply to this classic piece that was written three—nearly four—centuries ago." Already that encourages you.

At that point you have to make an effort to imagine the progress of the author if he had been given the possibility of living up to our times—in other words, to write that play today for us. So that is another big step, isn't it? If he were here, writing for the audience of America, the young kids of England, how would he express himself? What would he like for them to receive from him? Then you begin to work around this idea and, of course, it evolves from question and answer. That is why I like this kind of meeting, because from question and answer come ideas. A creator always questions himself and gives himself the answers.

Now, if you do *Romeo and Juliet* today, how old should they be? First answer: they should be the right age. Second, should it be costumed or contemporary? No, costumes. Because contemporary has already been done, and it just wouldn't work. Will we be adapting the dialogue or using the original dialogue? Well, I think the original dialogue is pretty good. So, we begin working that way. Once you start, it comes. Sometimes it succeeds; sometimes it doesn't. If it doesn't, it's interesting later to go back and find the mistake—like in a computer where there has been a fouling. There is always a moment where you made the wrong choice and that has jeopardized the whole operation. I was blessed in *Romeo and Juliet*, saved from making some crucial mistakes—though there were some.

QUESTION:

You are interested in *Troilus and Cressida* and *Much Ado*. Can I start with a basic question—why? I want to see what appeals to you in those plays and for what reason you want to turn over six months or a year or two years of your life to that work.

ZEFFIRELLI:

I have to give you two different answers. One is a practical one. I have done a production of *Much Ado About Nothing* at the National Theatre. I did it in 1965, and it was very successful, and I enjoyed tremendously doing it. A superb cast: Maggie Smith and Bob Stephens. Since then, I've always had this thing that I must do a film of it one day. I must do a film of this. Also, it will give me the opportunity of doing a Shakespeare without the English, being an Italo-American homage to Shakespeare. It's kind of a jolly answer to *The Godfather*. Another interesting angle is that it has never been done. Americans and Italians in chopped English, speaking your broad Brooklyn accent, but the Shakespearean text. That's what I asked the English actors to do at the National Theatre. Of course, it outraged the critics, but it worked. So, that's one answer for *Much Ado*.

Second, *Troilus and Cressida* fascinated me because it is the clash of two races. It's in the Mediterranean—the whites and the less white. The Greeks, invaders, civilized, sophisticated, corrupted, and this very solid patriarchal city where the king has 51 sons. They stole a beautiful Greek lady, and the whole thing started. I'd like to bring that in—I don't mean in contemporary terms, but the audience will get the message anyway, even if it's in the costume of the period. It's one idea of a picture that interests me very much. Apart from that, the play of Shakespeare is quite beautiful and again offers marvelous dialogue.

QUESTION:

In working with your actors, do you constantly refer to the total script, or do you just use the cut version? I imagine that you, as a director, constantly study images used in the entire script.

ZEFFIRELLI:

You have to be extremely flexible. Look, there is no one production that can be a permanent example, because a production is a combination of so many live and unpredictable elements. The actors: the actors bring their human life, as human beings, into this particular venture they are doing. So that girl who is supposed to say this kind of speech perhaps is not ready, either mentally or professionally, to do justice to it, although she is marvelous in other areas. If you cannot have the right performance of something which is essential to an understanding of the plot, if you can't do it, it's better to cut it out. If you cannot make it happen on the level of the rest, it is better to cut it out. I have cut out very valuable things sometimes because for some reason the chemistry didn't work. And there were moments where the attention really sagged. You jeopardize the value of what other good you have done. . . .

QUESTION:

But it always seems the essence of what was missing was still there, and I wonder if you had worked with them saying, "Well, let's remember this part that we're cutting out . . ."

ZEFFIRELLI:

You are talking about me? Specifically what? Like the potion scene?

QUESTION:

Well, for instance, yes. Do you constantly go back to the script with the actors and remind them that this is not what's here, but it will be implied, unsaid?

ZEFFIRELLI:

I went through three different stages. I had a much longer script when I shot, and some things were killed on the spot. "Can't do it; can't do it; can't do it." Or, "Try it again; try it again." I became convinced something didn't work, or we couldn't do justice to it, so we cut it. Other things were moderately successful, but not fully convincing, so I kept them in the first rough cut, and then for other reasons they were cut. The girl, Olivia, was not that good in the Potion Scene, so why spoil the girl with that scene when she is so good in the rest?

There were other things we just didn't put in. I mean, all that pestilence in Mantua; we didn't need that stuff. Or the clowns, or the many other parts which are very dull, or the speech of the prior at the end that tells the whole story all over again. But in Shakespeare's time, there was a very good reason why he tells the story all over again. The theatre audience was not concentrating on what was on stage. They were chatting and going away and coming back, so they lost track of the plot. At the end they had to be reminded what the play was about.

QUESTION:

You have spoken just now about content that was removed. Have you found anything that was impossible or at least very difficult to translate into film terms in Shakespeare?

ZEFFIRELLI:

No, everything can be done. No limit.

QUESTION:

What is the difference in staging the scene where the Nurse tells Juliet of Romeo's banishment and Tybalt's death in film terms and stage terms? I think I'm right in recalling that there was a lot of crying dubbed into that scene in order to sustain the grief and shock. It's very effective, but you certainly can't do that on stage. Do you try for a different result on stage?

ZEFFIRELLI:

No, we also did it on stage. Actually, on stage it's much longer. You have the two crying scenes come one on the top of the other. I cut to give meaning. Romeo in the cell: banishment, banishment—and Juliet: Tybalt, Tybalt: it goes on forever, and cinema really cannot bear it. It was hardly bearable in this cutting we did. In fact, certain audiences—not the young people—but certain adults and sophisticates laughed a bit: "Oh, the crying, it goes on again!" You see, cinema creates a different chemistry with the audience, a different taste, and the attention of the audience moves so fast. Really, fantasy gallops in the audience in movies. They know all before the image is finished. They say: "What's next? Give me more. Give me another idea—give me another feeling." You have to be very economical in cinema.

QUESTION:

Would you talk then about how you worked on that scene on stage? We just finished doing the play, and that scene was enormously difficult.

ZEFFIRELLI:

To begin with, the Nurse is a clown. She says, "Oh, give me my aqua vitae." She wants a drink. She again stretches out the news. We all know about it because we have seen it happen, but Juliet doesn't know, and the Elizabethan audience says, "Don't torture this girl." But the Nurse doesn't tell her yet; she makes her suffer, makes her wonder. It is very Elizabethan that scene—I mean the clowning in the dramatic moment. Today you have to be very careful. If you go for the cultural experience, the audience says, "I want to see the full text of *Romeo and Juliet* as they've done it in Stratford." Very well—five-and-one-half hours! That's the purpose of a National Theatre: to give the full text. But if you go for a public success, I mean not in terms of money or glamour, but to make the audience be there with their guts and heart and feeling, you cannot give them this. So, if it means surgery on the text, even on its great values, you'd better do it. Sometimes it is better to do without certain things than jeopardize rapport. It's always a matter of choice, depending on the opportunity and occasion. If a school wants to do a straightforward presentation of the play, it decides to go in that direction. Then you inform your audience that this is it, but don't expect them to cry with you—they might laugh, as a relief.

QUESTION:

For me, *Romeo and Juliet*—your film—was a direct and beautiful experience. I would be interested in what you consider your mistakes.

ZEFFIRELLI:

You trapped me because, as I said before, really I don't consider anything a mistake. No, there were a lot, but we won't talk about that.

QUESTION:

Would you say that film presents a very accurate delineation of space and place, whereas on stage it is suggested? Or would it be that film is a two-dimensional medium, compared to the three-dimensional medium of the stage?

ZEFFIRELLI:

You are touching the difference of theatre—the live performance— and film. I perceive that theatre is the basis of everything, and the attitude of others towards the theatre is a ritual attitude. You perform a rite between the actors and the audience. They are equally important—there is a kind of a Mass. That's how theatre started, a celebration in common. In being part of a live performance, you give not so much attention to your fantasies as to the ritual of being together—the bodies there, our souls together, celebrating this event for us.

In cinema this problem has fascinated me. Your fantasies are completely loose. You don't have any direct responsibility of contact with what is there except in your feelings and in your fantasies. Your fantasy runs much faster in cinema—actually cinema is a fantasy itself. You don't have any physical problem in following, in that it's all there, and your mind flashes-flashes-flashes. That doesn't mean that you cannot hold. There have been marvelous masterpieces of cinema where the audience was nailed to the chair for three hours, looking at landscape or silent scenes for almost 10 minutes. The cleverness of the author is to hook your imagination in fantasy, helping you enter the minds of these characters and bring them into your mind.

Do you realize when the lights come up in cinema you feel like you're waking up from a dream? You have been in a really unique experience, which you don't get in a theatre. In theatre there is a live event you have not dreamed at all. You are seeing something; you have been together with someone who has given you something. In cinema, you wake up, and it takes some time to readjust. You go back home and fill your heads with dreams and thoughts; perhaps it stays with you for weeks and months. I don't know how to articulate it, especially in English, but it's very much like that. Also, we are very much conditioned by television—a different medium which is information, information. We change channels and try every other thing, but that idea of the moving images has very much shaped our minds to a medium that has formed our tastes.

QUESTION:

I have a very small personal question I have wanted to ask you for years.

ZEFFIRELLI:

Don't ask my age.

QUESTION:

Just a curiosity of mine about *Romeo and Juliet*. I've seen it ten times, always with increasing admiration and love. Were you at all unhappy because the story-line actually forces Friar Laurence's exit at the end. Wasn't it a bit hard to justify, having made him such a marvelous character? Were you unhappy about that?

ZEFFIRELLI:

The character of Friar Laurence disintegrates and rightly so. He is introduced in the beginning as a man who believes in drugs and spells and magic. He thinks the answer to the problems of life lies in these kinds of solutions. He is a man haunted by a wrong idea. He is not a rich man at all: someone who believes in chemistry, one of those Renaissance alchemists. He's punished at the end because the poison he has given to Juliet hits him like a boomerang. I don't think Shakespeare has made a mistake there in punishing him at the end. I think it's perfectly reasonable.

QUESTION:

My 15-year-old daughter agrees with what you're saying. But I found it the only thing that one couldn't totally justify.

ZEFFIRELLI:

I can. You know, to put them together, to marry them on such short notice—they met last night; tomorrow midday marry them—he makes a mistake. In fact, he makes one mistake after another. He should have taken the two children to the families, to the Prince, and said, "This is it. I'll marry them in public in the square." Everything would have been all right. Instead there is this tedious, "Yes, I'll marry them and then I'll keep them apart and then I'll bring out the news so the two families will have to accept everything." It was all very gadgety and tedious. In the end, it couldn't work. The tragedy is these poor kids who believed so genuinely.

QUESTION:

Having seen your films of *Taming of the Shrew* and *Romeo and Juliet*, I am impressed with the lushness of color, the soft colors that suddenly made that period seem more vibrant, but I was also impressed with the sounds that you added—noises made by people and the street. The operatic influence is very strong in the music that was added, especially in *Romeo* but also in *Shrew*. I feel that as far as you're concerned, it would be difficult for Shakespeare's plays to exist without music; so that you almost add the music yourself . . .

ZEFFIRELLI:

Of course, you know Shakespeare's productions had a lot of music. They always had musicians. The audience would have made an outcry if there had been a play without musicians. In these plays, today you normally cut out those parts, but there were moments when they came on stage and sang.

In *Romeo* particularly, the music works dramatically. I imagined that party when the boy was singing behind the shoulders of the adults when the kids met. That was a particular case in which I used music for a certain dramatic purpose. Otherwise, it was all incidental, as in any other production. The scores for these two films were very good. I needed a lot in both cases. Normally, I haven't seen anything without music in it, especially Shakespeare.

QUESTION:

Were there any specific times of day you just had to wait for, like when he's leaving from the balcony in the morning fog? Or would you have them rearrange the woods?

ZEFFIRELLI:

We always rearranged everything. You are talking in terms of scenery? We rearranged a lot. The square was rebuilt entirely, and the background for the church tower. The first part of the duel was done in Gubbio, which is a beautiful city in Umbria. We had to close a few windows and doors and make it look the way it was. We fixed the real exteriors very much.

QUESTION:

And the times of day?

ZEFFIRELLI:

Well, again the cameraman does a lot. But when they part at dawn—the rooster and all of that, and they see dawn— that was done at the end of one night's shooting, at the crack of dawn.

QUESTION:

Would you talk about the way you collaborate with yourself when you design as well as direct the play? Do you ever fight?

ZEFFIRELLI:

Oh, I curse the designer Zeffirelli: "What an idiot!" I do, yes! Well, generally it happens on good terms—a good collaboration between the two. But sometimes I find that the designer has put the director in trouble, although I don't tell the producers. Other times the designer helps tremendously. I consider designing for yourself integrated. But even when I have some other designer do a show for me, the basic points of what I know I'm going to face on stage are fully expected and indicated. Designers work on this kind of structure as any director does. I have this bad habit of designing most of my shows, because I started as a designer.

QUESTION:

How was the film of *Romeo and Juliet* financed?

ZEFFIRELLI:

Financing of *Romeo and Juliet* in cinema is one of the most historical mistakes of the industry. No major company wanted to finance it. No one. I knocked at all doors—I could name all of them—but they are ashamed. They told me, "Oh, Shakespeare—no, no! Not even one penny." I said that I had proved it could come back to life. I proved that in London, and we toured America. Wherever the production of *Romeo and Juliet* played all through America—that was in 1961-1962—we had the same kind of reaction. "So, please give me credit that I can do something; that you won't lose your money at least!" No one wanted to listen.

I finally ended up by offering it as a television special. Italian and English television joined hands, but television was not ready to spend much money, and the English were not very rich either. We had a budget of only $200,000. Finally, a marvelous man who was at the time the chief of the European production of Paramount financed it. He had seen my play with the young people in London. He said, "Well, I think it's possible. I know on the coast they don't want to hear about it, but you might as well take half a million dollars. Add it to the rest, and you'll have $700,000—so let's start." As soon as I had something to show, I went to London and screamed, "You must give me more money, because it is a crime to make this for television." So, a drop here, a drop there.

Fortunately, Paramount's chief, Charles Bludhorn, came to Rome to Cinecitta. He liked Olivia Hussey very much. His son was with him. He was thirteen at the time. His son saw the duel scene and the balcony scene and was all excited. Bludhorn looked at his son and said, "Paul, do you like it? You really like it—you understand it?" The boy said, "Yes, I like it. I want to see more." "Well, Franco, you've got it—how much money do you want?"

It was hell to put it together—I promise you, it was hell. Now, *Troilus and Cressida* and *Much Ado About Nothing*! These people don't learn that there is an audience of good people in the world: millions of youths and adults who like to go back to the sources of culture and rediscover the classics, instead of seeing the kinds of commercial productions that are normally offered. They don't seem to realize that even commercially, Shakespeare is still a best-seller.

QUESTION:

Is that why you dropped *Camille*? I had read that you were going to do a version of *Camille* and go back to the book.

ZEFFIRELLI:

Yes, I have a destiny with *Camille*.[1] I did an ill-fated production of *La Traviata* at La Scala. Honestly, it was the most beautiful production I have ever done—Von Karajan conducting and all of that. It failed promptly because the soprano missed the top note at the end of Act I. We didn't even get a second production. Then I came to Broadway with *Camille* in 1963; it didn't work at all. Every time I am attracted by this property— because I like this woman. I'd also like to prove that she has been badly illustrated by Garbo. I think that Garbo didn't know the story altogether, and she told us the story of a retired whore who turned up with a kid. Instead, the story is that Marguerite Gautier died when she was twenty-one and her mother, thirty-five. Again, it is the story of young people abused by society. Again, it's *Romeo and Juliet.*

QUESTION:

Would you ever consider doing *King Lear*? If so, how would you approach it?

ZEFFIRELLI:

I am too young to do it. No, really, I've been offered it several times. I can't understand that kind of cruelty and the problems of nagging old men. It's marvelous, but there are many other things that I would like to do of Shakespeare.

QUESTION:

As a musician, I noticed that during the ball scene the viol and the recorder were holding sustained notes, but the musicians' fingers were fiddling around. I know the music was recorded afterwards, but do you get any questions or concern from other people about this?

ZEFFIRELLI:

Yes, that shot of the players was done at the end of the day with the unions pushing us, and we had to throw in the musicians. I said, "Do whatever you want, and we will fix it." But we couldn't fix it. You are absolutely right.

QUESTION:

I always think of Zeffirelli as a lot of scenery. Is there something unique in your approach, particularly to Shakespeare? That is, you start away from the word, when most of the people have been stressing the text first—the sanctity of the text?

ZEFFIRELLI:

Everyone has his own tastes. I don't like to see bare productions. You have to offer some kind of total experience to the audience, not only through the ears but also through the eyes—I think we are so visual. Sometimes an actor cannot hold the stage alone; he needs to be helped by some kind of illusion around him—a beauty around him—that helps. It becomes a kind of additional character.

Also, I like to go to the theatre and see a picture when the curtain goes up. Even those people who preach no scenery create another kind of scenery which is lights and elements. Again, this is scenery—more sparing perhaps, but it doesn't create a kind of: "Only acting is important." Your other senses are involved just the same. It is another style altogether, like Josef Svoboda, who is a spare designer. But I wouldn't call him "lack of scenery." He creates very important pictures, though they are so stark. He has his own style in whites and blacks, and he has his vision which is rich and turgid. Again, in theatre and movies, the senses are most important. I admit I indulge in scenery a lot!

QUESTION:

Sir Rudolf Bing has suggested that you do have scenic problems sometimes. You may not care to answer this, but could you discuss the problems with the scenery for *Antony and Cleopatra* at the Met? It was headline news.

ZEFFIRELLI:

I should discuss other problems about that, before scenery, but . . . It was one of those cakes that didn't come up: for many reasons, including my responsibility. I misunderstood the whole point. I thought that it was an opening of a new house and the most important house in the world. It was a beautiful building; there was a lot of glitter and power, and Americans wanted to see that they could do great things on stage. But I loaded the production down too much, I must say. And I wasn't sure about the libretto, the music, and you know when you begin to feel insecure, you rely upon your own tricks. It's a pity because there was enough material there for three *Aidas*!

* * *

[1]Zeffirelli fulfilled it with his cinema version of Verdi's *La Traviata* in 1982, and again in 1989, in a new Metropolitan Opera staging, both starring Teresa Stratas.

BIBLIOGRAPHY

Adams, John Cranford. *The Globe Playhouse: Its Design and Equipment*. Cambridge, MA: Harvard University Press, 1942.

Beckerman, Bernard. *Shakespeare at the Globe*. New York: Macmillan, 1962.

Bradbrook, M. C. *Elizabethan Stage Conventions*. London: Cambridge University Press, 1932.

———. *Shakespeare and Elizabethan Poetry*. London: Chatto & Windus, 1951.

———. *Shakespeare and the Craftsmen*. Cambridge: Cambridge University Press, 1969.

Brustein, Robert. *Revolution as Theatre*. New York: Liveright, 1971.

———. *The Third Theatre*. New York: Knopf, 1969.

Clinton Baddeley, V. C. *Words for Music*. Cambridge: Cambridge University Press, 1941.

Harbage, Alfred. *The Complete Pelican Shakespeare*. Baltimore, MD: Penguin, 1969.

———. *Shakespeare and the Rival Traditions*. New York: Macmillan, 1952.

———. *Shakespeare's Audience*. New York: Columbia University Press, 1941.

Hodges, C. Walter. *The Globe Restored*. London: Ernest Benn, 1953.

———. *Shakespeare's Second Globe: the Missing Monument*. London: Oxford University Press, 1973.

Hosley, Richard, ed. *Shakespeare's Holinshed*. New York: Capricorn, 1968.

Hotson, Leslie. *Shakespeare's Wooden O.* London: Rupert Hart-Davis, 1959.

Houseman, John. *Front and Center.* New York: Simon & Schuster, 1979.

————. *Run-Through.* New York: Simon & Schuster, 1972.

Kantorowicz, Ernst. *The King's Two Bodies.* Princeton, NJ: Princeton University Press, 1961.

Kott, Jan. *Shakespeare Our Contemporary.* Garden City, NY: Doubleday/Anchor, 1966.

Loney, Glenn. *Peter Brook's Production of "A Midsummer Night's Dream."* Chicago: Dramatic Publishing Co., 1974.

Loney, Glenn, and MacKay, Patricia. *The Shakespeare Complex.* New York: Drama Book Specialists, 1975.

Nagler, Alois. *Shakespeare's Stage.* New Haven, CT: Yale University Press, 1981.

Poel, William. *Shakespeare in the Theatre.* New York: Benjamin Blom, 1968.

Righter, Anne. *Shakespeare and the Idea of the Play.* New York: Barnes & Noble, 1962.

Smith, Irwin. *Shakespeare's Globe Playhouse.* New York: Scribner's, 1956.

Thomson, Virgil. *Music Right and Left.* New York: Henry Holt, 1951.

————. *Virgil Thomson.* New York: Knopf, 1966.

Wickham, Glynne. *Shakespeare's Dramatic Heritage.* New York: Barnes & Noble, 1969.

INDEX